THE POWER OF PARABLE

THE POWER OF PARABLE

HOW FICTION BY JESUS
BECAME FICTION ABOUT JESUS

JOHN DOMINIC CROSSAN

HarperOne
An Imprint of HarperCollins*Publishers*

HarperOne

HarperCollins books may be purchased for educational, business, or sales promotional use. For information please write: Special Markets Department, HarperCollins Publishers, 10 East 53rd Street, New York, NY 10022.

HarperCollins website: http://www.harpercollins.com
HarperCollins®, ®, and HarperOne™ are
trademarks of HarperCollins Publishers.

FIRST EDITION

Library of Congress Cataloging-in-Publication Data
Crossan, John Dominic.
  The power of parable : how fiction by Jesus became fiction about Jesus / John Dominic Crossan. —1st ed.
    p. cm.
  ISBN 978–0–06–187569–4
  1. Jesus Christ—Parables. 2. Storytelling—Religious aspects—Christianity. 3. Bible. N.T. Gospels—Criticism, interpretation, etc. 4. Jesus Christ—Person and offices. I. Title.
BT375.3.C76   2012
232.9'54066—dc23   2011032682

12 13 14 15 16 RRD(H) 10 9 8 7 6 5 4 3 2 1

To dear friends
Myra Wells
and
Drew Gribble

Those images that yet
Fresh images beget.

W. B. Yeats, Byzantium

Contents

Prologue *Story and Metaphor*   **1**

Part I
Parables Told by Jesus

1 Riddle Parables   **13**
   So That They May Not Understand

2 Example Parables   **29**
   Go and Do—or Don't Do—Likewise

3 Challenge Parables: Part I   **45**
   Down from Jerusalem to Jericho

4 Challenge Parables: Part II   **65**
   The Word Against the Word

5 Challenge Parables: Part III   **89**
   Let Anyone with Ears to Hear Listen!

6 The Kingdom of God   **113**
   The Challenge of Collaboration

Interlude

The Lure of Parabolic History   141
Caesar at the Rubicon

Part II
Parables Told about Jesus

7 A Hymn for the Nameless   157
The Parable Gospel according to Mark

8 Rhetorical Violence   177
The Parable Gospel according to Matthew

9 Rome as the New Jerusalem   197
The Parable Gospel according to Luke-Acts

10 The Visionary Dream of God   219
The Parable Gospel according to John

Epilogue   *History and Parable*   243

Scripture Index   253

Story and Metaphor

IN THE SUMMER OF 1960 I was a monk and a priest in the Servite monastery high on the Janiculum hill in Rome and halfway through two years of postdoctoral research at the downtown Pontifical Biblical Institute. Rome was preparing for the Olympic Games in late August and so, apart from its standard heat, the city promised too much construction and too many people. (Even the pope abandons the Vatican in August for cool Castel Gandolfo among the Castelli Romani in the nearby Alban Hills—a sure if minor proof of his infallibility.)

That August I was grateful to receive an "obedience"—the monastic equivalent of a soldier's "orders"—to leave Rome for Lisbon, meet an American group there, and chaplain them around the major Roman Catholic pilgrimage sites in western Europe. These included Fatima and Lourdes for the Virgin Mary, Lisieux for St. Thérèse, Monaco for Grace Kelly, and Castel Gandolfo for John XXIII. And then it happened.

As our group traveled slowly by bus from Rome to Paris for its homeward flight, we stopped at Oberammergau in the foothills of the Bavarian Alps to attend its Passion play, a five- to six-hour dramatization of Jesus's final week on earth. It is performed by the villagers every decade on the decade in gratitude for deliverance from bubonic plague in 1634. It was not performed, of course, in 1940, but it returned in 1950 with both Chancellor Adenauer and General Eisenhower in attendance.

In other words, what we saw in 1960 was the unchanged play that Hitler saw before his election in 1930 and again after it in 1934, for its special three hundredth anniversary. But that early September day in 1960 I had not yet read Hitler's enthusiastic comment about it:

> It is vital that the Passion Play be continued at Oberammergau; for never has the menace of Jewry been so convincingly portrayed as in this presentation of what happened in the times of the Romans. There one sees in Pontius Pilate a Roman racially and intellectually so superior, that he stands out like a firm, clean rock in the middle of the whole muck and mire of Jewry.

That obscene review came in July 1942, about the time the German armies were beginning their fateful push toward Stalingrad. But, if I did not know of Hitler's commentary, I certainly knew the sequence of what happened in Christianity's Holy Week from both monastic liturgy and biblical study.

What I did not expect was that a story I knew so well as written *text* was so profoundly unconvincing as enacted *drama*. The play started early in the morning with Palm Sunday, and the huge stage was filled with a crowd shouting approval and acclamation for Jesus as he entered Jerusalem. But by late afternoon the play had progressed to Good Friday, and that same huge crowd was now shouting condemnation and demanding crucifixion. But nothing in the play explained how the crowd had changed its mind so completely.

I wondered if that infamous scene in which the crowd claims responsibility for Jesus's death by shouting, "His blood be upon us and upon our children," was fact or fiction. It did not seem convincing as history. What was the reason for the crowd's change of attitude from acceptance to rejection? Could this story function more as parable than history?

This insight led to others. If it were parable, that is, a fictional story invented for moral or theological purposes, then there were not only parables *by* Jesus—like that of the Good Samaritan—but parables *about* Jesus—like that of the lethal crowd in this Passion play. And, further, there were not only parables of light, but parables of darkness. The factual history of Jesus's crucifixion had become parable—parabolic history or historical parable, if you wish, which I'll return to in more detail later—and from it, in the terror of time, theological anti-Judaism would spawn racial anti-Semitism.

In June 1967, I returned from a two-year sabbatical at the French School of Archaeology just north of the Damascus Gate of Old Jerusalem. I left—the technical term is "fled"—just before Old Jerusalem passed from Jordan to Israel in the Six-Day War. During the next two years, before I left monastery and priesthood for DePaul University in 1969, I was teaching at two seminaries in the Chicago area. One of my courses was on the parables *by* Jesus and the other was on the resurrection stories *about* Jesus.

With these courses I was back to exploring—as before at Oberammergau—the interface of parable and history. I had observed that the parabolic stories *by* Jesus seemed remarkably similar to the resurrection stories *about* Jesus. Were the latter intended as parables just as much as the former? Had we been reading parable, presuming history, and misunderstanding both, at least since literalism deformed both pro-Christian and anti-Christian imagination in response to the Enlightenment? Think, for example, of the Jerusalem to Jericho road with its Good Samaritan and the Jerusalem to Emmaus road with its Incognito Jesus after the resurrection. Most everyone accepts the former (Luke 10:30–35) as a fictional story with a theological message, but what about the latter (Luke 24:13–33)? Is the latter story fact or fiction, history or parable? Many would say this latter story actually happened. But why is that so, when just a few chapters earlier a similar story is considered pure fiction, completely parable? We need to look at that question a little closer.

A first clue that the Emmaus road story was meant as parable and not history is that when Jesus joins the couple on the road, they do not recognize him. He is, as it were, traveling incognito. A second clue is that even when he explains in detail how the biblical scriptures pointed to Jesus as the Messiah, they still do not recognize him. But the third and definitive clue to the story's purpose is in the climax, and it demands full quotation:

> As they came near the village to which they were going, he walked ahead as if he were going on. But they urged him strongly, saying, "Stay with us, because it is almost evening and the day is now nearly over." So he went in to stay with them. When he was at the table with them, he took bread, blessed and broke it, and gave it to them. Then their eyes were opened, and they recognized him; and he vanished from their sight. They said to each other, "Were not our hearts burning within us while he was talking to us on the road, while he was opening the scriptures to us?" (Luke 24:28–32)

That is parable, not history. The Christian liturgy involves both *Scripture* and *Eucharist* with the former as prelude and prologue to the latter. So also with the twin components of the Emmaus story. First comes the *Scripture* section, but even with Jesus as its interpreter the result is "burning hearts," that is, hearts ready to do—but to do what? In the *Eucharist* section we get the answer to that question. It is to treat the stranger as oneself, to invite the stranger into one's home, to have the stranger share one's meal. And it is precisely in such a shared meal that Jesus is recognized as present—then, now, always. That is why the key verbs "took, blessed, broke, and gave" in the Emmaus story's climax were also used in the Last Supper's Passover meal before Jesus's execution (Mark 14:22).

That story is a parable about loving, that is, feeding, the stranger as yourself and finding Jesus still—or only?—fully present in that encounter. That was very clear to me decades ago, and I summed up the ancient Christian intention and modern Christian meaning of that parable by saying that, "Emmaus never happened. Emmaus always happens." That is, by the way, an introductory definition of a parable: a story that never happened but always does—or at least should.

All of that preceding section introduces the basic questions of this book. If there was at least one dark parable in the crucifixion details and one bright parable in the resurrection accounts, how many other parables were there as well? Are some, many, or most of the recorded events of Jesus's last week—the Christian Holy Week— parable rather than history, or again, parabolic history or historical parable? You can see already that, although parables *by* Jesus invented both characters and stories about them—for example, the Good Samaritan, the Prodigal Son, the Unjust Steward—parables *about* Jesus presumed historical characters—for example, John and Jesus, Annas and Caiaphas, Antipas and Pilate—but invented stories about what they said and did.

Where does factual history end and fictional parable begin? Does that interaction of fact interpreted by fiction, of history interpreted by parable, of human event interpreted by divine vision extend to the full content of a gospel? Could that be why we have only one gospel given in multiple versions, in four "according to"s as they are properly and correctly entitled: the Gospel *according to* Matthew or Mark or Luke or John? Those are the generative questions that inspire the sequence of this book, and I now provide a structural outline of the chapters to follow.

The book has two main parts of equal size. Part I concerns parables *by* Jesus—involving *fictional* events about *fictional* characters. Part II concerns parables *about* Jesus—involving *fictional* events about *factual* characters. In between those two parts is a very important interlude to emphasize and exemplify that shift from pure fiction to fact-fiction mixture. My chosen case study is Julius Caesar and his crossing of the Rubicon to invade Italy and start twenty years of Roman civil war in 49 CE. It is factual history that he did so, but all the ancient stories about it—maybe even his own?—are parables.

They do not give us pure history, but historical parable or parabolic history, which helps us understand, in Part II, the shift to historically parabolic stories *about* Jesus.

Part I, on parables *by* Jesus, has six chapters. In Chapters 1 and 2 I propose a basic twofold typology for Jesus's parables, namely, *riddle parables* and *example parables*. I show that those two ways of understanding the point of parables were already present in the biblical tradition before Jesus. But I also indicate problems with applying either of them to Jesus's own parabolic vision.

In Chapter 3 I suggest enlarging that twofold to a threefold typology by adding a third type I call *challenge parables*. That involves two additional steps in the following chapters. Chapter 4 argues that challenge parables already existed—powerfully—in that pre-Jesus biblical tradition. Then, in Chapter 5, I show how many of Jesus's parables were challenge parables rather than either riddle or example parables. Challenge fits well with Jesus's rhetorical purpose and parabolic intention.

To conclude Part I, I ask in Chapter 6 why Jesus chose challenge parables as his major pedagogical style and major teaching tool. If the medium is the message, what is the special relationship between his message of the kingdom of God and his medium of parabolic challenge? Why did Jesus "not speak to them except in parables," as Mark 4:34 puts it?

Part II, on parables *about* Jesus, has four chapters. Each chapter corresponds to one of the four gospel versions: Mark in Chapter 7, Matthew in Chapter 8, Luke-Acts in Chapter 9, and John in Chapter 10. In each chapter and for each gospel I focus on one important part of the gospel to propose it as parable rather than history. I then widen out from that case to think of each entire gospel version as a book-length *megaparable* about the life, death, and resurrection of the historical character Jesus of Nazareth. There is also, however, another unifying theme across those four chapters.

Throughout those four gospel versions we find not only challenge parables *about* Jesus but also a fourth type of parable not investigated so far in this book's threefold typology. I call it an *attack parable*, that is, a story in which Jesus not only challenges his hearers, but attacks them—by, for example, calling them names, doubting their sincerity, or impugning their integrity. The major thematic question running through Chapters 7 to 10 and all four gospel versions as megaparables *about* Jesus is this: Were attack parables—as distinct from challenge parables—characteristic of the historical Jesus?

In this book I concentrate exclusively on parables in the Christian biblical tradition of Old and New Testaments, and you now have a map of the terrain ahead. But there is still one obvious question with which to conclude this Prologue. What *is* this thing "parable" that we have been discussing? Apart from this type or that type, apart from riddle or example, challenge or attack, what is a parable, all by itself, as it were, before any such distinctions?

"The basic challenge of the parable is to write a good story in as short a space as possible" writes Howard Schwartz in the preface to *Imperial Messages*, his superb collection of one hundred modern parables.* But that definition seems both a little inaccurate and a lot inadequate. Granted that a parable is definitely a *story*, is it to be recognized only by length and judged only by word count? Is Jesus a famous parabler because—at least in Luke's Greek—his Good Samaritan had around a hundred words and his Prodigal Son around four hundred?

I do not accept *brevity* as the defining characteristic of a parable. On the one hand, Julius Caesar recorded his victory of 47 BCE at Zela, inland from Turkey's mid-southern Black Sea coast, with the lapidary Latin *Veni, Vidi, Vici*—"I came, I saw, I conquered," but we do not usually think of that as the perfect—because minimalist—parable. On the other, John Bunyan's *Pilgrim's Progress* and Herman Melville's *Moby Dick* are certainly very long stories. Yet we think of them as parables.

---

* Howard Schwartz, ed., *Imperial Messages: One Hundred Modern Parables* (Woodstock, NY: Overlook Press, 1991), p. xix.

But, even if we accepted brevity as an important characteristic of parabling, is that all we need to identify a parable? Do *brevity* and *narrativity* constitute a parable? I propose, instead, to bracket brevity as a possible, but not necessary, characteristic of parable and to define parable as follows:

Parable = Metaphoricity + Narrativity

A parable—whether it is short, medium-length, or long—is a metaphor expanded into a story, or, more simply, *a parable is a metaphorical story*. But what is a metaphor, what is a story, and how does their combination as metaphorical story differ from any other type of story—from, say, the novel you have just read or the film you have just seen?

Metaphor. The term "metaphor" comes from two Greek roots; one is *meta*, "over" or "across," and the other is *pherein*, "to bear" or "to carry." Metaphor means "carrying something over" from one thing to another and thereby "seeing something as another" or "speaking of something as another." Think of a simple, everyday clichéd example: "The clouds are sailing across the sea." That description is metaphorical, because it *sees* the blue sky *as* the blue sea and it *sees* the white clouds *as* white-sailed ships. A metaphor is "seeing as" or "speaking as."

We have, of course, no problem with recognizing *small* metaphors like the one just given or all the other tiny ones that crowd our ordinary speech—especially, for example, in proverbs. It is the *big* ones that are as dangerous as they are inevitable. When a metaphor gets big, it is called "tradition"; when it gets bigger, it is called "reality"; when it gets biggest of all, it is called "evolution" or even "god." The problem is not that we use metaphors all the time, but that we tend to forget or ignore their presence. They are, however, the tectonic plates of language, and it is never wise to forget or ignore tectonic plates. (That's a metaphor.)

Story. A story or narrative is a sequence of linked events with a beginning, middle, and end. As I write this Prologue, *The King's Speech* has just received four of the 2011 Oscars. It is a story, because it has a tensive sequence with a *beginning*, when King George VI ascends England's wartime throne incapacitated for public speaking by a stutter; a *middle*, when a speech therapist, as kind as he is draconian, works to cure him; and an *end*, when the king gives a fully successful Christmas radio address to the embattled British Empire.

Metaphorical Story. An *ordinary story*—think of that one just given—wants you to focus *internally* on itself, to follow the development of character and plot, to wonder what will happen next and how it will all end. It wants you to get *into* the story and not *out* of it. A story fails when we say, "I just can't get into it," or "It never held my attention." In fact, a standard novel or film may want you *not* to wander outside itself, lest you realize how unlikely and unbelievable the whole thing is.

On the other hand, a parable, that is, a *metaphorical story*, always points *externally* beyond itself, points to some different and much wider referent. Whatever its actual content is, a parable is never about *that* content. Whatever its internal subject, a parable always points you toward and wants you to go to some external referent.

That is why Franz Kafka's parable "My Destination" is also a paradigmatic parable of parabling. In that very, very short story, when the servant asks his master where he is going, he replies:

> "I don't know . . . only away from here, away from here. Always away from here. Only by doing so can I reach my destination."
>
> "Then you know your destination?" [the servant] asked.
>
> "Yes," [he] said. "I have already said so. Away-from-here, that is my destination."

From literal to metaphorical register and from specific microcosm to general macrocosm, "away-from-here" is the destination of any parable.

Think, for example, of Jesus's parable about the Sower in Mark 4:3–9. It tells the story of a farmer spreading seed on different kinds of soil. But the earliest hearers and the latest readers know immediately that, whatever it is about, it is *not* about sowing. Jesus is not trying to improve the agricultural yield of lower Galilee. It is about "away from sowing." But whither and why? The Greek roots of "parable" combine *para*, "with" or "alongside," and *ballein*, "to put" or "to throw." In Jesus's parable, "sowing" is cast alongside and compared with some other activity—but what is that other activity? And that question leads directly into the next chapter, where we will consider that Sower parable in much greater detail. We will see there how Mark tells us what—*positively*—it is about, granted that—*negatively*—it is not "about," but "away from" sowing seed in the ground.

Parables Told by Jesus

CHAPTER I

Riddle Parables

So That They May Not Understand

Nessun dorma—"Nobody sleeps tonight"—proclaims the Princess Turandot in Giacomo Puccini's final opera, *Turandot*, unfinished at his death in 1924. Nobody can sleep because a riddle must be solved before the dawn. Here is Princess Turandot's tale.

In the long distant past, her ancestor, the Princess Lo-u-Ling, ruled wisely and well until she was raped and killed by an invading prince. In revenge, her descendant, Princess Turandot, decreed that any man who wished to marry her must answer three riddles—failure would entail beheading, and success, betrothing. Even as the opera opens, the handsome young Prince of Persia goes to his execution with Princess Turandot's gleeful consent. Despite that, the newly arrived Prince of Tartary declares himself ready for the three riddles. This is the first one:

Princess Turandot: "What is born each night and dies each dawn?"
Prince of Tartary: "Hope."

He is correct, and then comes this next riddle:

> Princess Turandot: "What flickers red and warm like a flame,
> but is not fire?"
> Prince of Tartary: "Blood."

Again he is correct, and it is time for the final riddle:

> Princess Turandot: "What is like ice, but burns like fire?"
> Prince of Tartary: "Turandot!"

He has won the contest, but offers the princess one final way out of the marriage. If she can guess his name by morning, he will be executed and she will be liberated. Otherwise, they will marry. And so nobody is to sleep that night, as all must seek to solve the riddle of the prince's true name.

Princess Turandot tortures the servant Liu, who alone knows the prince's name, but Liu kills herself to protect his secret. But the prince himself tells Princess Turandot that his name is Calaf and leaves his fate in her hands. Finally, then, she announces she knows his name. It is "Love" and they live happily ever after.

We think today of riddles as "gotcha games," as puns or plays on words more appropriate between children or between children and adults, where the latter must say they don't know even when they do. But in folklore—as with Princess Turandot's story—they were often lethal contests in which failure to guess correctly could get you a coffin and success could gain you a kingdom. They were archetypal struggles between ignorance and knowledge and, as so often in life itself, ignorance could get you killed.

FOUR QUESTIONS STRUCTURE THIS chapter, and each leads onward from the preceding one's answer. First, did lethal riddle parables— like those in *Turandot*—exist in the Mediterranean world *before* Jesus. Second, are Jesus's own stories best seen as such riddles with potentially profound consequences—either negative or positive? The answer to that question involves a close reading of Mark 4—as promised at the end of the Prologue—and Mark clearly answers it affirmatively. Third, why did Mark interpret Jesus's parables as riddle parables. Finally, was that understanding actually the intention of Jesus or only the (mis)interpretation of Mark?

THIS CHAPTER'S FIRST QUESTION is whether such potentially fatal linguistic contests as just seen in *Turandot* existed within Jesus's own Greek and Roman environment or his own Jewish and biblical tradition. Two very famous cases answer that question with a very definite and very emphatic affirmative response.

The first case is that of *Oedipus and the Sphinx*. Sophocles's ninety-year life spanned the entire fifth century BCE at Athens. The greatest play of this great tragedian is—in Aristotle's famous judgment—*Oedipus the King*, of 429 BCE.

The great Oracle at Delphi warns King Laius and Queen Jocasta of Thebes that their son will kill his father and marry his mother. Laius orders a servant to kill their newborn son, but the servant simply abandons him on a hillside. He is saved and reared by some shepherds and later adopted by the king and queen of Corinth. When he eventually discovers that they are not his real parents, he consults that ever helpful Delphic Oracle, who gives him the same warning about killing his father and marrying his mother. He accordingly decides not to return to Corinth, but heads instead—you got it—for Thebes.

On the way there he has a row with another man and kills him. All unknown to him, he has just murdered his father, Laius. And so, halfway into his terrible destiny, he arrives at the gates of Thebes. The entrance is protected by the Sphinx, a human-headed lioness, who poses a riddle to every traveler wishing to enter the city. The penalty for incomprehension is to be eaten alive by the monster. That was clearly bad for trade, so the city grew lean as the Sphinx grew fat. Here is that lethal contest:

Sphinx's riddle: "What walks on four feet in the morning, two in the afternoon, and three at night?"

Oedipus's response: "Human beings: as infants, they crawl on all fours, as adults, they walk on two legs, and, in old age, they rely on a walking stick."

He is, of course, correct, and the Sphinx immediately kills herself. Thebes is liberated, Oedipus marries the newly widowed Queen Jocasta, thus having unknowingly killed his father and married his mother. Sophocles's great play opens on the tragic outcome for all concerned.

That is the most famous riddle in the Greek tradition and, indeed, it is hard to decide whether success or failure in solving it would have been the better fate for Oedipus, Jocasta, and all of Thebes. But, one way or another, riddle parables are not childish games, but lethally serious adult contests. Success means great gain; failure means great loss. And, as we see next, the same fatal threat hangs over riddle parables in the biblical tradition.

The second case, then, is that of *Samson and the Lion.* The story of Samson appears in Judges 13–16 and is, among other things, a severe warning against intermarriage between Israelites and non-Israelites. "Is there not a woman among your kin, or among all our people," said his father and mother, "that you must go to take a wife from the uncircumcised Philistines?" (14:3). Samson was a Hercules-like figure who protected his people from threats and dangers, but was, unfortunately, a terribly slow learner when it came to women—not to speak of having a problem with anger management. At that time Israel's particular enemies were the Philistines, who invaded Egypt possibly from Mycenean Crete in 1190 BCE. Repulsed by Egypt, they settled on the southern coast of Canaan and eventually became a serious military threat to Israel—despite what David's slingshot did to their Goliath in single combat between the assembled armies.

Samson's preference for Philistine women involved, first, the unnamed woman of Timnah (14:1); then, the unnamed prostitute of

Gaza (16:1); and, finally, Delilah of Sorek (16:4). I focus here on that first woman and, once again, a riddle contest results—eventually—in death. On his way to propose to the woman of Timnah, Samson was attacked by a young lion, but "he tore the lion apart barehanded as one might tear apart a kid" (14:6). Later, when he went back to marry his betrothed, he found that bees had made honey in the lion's carcass, and he scooped it up and ate it on his way.

His Philistine in-laws gave Samson thirty companions for the wedding feast. "Let me now put a riddle to you," Samson said to them. "If you can explain it to me within the seven days of the feast, and find it out, then I will give you thirty linen garments and thirty festal garments. But if you cannot explain it to me, then you shall give me thirty linen garments and thirty festal garments" (14:12–13). Here is the riddle:

Out of the eater came something to eat.
Out of the strong came something sweet. (14:14)

Not exactly a fair riddle, by the way, as it involved private information they could never have guessed.

So, "on the fourth day they said to Samson's wife, 'Coax your husband to explain the riddle to us, or we will burn you and your father's house with fire. Have you invited us here to impoverish us?'" (14:15). Samson eventually succumbs to her insistence, and his thirty wedding companions triumphantly ask:

What is sweeter than honey?
What is stronger than a lion? (14:18)

Samson knows that they have cheated by using his wife against him. The result is that "the spirit of the Lord rushed on him, and he went down to Ashkelon. He killed thirty men of the town, took their spoil, and gave the festal garments to those who had explained the riddle" (14:19). Even after that, the riddle's lethal effects continue.

Samson, however, considers the woman of Timnah to be his wife and, finding that her father had given her to his best man instead, he "burned up the shocks and the standing grain, as well as the vineyards and olive groves" of the Philistines (15:5). They, in turn, burned the woman of Timnah and her father (15:6). And, in revenge, Samson "struck them down hip and thigh with great slaughter" (15:8). Widely throughout folklore and legend riddles carry with them the smell of death.

With *Turandot*, Oedipus, and Samson we have stories that contain riddles rather than riddle stories. Those riddles are crucial to, but simply imbedded in wider narratives. But what if a riddle expanded to fill the entire story, so that its major point and even the minor points within it all presented hearers or readers with riddle upon riddle upon riddle? A riddle—as seen in those three cases—is usually just a one-sentence puzzle or mystery. When a one-sentence *riddle question* is expanded into a *riddle narrative*, not only the general story itself, but even its multiple parts each and all point elsewhere. Such riddle parables are also called *allegories*—from the Greek roots for "other" and "speak." In riddle parables or allegories the whole story and also each of its component parts "speak" of something "other." With them, not only the whole story, but all its elements must be decoded.

The answer to this chapter's first question, therefore, is that potentially lethal riddles existed both outside and inside the biblical tradition in the Mediterranean world before Jesus.

I TURN NOW TO this chapter's second question. Are some, most, or all of the parables of Jesus to be understood as riddle parables—also called allegories, as mentioned above? Is *riddle parable* the major type of parable preferred by Jesus? An emphatically positive answer is found in the Gospel according to Mark, and, since Mark is the earliest of the four gospels in our present New Testament, that answer demands careful study.

First, Mark gives us Jesus's Sower parable and interprets it item by item as a riddle parable (4:1–20). He also cites it as a model or paradigm for the other parables of Jesus, so that all are taken as riddle parables. Finally, in the best riddling tradition, those parables have profoundly important consequences. Success in understanding them gains you the kingdom of God. Failure to understand them results not in physical, but in spiritual death. Here, then, is Mark on Jesus's Sower parable—as a short drama in two acts.

The first act opens at the Sea of Galilee. Jesus "got into a boat on the sea and sat there, while the whole crowd was beside the sea on the land." He taught them "many things in parables" (4:1–2). Notice, immediately, that plural use of "parables." It's worth noting because only the single parable of the Sower follows in 4:3–8 before the disciples ask him "about the parables," again in the plural, in 4:10.

Why that sequence of first *plural* "parables," then the *single* Sower parable, and finally, once again, that mention of *plural* "parables"? Mark is emphasizing that this single example of the Sower is a *paradigm* for parables, a model for all the others. If you understand this one parable, he says, you will understand all parables. If not, you will not understand any of them.

Here, then, is that paradigmatic parable (my numbers added):

A sower went out to sow.

[1] And as he sowed, some seed fell on the path, and the birds came and ate it up.

[2] Other seed fell on rocky ground, where it did not have much soil, and it sprang up quickly, since it had no depth of soil. And when the sun rose, it was scorched; and since it had no root, it withered away.

[3] Other seed fell among thorns, and the thorns grew up and choked it, and it yielded no grain.

[4] Other seed fell into good soil and brought forth grain, growing up and increasing and yielding thirty and sixty and a hundredfold. (4:3–8)

No further explanation of that parable is given to the crowd before the first act ends.

The second act opens with Jesus leaving the crowd and speaking privately with his disciples. Then, "while he was alone, those who were around him along with the twelve asked him about the parables" (4:10). There is that second *plural* use of "parables." The Sower is a parable for all parables, a parable about parables and parabling. What does Jesus say in response to the disciples' question?

Their first query was not just about the Sower, but "about the parables." Why, they ask, use such images, figures, metaphors? Why parables? Why not open, literal, straightforward teaching? The answer from Jesus is rather shocking:

"To you has been given the secret of the kingdom of God, but for those outside, everything comes in parables; in order that

'they may indeed look, but not perceive,
may indeed listen, but not understand;
so that they may not turn again and be forgiven'"
(Isa. 6:10)

And he said to them, "Do you not understand this parable? Then how will you understand all the parables?" (4:11–13)

Those are surely some of the most stunning words ever uttered by Jesus. You could take them in two ways—one malign, one benign, but both bad.

It is possible to give that declaration a somewhat benign reading by saying that the effect of Jesus's riddle parables is cited as their purpose. The incomprehension of the audience is recorded as if were the intention of Jesus.

You find that same structure, for example, in the book of Exodus, as Moses attempts to liberate the enslaved Hebrews from Egyptian bondage and Pharaoh keeps refusing. Watch how the causality shifts from what Pharaoh did to God and becomes what God did to Pharaoh:

Pharaoh hardened his heart. (8:15, 32; 9:34)

Pharaoh's heart was hardened. (7:13–14, 22; 8:19; 9:7, 35)

God hardened Pharaoh's heart. (9:12; 10:1, 20, 27; 11:10; 14:8)

What Pharaoh did to God as effect, result, and consequence becomes attributed to God as cause, intention, and purpose.

Mark, however, does not seem to want any such benign reading. He is not saying that the unintended result of Jesus's parables was incomprehension. He is saying that incomprehension was already there in response to Jesus's message and Jesus therefore used riddle parables to increase and punish that incomprehension. According to Mark, prior rejection of Jesus by his listeners begets counter-rejection by Jesus of those listeners—through riddle parables. Mark's interpretation, therefore, is that Jesus's parables were deliberately intended to be incomprehensible to outsiders, the opponents, but comprehensible—with special interpretation from Jesus—to insiders, the disciples.

THAT BRINGS US TO the third question for this chapter. Why did Mark interpret Jesus's parables as punitive riddle parables for his opponents that required private interpretation for his followers? My answer derives from specific passages in Mark—in Chapters 3 and 4 as well as in Chapters 7 and 12.

I begin with Mark 3. Here is Mark's vision of the gospel: "After John was arrested, Jesus came to Galilee, proclaiming the good news of God, and saying, 'The time is fulfilled, and the kingdom of God has come near; repent, and believe in the good news'" (1:14–15). But from 2:1 onward, Jesus meets with repeated opposition, which reaches a climax when "the Pharisees went out and immediately conspired with the Herodians against him, how to destroy him" (3:6).

Next comes this incident: "His family . . . went out to restrain him, for people were saying, 'He has gone out of his mind.' And the scribes who came down from Jerusalem said, 'He has Beelzebul, and by the ruler of the demons he casts out demons'" (3:21–22). It is in immediate response to that absolute insult that Mark first mentions Jesus's use of parables:

> He called them to him, and spoke to them in *parables*, "How can Satan cast out Satan? If a kingdom is divided against itself, that kingdom cannot stand. And if a house is divided against itself, that house will not be able to stand. And if Satan has risen up against himself and is divided, he cannot stand, but his end has come. But no one can enter a strong man's house and plunder his property without first tying up the strong man; then indeed the house can be plundered." (3:23–27)

After that inaugural use of parables in 3:23, it is not surprising to find them understood in Mark 4 as Jesus's rejection of rejection, as riddle parables intending to extend and condemn prior rejection.

I return to Mark 4 and have already mentioned that when a *riddle query*—as with Samson, Oedipus, or Turandot—is expanded by narrative into a *riddle parable*, it is usually called an *allegory*. Here is how Mark's Jesus explains the riddle parable or allegory of the Sower when he is alone with the disciples (my numbers, as before):

The sower sows the word.

[1] These are the ones on the path where the word is sown: when they hear, Satan immediately comes and takes away the word that is sown in them.

[2] And these are the ones sown on rocky ground: when they hear the word, they immediately receive it with joy. But they have no root, and endure only for a while; then, when trouble or persecution arises on account of the word, immediately they fall away.

[3] And others are those sown among the thorns: these are

the ones who hear the word, but the cares of the world, and the lure of wealth, and the desire for other things come in and choke the word, and it yields nothing.

[4] And these are the ones sown on the good soil: they hear the word and accept it and bear fruit, thirty and sixty and a hundredfold. (4:14–20)

Birds as Satan? Rocks as temptations? Thorns as desires? That certainly seems to be a riddle story intending, first, incomprehension and, then, condemnation: "*in order that . . . so that* they may not turn again and be forgiven." Even if you guessed that "sowing" meant "teaching," how could you ever get all those other details correct? And a riddle demands that you get *all* its details correct: for Oedipus, "four" means infancy, "two" adulthood, and "three" senility; for Mark, "birds" mean Satan, "rocks" persecution, and "thorns" temptation. Get all or you get none.

I turn next to Mark 7. A situation similar to the one in Mark 4 appears in Mark 7. "When the Pharisees and some of the scribes who had come from Jerusalem gathered around him," they criticized some of his disciples (7:1–5). Jesus responds by calling them "hypocrites" who "abandon the commandment of God and hold to human tradition" (7:6, 8). It is, once again, in that confrontational situation that Jesus first speaks publicly to "the crowd" (7:14) and then, "when he had left the crowd and entered the house, his disciples asked him about the parable" (7:17). For Mark, parables intend to reject those who have already rejected Jesus.

My final focus is Mark 12. That inaugural series of bitter controversies at the start of Jesus's public life in Mark 2–3 looks to that other series at its end in Mark 11–12. And, once again, we find Jesus speaking "parables" in the midst of lethal confrontation:

He began to speak to them in parables. "A man planted a vineyard, put a fence around it, dug a pit for the wine press, and built a watchtower; then he leased it to tenants and went to another country. . . ." When they [the chief priests, the scribes, and the elders of 11:27] realized that he had told this parable against them, they wanted to arrest him, but they feared the crowd. So they left him and went away. (12:1, 12)

For Mark, from 3:23–27 through 4:11–13 and 7:17 into 12:1, 12, Jesus tells "parables" in the midst of rejection by hearers as his own counterrejection of those hearers.

ALL OF THAT IS clear enough—for Mark. But that leaves us with the fourth and final question for this chapter. Were incomprehensible riddle parables Jesus's deliberate punishment for prior incomprehension, his counterrejection for prior rejection? Was that Jesus's intention or Mark's (mis)understanding?

I do not consider that counterrejection was Jesus's purpose for his parables—even if you consider them riddles or allegories. The main reason is that Mark contradicts himself on the function of parables as creating incomprehension and thereby guaranteeing condemnation. Here are five examples from Mark 4 itself.

First, Mark's interpretation contradicts his own opening emphasis at the start of this chapter of parables. "Jesus began to *teach* beside the sea. . . . He began to *teach* them many things in parables, and in his *teaching* he said to them" (4:1–2). The parable of the Sower follows. But what teacher teaches *in order to* create incomprehension? Teaching may often result in incomprehension, but that is usually not the intention of teachers; rather, they usually teach in order to bring clarity and understanding.

Also, Mark's interpretation even contradicts the framing words used by Jesus for the Sower parable itself. He opens with "Listen" and closes with "Let anyone with ears to hear listen!" Fair translations would be: "You have ears, use them! Listen! Think! Respond!

Comprehend!" Why would Mark emphasize listening, if he believed incomprehension was the goal?

Next, what about the parable of the Lamp a few verses later? "Is a lamp brought in to be put under the bushel basket, or under the bed, and not on the lampstand? For there is nothing hidden, except to be disclosed; nor is anything secret, except to come to light. Let anyone with ears to hear listen!" (4:21–23). That is not a program for incomprehension and, once again, it concludes with that challenge to use your ears.

Furthermore, Mark ends this chapter of parables with this summary: "With many such parables he spoke the word to them, as they were able to hear it; he did not speak to them except in parables, but he explained everything in private to his disciples" (4:33–34). So "they," that is, the crowd, were able "to hear" some of the parables?

Finally, the parable of the Sower *itself* in Mark 4:3–9 and its detailed *interpretation* in 4:14–20 contradict Mark's reading of Jesus's purpose for this particular parable as a paradigm for all parables. Think about it this way.

Jesus gave not only three types of bad soil, but also three types of good soil in Mark's version of the riddle parable. Thus there are three types of loss but also three degrees of gain: "Other seed fell into good soil and brought forth grain, growing up and increasing and yielding thirty and sixty and a hundredfold" (4:8). Good soil yields thirty, better soil yields sixty, and the best soil yields a hundredfold. That is later explained allegorically: "These are the ones sown on the good soil: they hear the word and accept it and bear fruit, thirty and sixty and a hundredfold" (4:20).

The three types of bad soil get extensive commentary, but nothing more is said about the three types of good soil. They are not interpreted allegorically. Are they not important? One of Mark's most careful and most critical early readers was Luke. He saw that problem and rewrote Mark to avoid it. He ends the parable with this: "Some fell into good soil, and when it grew, it produced a hundredfold" (Luke 8:8). And the interpretation reads like this: "As for that in the good soil, these are the ones who, when they hear the word, hold it fast in an honest and good heart, and bear fruit with patient endurance" (Luke 8:15). Luke gives three modes of failure, but only one of success.

Does not that balance of three modes of failure with three degrees of success *inside* the parable itself negate that outside interpretation of its purpose as incomprehension—with or without condemnation? If the audience easily recognizes the three degrees of failure (birds, rocks, thorns), how would it interpret those three degrees of success (thirty, sixty, hundredfold)—even in the literal microcosm of sowing? Jesus's parable seems quite ready to expect and accept degrees of failure and of success. I conclude that, at least pending further investigation, Mark's interpretation of Jesus's parables as riddle parables intending incomprehension and thereby generating condemnation is not appropriate or adequate to the intention of Jesus.

THIS CHAPTER'S SUBTITLE, "So That They May Not Understand," is a motto or mantra for riddle parable as a whole. I began the chapter with the opera *Turandot* as a modern overture to emphasize that, in the ancient world, riddles were not childish word games, but potentially lethal word contests. That opening was followed by answers to four questions.

The first question asked whether such lethal word duels existed in the Mediterranean world of Jesus. Oedipus's sphinx story and Samson's lion story gave us a resoundingly affirmative answer. Lethal riddle parables were there, in other words, as possible models for Jesus's own parables.

The second question was whether those parables of Jesus were best seen as riddle parables—not just stories with riddles in them, but riddles with stories in them. Mark's interpretation of the Sower parable as paradigm for all the rest gave us another resounding yes.

The third question asked why Mark chose the Sower as a punitive riddle parable and, indeed, as his master model for all the parables of Jesus. Why did he think that Jesus intended public incomprehension for the many, mitigated only by private interpretation for the few? Because, for Mark, rejection *of* Jesus by hearers begot counterrejection *by* Jesus of those hearers.

The final question was whether Mark was correct in that understanding of Jesus's parabolic intention. My response was strongly negative, because it is contradicted by the very context of Mark 4, with, for example, its parable of the Lamp. Parables are no more meant for noncomprehension than a lamp is intended for nonlight.

Granted, from this chapter, that Jesus's parables were not intended as riddle parables for punitive incomprehension, were they intended as example parables for ethical admonition? That will be the basic question for the next chapter, and I will detail its structure and sequence after the chapter's introduction.

CHAPTER 2

Example Parables

GO AND DO—OR DON'T DO—LIKEWISE

ONCE UPON A TIME, LONG, long ago, theologians used to debate whether God was all-present, all-knowing, and all-powerful. That, of course, is not God, but Google. If you look up "parable" in that ethereal omniscience, it refers you to *Wikipedia*, which defines parable as "a brief, succinct story, in prose or verse, that illustrates a moral or religious lesson. It differs from a fable in that fables use animals, plants, inanimate objects, and forces of nature as characters, while parables generally feature human characters." That is a very common definition of parables, but I cite it here to qualify it in the light of my own different definition in the Prologue.

First, the distinction between *fables* as unrealistic and impossible examples (think about animals or trees talking to one another) and *parables* as realistic and possible examples (think about servants and masters talking to one another) goes back to Aristotle's *Art of Rhetoric* (2.20) from the fourth century BCE. I will not make any use of it in this book, although, of course, Jesus uses parables rather than fables—in Aristotle's sense. Aesop, for example, who lived between 620 and 560 BCE and is cited by Aristotle, told fables about animals, people, and people with animals. I would simply call all of those stories in *Aesop's Fables* example parables.

Second, *Wikipedia* gives us a very common interpretation of parables that, unfortunately to my mind, defines the genre of parable by identifying it with one—but only one—of its types. In other words, *parables are identified and equated with example parables.* I do not accept that equation in this book. Instead, I use the term *example parables* for one—but only for one—perfectly valid type of parable. In this book, example parables are moral models or ethical stories that consciously and deliberately point metaphorically beyond themselves from literal microcosm to macrocosm, from one clear content to far, far wider implications and applications.

FOUR QUESTIONS WILL, ONCE again, structure the sequence of this chapter. First, what exactly are example parables? I answer by looking at two stories from the Jewish tradition *after* the time of Jesus. Second, did example parables exist in the biblical tradition *before* the time of Jesus. I answer affirmatively and give several instances, some short, some long. Third, are example parables—as seen, for example, in Luke's gospel—the best model for some, most, or all of Jesus's parables? Finally, does this understanding of Jesus's parables as example parables represent the actual intention of Jesus or only the (mis)interpretation of Luke?

I BEGIN, THEN, IN answer to this chapter's first question, with two case studies to indicate the style and mode of what I mean by example parables. The first case study is from rabbinic Judaism in the Babylonian Talmud, that great compendium of Jewish law and wisdom, ethics and thought, history and tradition, first published around 500 CE. The parable of the Blind and the Lame is cited in *Sanhedrin* 91b and attributed to Rabbi Judah ha-Nasi from the end of the second century CE. It ponders what God would do if, on the day of judgment, Soul and Body blamed each other and declared their own innocence. Body blames Soul, and Soul blames Body. Each says it was the other that sinned and, now that they have been separated by death, each claims no responsibility for evil. Each claims innocence!

The problem is solved in this example parable by illustrating how a human ruler would handle it. A king appointed two guards—one blind and one lame—to protect his beautiful fig orchard. The lame man saw the figs, got up on the blind man's shoulders, and together they ate the figs. When the figs were discovered missing, each guard claimed innocence. "I could not see any figs," said the blind one. "I could not get to them," said the lame man. The king's solution was to simply put the lame man back on the blind man's shoulders and punish them both at the same time. The parable concludes with this application: "So the Holy One, blessed be He, will bring the soul and place it in the body and judge them both as one." It is quite clear that, in this parable, what the human ruler did is a metaphorical, micro-cosmic, and illustrative *example* of what the divine ruler will do.

The second case study of an example parable is from Hasidic Judaism, that mystical tradition of joyful popular devotion emphasizing song, dance, and story that was founded by Rabbi Israel ben Eliezer, known as the Baal Shem Tov, or "Master of the Good Name." It is the parable of the Rooster Prince and it comes from his great-grandson, Rabbi Nachman of Breslov, who lived from 1772 to 1810, in what is now the Ukraine.

"Once there was a prince," starts the parable, "who went mad and insisted he was a rooster." He took off all his clothes, started to cluck, and ate his food off the floor under the table. Nothing and nobody could cure him until a Hasidic rabbi arrived at the palace. He took off all his own clothes and got to know the prince by sitting naked under the table as another rooster.

Then one day the rabbi started to put on pants. The prince protested that roosters did not wear pants. "But," responded the rabbi, "why cannot roosters be just as warm and comfortable as human beings?" The prince agreed and put on pants. Next, the rabbi put on a warm shirt and, when the prince protested, he gave him the same answer—with the same result. Finally, the prince followed the rabbi into a full complement of clothes, human manners, and use of table utensils, so that he was completely cured.

Both of those stories are example parables and demonstrate—in answer to this chapter's first question—what I mean by that style of parable. The Talmudic one is explicitly framed with application and interpretation. It uses human action as an illustrative example for divine action. It tells you exactly what it means. The Hasidic one does not give any framing interpretation, but it offers one case of human action and leaves it open for hearers or readers to apply it across a wide spectrum of how anyone—from the divine to the human—could and should act. Example parables are metaphorical and microcosmic models, illustrations, paradigms, or examples of religious theory, moral practice, or, indeed, any wider mode of action or style of life.

I NOW MOVE TO this chapter's second question. We have just seen two Jewish example parables from many centuries *after* the time of Jesus. But what about *before* it? The question now is whether example parables existed in the biblical tradition before Jesus. It is clear that they did from the following two instances.

My first case study comes from the biblical book of Judges, which tells how Israel, having escaped from lethal slavery in Egypt and trekked through the Sinai desert, entered the land of Canaan—inhabited, of course, by Canaanites. During the two centuries from around 1200 to 1000 BCE individual tribes—and not a unified people—struggled slowly but successfully against local or regional opponents such as the Canaanites, Moabites, Ammonites, Amalekites, Midianites, and Philistines.

In those early years, tribal leadership was charismatic and temporary rather than institutional and permanent. The separate tribes depended on "deliverers" in wartime and "judges" in peacetime. They had—quite happily—no kings with established dynastic succession.

Their ancient stories were initially passed down orally—warts and all—as sagas of tribal defeat and tribal triumph.

My present interest is with one of those ancient tribal tales, this time in Judges 9, and especially with the parable in 9:8–15. It concerns the heroic leader Jerubbaal (Gideon), who had many wives and concubines and seventy sons, the youngest of whom was named Jotham. He also had a son named Abimelech by a slave woman who was probably a Canaanite.

Abimelech killed all of Jerubbaal's other sons except Jotham, and he proposed that his fellow Canaanites make him not just tribal chieftain, but king over his native city-state of Shechem (9:1–3). But Jotham, the only other surviving son of Jerubbaal, counters his half brother's proposal using this parable of the Trees.

Once upon a time the other trees invited first the olive, next the fig, and then the vine to "reign over" them. They all refused, since producing oil or fruit or wine was a far more important function than starting "to sway over the trees." Finally, therefore, the trees had to appeal to the bramble:

> And the bramble said to the trees, "If in good faith you are anointing me king over you, then come and take refuge in my shade; but if not, let fire come out of the bramble and devour the cedars of Lebanon." (9:15)

It is very easy to understand that parable—with or without its context—since "reign" and "king" give it away immediately. Those who are gracious and productive are too busy to rule over others; only those who are unproductive and dangerous have time to do so.

Furthermore, the bramble that easily spreads fire is a perfect symbol for Abimelech. Later, when enmity breaks out between Abimelech and the Shechemites, he fires "brushwood" to destroy their citadel (9:49). Later still, when Abimelech attempts the same fire attack on the citadel of Thebez, Shechem's nearby ally, "a certain woman threw an upper millstone on Abimelech's head, and crushed his skull" (9:53).

The driving force behind that parable is both antimonarchical and anti-ecumenical. First, it is antimonarchical, because it is in favor of charismatic tribal leaders certified by military success or judicial prowess and not the fire-prone "bramble" of monarchy. Second, it is anti-ecumenical, because it is in favor of completely separating Israelites from Canaanites. The Israelite Jerubbaal and a Canaanite slave woman were the parents of Abimelech and, says the parable, look what happened! It is a warning example parable of what *not* to do.

My second case study of an example parable from the Old Testament is in 2 Samuel 12:1–4. It dates to the time when dynastic kings had replaced charismatic judges as Israel's official leaders. The parable of the Trees, apparently, had no lasting effect! The immediate context of the parable is the reign of David as the 1000s turned into the 900s BCE.

It was, so the story starts, "the spring of the year, the time when kings go out to battle" (2 Sam. 11:1); but David, king of Israel, did not lead his army himself. Instead, he ordered his commander, Joab, to attack the Ammonites and besiege their capital city of Rabbah or Rabbath Ammon—today's Amman, the capital of the Hashemite Kingdom of Jordan.

From his palace in Jerusalem David saw a beautiful woman bathing on the flat roof of a nearby house. She was "Bathsheba, daughter of Eliam, the wife of Uriah the Hittite" (11:2–3), a foreign captain serving under Joab before the walls of Rabbah. David had intercourse with Bathsheba, she conceived, and, as so often since, a cover-up causes the plot to thicken—and sicken.

David orders Uriah home on leave, gives him a present, and tells him to "go down to his house" and "wash his feet" (11:8). But, out of respect for the rest of the army fighting away from homes and wives, Uriah remains apart from Bathsheba. David then invites him back to eat in the palace and gets him drunk, but still Uriah will not go home to his wife. Finally, David sends Uriah back to the siege and orders

Joab to "set Uriah in the forefront of the hardest fighting, and then draw back from him, so that he may be struck down and die" (11:15).

God's response is immediate. The prophet Nathan comes to David and tells him this parable of the Poor Man's Lamb:

> There were two men in a certain city, the one rich and the other poor. The rich man had very many flocks and herds; but the poor man had nothing but one little ewe lamb, which he had bought. He brought it up, and it grew up with him and with his children; it used to eat of his meager fare, and drink from his cup, and lie in his bosom, and it was like a daughter to him. Now there came a traveler to the rich man, and he was loath to take one of his own flock or herd to prepare for the wayfarer who had come to him, but he took the poor man's lamb, and prepared that for the guest who had come to him. (2 Sam. 12:1–4)

Although a ruler should always be apprehensive at the approach of a prophet, David walks right into Nathan's parabolic trap:

> Then David's anger was greatly kindled against the man. He said to Nathan, "As the Lord lives, the man who has done this deserves to die; he shall restore the lamb fourfold, because he did this thing, and because he had no pity."
> Nathan said to David, "You are the man!" (2 Sam. 12:5–7a)

The rich man took the "one little ewe lamb" of the poor man and therefore, says David, he deserved death. But at least he did not murder him as David had murdered Uriah, so David judges himself deserving of worse than death. Nathan then recounts all that God will do to punish David, saying, "The sword shall never depart from your house" (12:10), and David has the grace—finally—to acknowledge, "I have sinned against the Lord" (12:13)—not to mention against Bathsheba and Uriah.

Once again, that example parable is easily decoded—at least for us at this safe distance. David is the rich man with "very many herds and flocks," that is, his own wives and concubines. Uriah is the poor man with "one little ewe lamb," that is, his wife Bathsheba. And so the rich man "takes" the poor man's only lamb. It is simple enough to move from the literal to the metaphorical register and from the microcosmic to the macrocosmic level.

Those two example parables are very short paragraph-length ones, even if their contexts are quite involved. But the biblical tradition also contains chapter-length and even book-length example parables before the time of Jesus.

The best known chapter-length example parables are in Daniel 1–6. Those example parables imagine Jewish sages as royal courtiers under the Babylonian or Median emperors in the 600s and 500s BCE. The most famous ones are the example parables about the three youths in the fiery furnace under the Babylonian ruler Nebuchadnezzar (Dan. 3) and Daniel in the lions' den under the Median monarch Darius (Dan. 6).

Their moral message is very clear. Those Jews who remained faithful to their ancestral traditions and covenantal commitments were magnificently successful as courtiers in the royal palace. The *message by example* is that Jewishness is an asset and not a liability because, if you stay faithful to God, God will protect you and all will be well.

Longer book-length example stories are found both in the Hebrew and Protestant canons of the Bible and also outside them in those of the Roman Catholic and Greek Orthodox traditions. Among the latter are such example parables as the book of Judith, named after its heroine, who is imagined as saving her people by killing a general named Holofernes, sent against her people by Nebuchadnezzar of Babylon.

An alternate mode of resistance to Assyrian oppression is depicted by the example parable of the book of Tobit, named after its main character, Tobit, who was exiled to Nineveh after the Assyrian destruction of northern Israel in the late 700s BCE. Before and after

Tobit's deportation he remained absolutely faithful to God and everything worked out for the best, despite his own many difficulties and his family's many dangers.

Finally, the book-length example parable of Esther is found in all those varied canons. It is named after the heroine who saved her people under the Persian monarch Ahasuerus/Xerxes. All three of those example-parable books show that living with great courage, covenantal fidelity, and traditional piety always ensures a happy ending.

WE HAVE JUST SEEN that example parables are well known in the biblical tradition before Jesus—with paragraph-length, chapter-length, and even book-length versions. That answers affirmatively this chapter's second question and brings me to its third question. Are example parables the best model for Jesus's parables—for some, most, or all of them? I do not ask, by the way, whether there are positive or negative examples *in* the parables of Jesus, but were such examples their primary focus, purpose, and intention?

If Mark thinks of Jesus's parables as riddle parables, Luke thinks of them as example parables, and he has been much more successful than Mark in making that understanding normative for most of later Christian interpretation. Luke's example parables are models of how God or Jesus does or does not act. They can also be models of how we should or should not act. Their theme is: "Go and do—or do not do—likewise." Think, for example, of the three parables in Luke 15.

That chapter opens like this: "All the tax collectors and sinners were coming near to listen to him. And the Pharisees and the scribes were grumbling and saying, 'This fellow welcomes sinners and eats with them'" (15:1–2). The three parables that follow are examples that illustrate and justify the actions of Jesus and thereby refute and negate the accusations of his opponents. They are everyday examples metaphorically and microcosmically supporting what Jesus is doing and opposing what his critics are saying.

The first two parables are a deliberate pair. The parable of the Lost Sheep uses an example from male experience, and the parable of the Lost Coin is taken from female experience:

> Which one of you, having a hundred sheep and losing one of them, does not leave the ninety-nine in the wilderness and go after the one that is lost until he finds it? When he has found it, he lays it on his shoulders and rejoices. And when he comes home, he calls together his friends and neighbors, saying to them, "Rejoice with me, for I have found my sheep that was lost." Just so, I tell you, there will be more joy in heaven over one sinner who repents than over ninety-nine righteous persons who need no repentance. (15:4–7)

> Or what woman having ten silver coins, if she loses one of them, does not light a lamp, sweep the house, and search carefully until she finds it? When she has found it, she calls together her friends and neighbors, saying, "Rejoice with me, for I have found the coin that I had lost." Just so, I tell you, there is joy in the presence of the angels of God over one sinner who repents. (15:8–10)

Those are stories of finding a lost article, whether it is a sheep by a man outside the house or a coin by a woman inside it. Once found, of course, the items are no longer lost—hence communal rejoicing is the appropriate response from all concerned. By analogy, says the Lukan Jesus, that is what I am doing—I am finding/saving the lost ones—"tax collectors and sinners"—and, once found/saved, nobody should grumble, but rather all should rejoice.

Luke then moves from the Lost Sheep and the Lost Coin to the Lost Son, to what we traditionally call the parable of the Prodigal Son. Jesus begins, "There was a man who had two sons" (15:11), and the parable goes on to tell first about the younger son (15:12–24) and then about the elder son (15:25–32).

The younger son asks for and receives "the share of the property that will belong to" him, but then goes into a distant country and wastes his inheritance "in dissolute living." Later, starving in the midst of famine, he feeds pigs that eat better than he does. He decides to return home, where his father welcomes him with open arms, clothes him, and organizes a feast for him, saying, "For *this son of mine* was dead and is alive again; he was lost and is found!" (15:24).

The elder son returns from working in the fields, and the servants tell him about the feast in progress. Angry, he refuses to enter, and complains to his father: "For all these years I have been working like a slave for you, and I have never disobeyed your command; yet you have never given me even a young goat so that I might celebrate with my friends" (15:29). The father responds: "You are always with me, and all that is mine is yours. But we had to celebrate and rejoice, because *this brother of yours* was dead and has come to life; he was lost and has been found" (15:31–32). The parable ends, and we are not told whether the elder son relents.

Once again, that parable fits well with Luke's opening context. The younger, prodigal, or lost son represents those "tax collectors and sinners" (15:1) and, like them, he has been "lost and is found" (15:24, 32). Hence, they had to "celebrate" (15:23, 32). The elder son, who "became angry and refused to go in" (15:28) to the feast, represents those Pharisees and scribes who "grumbled" because Jesus "welcomes sinners and eats with them" (15:2).

Indeed, all three parables—but especially that third one—metaphorically defend this earlier incident in Luke:

> Levi gave a great banquet for him in his house; and there was a large crowd of tax collectors and others sitting at the table with them. The Pharisees and their scribes were complaining to his disciples, saying, "Why do you eat and drink with tax collectors and sinners?" Jesus answered, "Those who are well have no need of a physician, but those who are sick; I have come to call not the righteous but sinners to repentance." (5:29–32)

The three parables of Luke 15 are example parables showing metaphorically and illustrating microcosmically that what Jesus is doing is just common sense and that what his opponents are saying is not the normal response to such situations. All involved should rejoice when "the lost" has been found again. Maybe, then, we can expand Luke's understanding in that chapter to all the other parables of Jesus? Maybe they are not riddle parables—against Mark 4—but example parables—with Luke 15?

THAT BRINGS ME TO this chapter's fourth question—and it echoes what I asked about Mark 4 in the preceding chapter. Is all we just saw—in Luke 15 and with other Lukan parables—Luke's own interpretation or Jesus's intention?

On the one hand, Luke 15 is all very convincing, and you can easily wonder if it is a parable of parabling, a model for all, most, many, or just some of Jesus's parables. On the other hand, I have one rather strong hesitation about Luke 15 even in itself, before it can become a paradigm for other parables.

First, that combination of interpretive context (15:1–3) followed by the three parables of the Lost Sheep (15:4–7), Lost Coin (15:8–10), and Lost Son (15:11–32) is found only in Luke and no other gospel. Next, the parable of the Lost Sheep—and only that one from among the Lukan threesome—is present in Matthew (18:12–14). But the context there is not the external one of Luke 15:1–3 concerning "grumbling" from opponents outside the community. In Matthew it is an internal one concerning "stumbling blocks" within the community. Watch, next, how differently Matthew interprets the Lost Sheep parable.

In Matthew, Jesus says, "Whoever becomes humble like this child is the greatest in the kingdom of heaven" (18:4). Next, he warns about "stumbling blocks" placed before "one of these little ones who believe" in him (18:6). Then he gives us this version of the Lost Sheep parable:

[1] Take care that you do not despise *one of these little ones;* for, I tell you, in heaven their angels continually see the face of my *Father in heaven.*

[2] What do you think? If a shepherd has a hundred sheep, and one of them has gone astray, does he not leave the ninety-nine on the mountains and go in search of the one that went astray? And if he finds it, truly I tell you, he rejoices over it more than over the ninety-nine that never went astray.

[3] So it is not the will of your *Father in heaven* that *one of these little ones* should be lost. (18:10–14)

For Matthew, in other words, the Lost Sheep is not about community outsiders criticizing Jesus as in Luke 15, but about Jesus criticizing community insiders. There is nothing wrong with either use of the same parable, but they are quite different ones. So any tight fit between context and parable in Luke 15 may be due to Luke and not Jesus. How sure can we be, then, that it was an example parable, let alone a model for all of the parables of Jesus?

Finally, the other known—and, in my judgment, independent—version of the parable of the Lost Sheep is in the *Gospel of Thomas,* a collection of the sayings of Jesus given without those narrative contexts present in the New Testament versions:

Jesus said, "The [Father's] kingdom is like a shepherd who had a hundred sheep. One of them, the largest, went astray. He left the ninety-nine and looked for the one until he found it. After he had toiled, he said to the sheep, 'I love you more than the ninety-nine.'" (107)

The overall theology of the *Gospel of Thomas* defends celibate asceticism as the Christian ideal. It imagines a return to the Garden of Eden not only before sin, but even before that inaugural "earthling" was split into female and male. The road back is through celibate asceticism, because by that discipline, says the Jesus of *Thomas,* "you

make the two into one, and when . . . you make male and female
into a single one, so that the male will not be male nor the female be
female . . . then you will enter" the kingdom of God (22).

Within that general theology, the "largest" sheep is that ideal
Christian celibate ascetic whom Jesus loves "more than the ninety-
nine" others. That is, to put it rather mildly, a very different interpretation of the Lost Sheep parable than those of Luke or Matthew. But
all of that means that Luke 15 is not *necessarily* an incident in the life
of Jesus, that those three parables are not *necessarily* connected to the
Lukan context or to one another, and that Luke 15 is not *necessarily* a
paradigm case for all the parables of Jesus as example parables.

I PAUSE NOW BOTH to review where we have been and to see what
comes next. What have we found here in Chapter 2 as well as in
Chapter 1, and how do those results structure the next four chapters
of Part I? Whence have we come and whither do we go?

In this chapter, my first question concerned the meaning of example parables—what are they? I answered with two instances or
case studies of Jewish example parables *after* Jesus. The next question
was whether such parables also existed in the biblical tradition *before*
him. A positive answer—with several instances of varying length—
led to the third question. Were some, most, or maybe even all of
Jesus's own parables best understood as example parables—as Luke
15 certainly indicated? The final question was whether that understanding of Jesus's parables as example parables came from Luke's
(mis)interpretation or from Jesus's intention. The conclusion was
that—despite Luke 15—Jesus's stories were not fully or even adequately interpreted as example parables.

Think now of both Chapters 1 and 2. In Chapter 1 we found that
riddle parables—potentially lethal or deliberately fatal tests—were
present in the world of Jesus, and that Mark 4 interpreted Jesus's own
parables in that paradigm, but that his interpretation was not at all
persuasive. In Chapter 2 we found that *example parables*—practical,

moral, or religious models—were present in the world of Jesus and that Luke 15 interpreted Jesus's own parables on that paradigm, but that his interpretation was not completely persuasive.

The parallel sequences and negative conclusions of those two chapters on riddle parables and example parables prepare for the positive focus on *challenge parables* in the rest of Part I. My generative proposal is, first, that *challenges* are a third type—apart from riddles and examples—among those metaphorical stories we call parables; and, second, that challenge parables are the best category within which to understand the intention and purpose of Jesus's stories. Those proposals will develop as follows through the next four chapters.

In Chapter 3, first of all, I pick up again the parable of the Prodigal Son. I look at a modern retelling of that classic story that turns it from its Lukan reading as an example parable into a challenge parable, that is, a parable that pointedly challenges the version in Luke 15. That retelling is my first paradigmatic instance of this proposed third type of parable.

Then, for the rest of Chapter 3, I focus on Jesus's Good Samaritan parable. With *riddles, examples,* and *challenges* established as our threefold typology for parables, my plan is to try out each of those readings on that most famous of all the parables of Jesus. My question is whether the Good Samaritan is best seen as riddle, example, or challenge parable.

Chapter 4 asks the next question. It is the same one asked in earlier chapters for riddles and examples. Did challenge parables exist in the biblical tradition before the time of Jesus? Or am I claiming that Jesus invented a new and special style of parable?

Chapter 5 continues from Chapter 4's strongly affirmative answer to the prior existence of challenge parables in the pre-Jesus biblical tradition. My question now is whether such challenges were intended in *all* of Jesus's original parables? Granted another affirmative answer to that one, there is only one question left for the final chapter of Part I.

Chapter 6 asks, Why did Jesus choose this third category of challenge—rather than riddle or example—for his parabolic vision of the kingdom of God? Is there some peculiarly appropriate interaction between the medium and the message, between Jesus's challenge parables and God's divine kingdom?

CHAPTER 3

Challenge Parables: Part I

DOWN FROM JERUSALEM TO JERICHO

THE FRENCH INTELLECTUAL ANDRÉ GIDE lived from 1869 to 1951. His search for honesty and integrity—a search at once sexual and social, political and religious—led him first to revere and then speedily to revile Russian Communism in the 1930s. It also resulted in his receiving Sweden's Nobel Prize for Literature in 1947 and the placing of his books on the Vatican's Index of Forbidden Books in 1952, just after his death.

Gide wrote "The Return of the Prodigal Son," his retelling of Luke's version, as several years of darkness and despondency were coming to a climax in 1907. At one point, in fact, he intrudes himself into the story to pray like a latter-day prodigal son: "Lord, like a child I kneel before you today, my face wet with tears. If I recollect and tender here Your urgent parable, it is because I understand Your prodigal son, it is because in him I see myself."

In Luke, Jesus says, "There was a man who had two sons" (15:11), but Gide's version expands that to a man who had three sons—and a wife. But it is no longer the prodigal's older brother, but this invented youngest brother who will be the climax of the retold parable. We already get a warning of his importance early in the retelling when Gide intrudes with the comment, "In a room next to the prodigal's,

I know that a boy, his younger brother, will seek slumber in vain all night long."

Gide develops the story through four longish dialogues between the returned prodigal and first his father, next his older brother, then his mother, and finally his younger brother. The *father* tells the prodigal about the older brother: "It is he who makes the law here. It was he who urged me to say to you, 'Outside of the house, there is no salvation for you.'" The *older brother* tells the prodigal about the father: "I am his sole interpreter, and whoever would understand the father must listen to me." The *mother* tells the prodigal about the youngest brother: "He reads too much, and . . . often perches on the highest tree in the garden from which, you remember, the country can be seen above the walls."

The *youngest* brother tells the prodigal about himself: "Brother! I am what you were when you left." He confesses, "I am leaving before the end of the night. Tonight. Tonight, before the sky pales." But unlike the prodigal, who left with his share of the inheritance, the youngest son claims, "I have no share in the inheritance. I leave with nothing."

The prodigal bids his younger brother farewell. He admits to him, "You are taking with you all my hopes," and tells him to forget his family and never return. The story concludes with some final words to the departing younger brother. "'Be careful on the steps' . . . cautions the prodigal."

How would you classify Gide's version of the parable in "The Return of the Prodigal Son"? It is, first and above all, an alternative version, a counterparable to that of Jesus. Even if you bracket Luke's interpretation of the younger son who returns home as "the tax collectors and sinners" and the older son who stays at home as "the Pharisees and the scribes," there are only two sons and two options in Jesus's story. One son leaves but returns; the other never leaves at all.

But Gide has three sons and three options: the oldest son never leaves home; the middle son leaves, but eventually returns; and the youngest son leaves, never to return. "Forget us, forget me," the prodigal tells him. "May you never return." The departure points metaphorically—like Kafka's "away-from-here"—to every life departure you can imagine. It is about leaving the security of home, garden, and walled-off spaces—in life and sex, in politics and religion, even in tradition and faith—for Gide and for all of us. But, of course and always, "Be careful on the steps."

With Gide's version as a paradigm, I call this proposed third type a *challenge parable* because, in its format and content, it quietly and gently challenges the version not only of Luke, but maybe even of Jesus. Gide does not applaud the prodigal's life abroad or suggest it should be imitated. That is why the youngest son leaves home "with nothing," with no inheritance to squander. "It is better that way," the prodigal tells him. But, for Gide, it is the third son, that youngest brother, who challenges us all far more than either of the other two could ever do.

It is a challenge parable because it challenges us to think, to discuss, to argue, and to decide about meaning as present application. Here is its basic challenge. If tradition is changed, it *may* be destroyed. If tradition is not changed, it *will* be destroyed. That is the *challenge* of this and of all other challenge parables. But be careful, be very careful on the steps. In summary, then, and with apologies to the apostle Paul for using his phrasing, riddle parables, example parables, and challenge parables abide, these three; and the greatest of these is challenge parables.

WHAT COMES NEXT in this chapter? I will focus, as promised, on the Good Samaritan parable of Jesus, with these three steps. First, I cite the full text, outline its context, and add a few comments for fuller discussion later. Second, I look at that text-in-context *indirectly* through three different interpretations: first as a riddle parable, next as an example parable, and finally as this newly proposed category of challenge parable. Third, I look at that text-in-context *directly*, through both literary context and social context, and argue that it is best seen as neither riddle nor example, but as challenge—at least from Jesus, even if not from Luke. I conclude by wondering whether all parabolic interpretations are equally valid or whether some are more appropriate than others.

HERE, TO BEGIN, IS the full *text* of the Good Samaritan parable in Luke—without any of the context before or after it. I give that context immediately but separately.

> A man was going down from Jerusalem to Jericho, and fell into the hands of robbers, who stripped him, beat him, and went away, leaving him half dead. Now by chance a priest was going down that road; and when he saw him, he passed by on the other side. So likewise a Levite, when he came to the place and saw him, passed by on the other side. But a Samaritan while traveling came near him; and when he saw him, he was moved with pity. He went to him and bandaged his wounds, having poured oil and wine on them. Then he put him on his own animal, brought him to an inn, and took care of him. The next day he took out two denarii, gave them to the innkeeper, and said, "Take care of him; and when I come back, I will repay you whatever more you spend." (10:30–35)

You can see how, in typical folklore fashion, it has two failures followed by a third and climactic success. But, even if you know that story's *text* quite well, it is even more important to recognize its Lukan *context* as a series of four interchanges between a lawyer and Jesus:

> [1a] *Lawyer to Jesus:* "Teacher," he said, "what must I do to inherit eternal life?" (10:25)
>
> [1b] *Jesus to lawyer:* "What is written in the law? What do you read there?" (10:26)

[2a] *Lawyer to Jesus:* "You shall love the Lord your God with all your heart, and with all your soul, and with all your strength, and with all your mind; and your neighbor as yourself." (10:27)

[2b] *Jesus to lawyer:* "You have given the right answer; do this, and you will live." (10:28)

[3a] *Lawyer to Jesus:* "And who is my neighbor?" (10:29)

[3b] *Jesus to lawyer:* Parable of the Good Samaritan. (10:30–35); "Which of these three, do you think, was a neighbor to the man who fell into the hands of the robbers?" (10:36)

[4a] *Lawyer to Jesus:* "The one who showed him mercy." (10:37a)

[4b] *Jesus to lawyer:* "Go and do likewise." (10:37b)

The actual parable in 10:30–35 is framed—and interpreted—by 10:25–29 before it and 10:36–37 after it. Could only the *text* be from Jesus and that framing *context* be from Luke? And how could you decide that question? I will return to those questions later in this chapter, but my next step now is to look at three readings of that parable—as a riddle, as an example, and finally as a challenge parable.

MY FIRST READING of the Good Samaritan is as a riddle parable by St. Augustine, one of Christianity's greatest theologians and a Roman citizen of North African Berber descent. Born in 354, he was consecrated bishop of Hippo Regius—now Algeria's Annapa—in 395, and he died amid the death throes of the western Roman Empire, with the Vandals already besieging his cathedral city in 430.

In his *Questions on the Gospels*, written between 399 and 400, Augustine takes the Good Samaritan as a riddle parable and provides one of the best-known allegorical readings given to any of Jesus's parables. It has also become an (in)famous instance of an interpretation that is at once brilliantly clever, but also brilliantly—what do I say—inadequate or incomplete or incorrect?

We have just read the text of the parable, and you can see—by my italics in what follows—how Augustine picks up and interprets its every part and almost its every word:

A certain man went down from Jerusalem to Jericho. Adam himself is meant. Jerusalem is the heavenly city of peace, from whose blessedness Adam fell. Jericho means "the moon" and signifies our mortality, because it is born, waxes, wanes, and dies.

Thieves are the devil and his angels; *who stripped him,* namely, of his immortality; *and beat him,* by persuading him to sin; *and left him half dead,* because insofar as man can understand and know God, he lives, but insofar as he is wasted and oppressed by sin, he is dead—he is therefore called half dead.

The *priest and Levite who saw him and passed by* signify the priesthood and ministry of the Old Testament, which could profit nothing for salvation.

Samaritan means "guardian," and therefore the Lord Himself is signified by this name. The *binding of the wounds* is the restraint of sin. *Oil* is the comfort of good hope; *wine,* the exhortation to work with fervent spirit. The *beast* is the flesh in which he deigned to come to us. The *being set upon the beast* is belief in the incarnation of Christ. The *inn* is the Church, where travelers are refreshed on their return from pilgrimage to their heavenly country. The *morrow* is after the resurrection of the Lord. The *two pence* are either the two precepts of love or the promise of this life and of that which is to come. The *innkeeper* is the Apostle [Paul]. The supererogatory payment [*whatever more you spend*] is either his counsel of celibacy or the fact that he worked with his own hands, lest he should be a burden to any of the weaker brethren when the Gospel was new, though it was lawful for him "to live by the Gospel" [2 Cor. 9:14]. (2.19)

Augustine takes Mark's allegorical interpretation of the Sower parable to its ultimate extreme with this reading of the Good Samaritan. But, of course, there is no mention about intended incomprehension for deliberate condemnation.

Here are some immediate questions. Does Augustine think we could or should read *all* of Jesus's parables allegorically as riddle parables? Or is Augustine quite aware that his reading is brilliantly clever, but also exegetically playful? Is his interpretation simply the freedom to be seriously playful and playfully serious at the same time? Be that as it may, it is quite clear that in his *Questions on the Gospels*, Augustine reads the Good Samaritan *allegorically as a riddle parable*.

I turn next to the Good Samaritan read as an *example parable* and, ironically enough, that alternative understanding also comes from St. Augustine. And it comes earlier than the one just seen—from his treatise *On Christian Doctrine* from 397. That is why I wondered if his riddle reading was simply serious play. I would, by the way, answer that question affirmatively.

In his work *On Christian Doctrine*, Augustine interprets the Good Samaritan not allegorically as a riddle parable, but ethically as an example parable. Furthermore, he had looked not just at the text of the parable itself, but also at that framing context we have just seen. Augustine cut down Luke's eight units of conversation between the lawyer and Jesus to only five units, but presented them in this elegantly reversed structure (titles and numbers added):

[A1] *Jesus to lawyer:* "When the man to whom our Lord delivered those two commandments, and to whom He said that on these hang all the law and the prophets,"

[B1] *Lawyer to Jesus:* "asked Him, 'And who is my neighbor?'"

[C] *Jesus to lawyer:* "He told him of a certain man who, going down from Jerusalem to Jericho, fell among thieves, and was severely wounded by them, and left naked and half dead. And He showed him that nobody was neighbor to this man except him who took pity upon him and came forward to relieve and care for him."

[B2] *Lawyer to Jesus:* "And the man who had asked the question admitted the truth of this when he was himself interrogated in turn."

[A2] *Jesus to lawyer:* "To whom our Lord says, 'Go and do thou likewise.'"

Then, immediately after that summary of text-in-context, Augustine makes his most significant comment. With that parable, he says,

> Jesus was teaching us that he is our neighbor whom it is our duty to help in his need, or whom it would be our duty to help if he were in need. Whence it follows, that he whose duty it would be in turn to help us is our neighbor. For the name "neighbor" is a relative [i.e., a bilateral one], and no one can be neighbor except to a neighbor. . . . Every one to whom we ought to show, or who ought to show to us, the offices of mercy is by right called a neighbor. (1.31, 33)

For the moment, pending more important discussion later in this chapter, I draw attention to two points in Augustine's analysis. One is that the italicized section in A1 above is not *from the lawyer to Jesus* in Luke 10:27, but *from Jesus to the lawyer* in Matthew 22:40. The other is that Augustine has solved the discrepancy of whether the *neighbor* is the one in the ditch or the one on the road, the one aided (10:29) or the aiding (10:37a). The term, says Augustine, is referential and reciprocal, and the parable is about the *mutuality* of the term "neighbor." The road from Jerusalem to Jericho is a two-way street. The neighbor is both whoever helps another and also that other who is helped. In *On Christian Doctrine*, therefore, Augustine reads the Good Samaritan *as an ethical example parable.*

We have just seen how this parable can be interpreted as first a riddle parable and then an example parable—even by the same writer. Granted that, I turn next to a third and final reading of the Good Samaritan—this time as a challenge parable. It is actually a retelling or paraphrase of that story with different characters in a very different setting over seventeen centuries after Jesus. But it is, to my mind, the most accurate "interpretation" ever given to that famous parable.

The full title of Henry Fielding's satirical novel of 1742 is *The History of the Adventures of Joseph Andrews, and of His Friend Mr. Abraham Adams, Written in Imitation of the Manner of Cervantes, Author of* Don Quixote. The title of chapter XII in volume I is equally full: "Containing many surprising adventures, which Joseph Andrews met with on the Road, scarce credible by those who have never traveled in a Stage-Coach." The incident begins like this:

> Joseph . . . had not gone above two miles . . . when he was met by two fellows in a narrow lane, and ordered to stand and deliver. He readily gave them all the money . . . [and] both together fell to belaboring poor Joseph with their sticks, till they were convinced they had put an end to his miserable being: they then stripped him entirely naked, threw him into a ditch, and departed with their booty.

Joseph began to "recover his senses as a stage-coach came by," and so the scene is set for the debate over poor, naked Joseph: to stop or not to stop, to help or not to help, to clothe or not to clothe, and to transport or not to transport him from ditch to inn.

The staff of the coach consists of a "postillion," a low-level servant who had to ride the lead horse as controller; a "coachman," who sat on the outside seat as driver; and an occupant's "footman," who probably had to ride somewhere on the outside as well. There are also three passengers inside the coach—a "lady" and two "gentlemen," one older and the other "a young man who belonged to the law."

(Recall that Fielding was a barrister who became London's Chief Magistrate.)

In other words, Fielding doubles Jesus's three characters—priest, Levite, and Samaritan—to six characters. But since his six are all present at the same time, he can have them argue with one another over what to do about the man in the ditch. But even more important, he sets up a sixfold ascending hierarchy from the three outside to the three inside the coach, from postillion, to coachman, to footman and from lawyer, to gentleman, to lady.

The postillion hears groans from the ditch and wants to stop, but the coachman does not, saying, "We are confounded late, and have no time to look after dead men." The lady wants to stop to see what the matter is, but when the postillion reports on Joseph's nakedness, "O J-sus!" cries the lady. "A naked man! Dear coachman, drive on and leave him." The older gentleman agrees: "Let us make all the haste imaginable, or we shall be robbed too." But then the lawyer intervenes—not from any motive of actual compassion or humanity, but from fear of any potential legal responsibility or accountability:

> He wished they had passed by without taking any notice; but that now they might be proved to have been last in his company; if he should die they might be called to some account for his murder. He therefore thought it advisable to save the poor creature's life, for their own sakes, if possible; at least, if he died, to prevent the jury's finding that they fled for it. He was therefore of opinion to take the man into the coach, and carry him to the next inn.

The lady objects that Joseph has no clothes to cover his nakedness, and the coachman objects that he has no money to pay his fare. The lawyer once again warns of possible legal consequences:

> But the lawyer, who was afraid of some mischief happening to himself, if the wretch was left behind in that condition, saying

no man could be too cautious in these matters, and that he remembered very extraordinary cases in the books, threatened the coachman, and bid him deny taking him up at his peril; for that, if he died, he should be indicted for his murder; and if he lived, and brought an action against him, he would willingly take a brief in it.

So the coachman, "perhaps a little moved with compassion at the poor creature's condition," agrees to take Joseph to the nearest inn. But Joseph is so admirably modest that he refuses to enter the coach without some covering for his naked body, "to prevent giving the least offence to decency." That final impasse is broken by this solution (my italics):

> Though there were several greatcoats about the coach, it was not easy to get over this difficulty which Joseph had started. The *two gentlemen* complained they were cold, and could not spare a rag; the man of wit saying, with a laugh, that charity began at home; and the *coachman*, who had two greatcoats spread under him, refused to lend either, lest they should be made bloody: the *lady's footman* desired to be excused for the same reason, which the *lady* herself, notwithstanding her abhorrence of a naked man, approved: and it is more than probable poor Joseph, who obstinately adhered to his modest resolution, must have perished, unless the *postillion* (a lad who hath been since transported for robbing a hen-roost) had voluntarily stript off a greatcoat, his only garment, at the same time swearing a great oath (for which he was rebuked by the passengers), "that he would rather ride in his shirt all his life than suffer a fellow-creature to lie in so miserable a condition."

Everyone refuses Joseph a greatcoat and, therefore, since he will not ride naked out of modesty, he at first has no hope of transportation to the safety of the inn.

Everyone refuses, that is, except the youngest, lowest-class, and prone-to-swearing member of the coach's staff. This "lad" was later to be "transported" for robbery—presumably to America, since Australia was not yet open for penal business. It was this lowest-class, oath-swearing, criminal-to-be who, alone of the coach's six occupants, "would rather ride in his shirt all his life than suffer a fellow-creature to lie in so miserable a condition." That is a classic case of a challenge parable—in which, of course, one out of three passersby has morphed into one out of six passersby, and the good Samaritan has morphed into the good postillion.

First of all, both Jesus and Fielding take it absolutely for granted that what should be done is to save the traveler beaten, robbed, stripped, and left for dead by the roadside. That is what makes it so easy to take the parable ethically as an example parable of truly moral behavior. Assistance, however, is the unspoken presupposition rather than the primary point of the parable.

Second, with both Jesus and Fielding, it is the respected ones who refuse to help and the disreputable one who does what is necessary. Jesus, accordingly, uses "the priest and the Levite," while Fielding works right down the coach's hierarchy from top to bottom. The upper-class lady and gentleman, the middle-class lawyer, and the lower-class coachman and footman all refuse to help. Only the youngest, lowest-class, oath-swearing criminal-to-be is the one who saves poor Joseph. This makes it a challenge parable, because it reverses the expectations and judgments, the presuppositions and prejudices of Fielding's hierarchically driven society. What happens to your world if a story records that your "best" people act badly and only your "worst" person acts well?

IN MY OPINION, AUGUSTINE got the Good Samaritan wrong— twice—and Fielding got it precisely correct. The next step is to show that—long before Augustine—the story of the Good Samaritan, which Jesus originally intended as a challenge parable, was changed by Luke into an example parable. But how am I so sure about that conclusion? What makes me think I can get behind the text of Luke and into the mind of Jesus? Is that claim anything more than sheer interpretive impertinence, sheer arrogant preference of now over then and here over there?

My conclusion that Jesus intended the Good Samaritan story as a challenge parable, but that Luke changed it into an example parable derives from the following two steps. First, I remove the story of the Good Samaritan in Luke 10:30–35 from the later *literary* context of Luke 10:25–29 and 36–37 and explain my reasons for that exclusion. Second, I return the now separate story to its earlier *social* context with Jesus and emphasize the results of that inclusion. I now take those two steps one after the other.

I begin with the Good Samaritan without its literary context. On the one hand, the story of the Good Samaritan is found nowhere else in the New Testament. We are dependent exclusively on Luke for its text, content, and any given interpretation. On the other hand, that dialogue between a questioner and Jesus about loving one's neighbor *is* found in Mark 12:28–34 and is copied from there into Matthew 22:34–40. (There is, by the way, a massive scholarly consensus that Mark's gospel is the primary source for Matthew and Luke.)

Furthermore, during Jesus's last week in Jerusalem, Mark has a series of debates between Jesus and others. This is where Mark locates the question and answer about loving God and one's neighbor. And Matthew follows him, using that same location. But Luke had to omit it from there, because he had used it earlier as the literary context for the Good Samaritan parable. Notice the vacant space in the last column as Luke copies Mark's three dialogues:

Marriage in Heaven	Mark 12:18-27	=Matthew 22:23-33	=Luke 20:27-40
Lawyer's Question	Mark 12:28-34	=Matthew 22:34-40	
David's Son and Lord	Mark 12:35-37	=Matthew 22:41-46	=Luke 20:41-44

The questioner, by the way, is "one of the scribes" in Mark 12:28, but "one of them [the Pharisees], a lawyer" in Matthew 22:34.

Finally, Mark had set up that question-and-answer as a double interchange between the scribe and Jesus:

[1a] *Scribe to Jesus:* "Which commandment is the first of all?" (12:28)

[1b] *Jesus to scribe:* "The first is, 'Hear, O Israel: the Lord our God, the Lord is one; you shall love the Lord your God with all your heart, and with all your soul, and with all your mind, and with all your strength.' The second is this, 'You shall love your neighbor as yourself.' There is no other commandment greater than these." (12:29–31)

[2a] *Scribe to Jesus:* "You are right, Teacher; you have truly said that 'he is one, and besides him there is no other'; and 'to love him with all the heart, and with all the understanding, and with all the strength,' and 'to love one's neighbor as oneself,'—this is much more important than all whole burnt offerings and sacrifices" (12:32–33)

[2b] *Jesus to scribe:* "You are not far from the kingdom of God." (12:34a)

In copying Mark, Matthew found that redundant and cut it back to a single interchange of *the lawyer to Jesus* in 22:34–35 and *Jesus to the lawyer* in 22:36–40. He also adds, "On these two commandments hang all the law and the prophets" in 22:40. You will recall from Augustine's earlier reading of the Good Samaritan in his *On Christian Doctrine* (1.31) that he—mistakenly?—slipped Matthew 22:40 into his summary of Luke 10:27.

It was Luke—and not Jesus—who *adopted* the dialogue about the double commandment of loving God and neighbor from Jesus in Mark as the context for the Good Samaritan parable. He also *adapted* it; he changed it from a questioner applauding Jesus with, "You are right, Teacher," in Mark 12:32 to Jesus applauding the questioner with, "You have given the right answer," in Luke 10:28.

It was Luke—and not Jesus—who interpreted the Good Samaritan parable by placing it in the middle of that interchange in which the lawyer asks Jesus, "Who is my *neighbor?*" (10:29) and Jesus asks the lawyer, "Which of these three, do you think, was a *neighbor* to the man who fell into the hands of the robbers?" (10:36). In summary:

Jesus and the lawyer	→	Good Samaritan parable	←	Jesus and the lawyer
(10:25–29, from Luke)		(10:30–35, from Jesus)		(10:36–37, from Luke)

My first argument is that Luke has brought together two independent units of the Jesus tradition—the *dialogue* about the double commandment and the *parable* about the Good Samaritan—and used the former to interpret the latter. But by doing so he turned a challenge parable into an example parable.

That is, of course, relatively easy to do, because *almost any* challenge parable presumes that its core action is the right, moral, and ethical thing to do. Jesus and Fielding take it absolutely for granted that one *should* stop and help an unfortunate person robbed, beaten, and left almost dead by the roadside. But the point of a challenge parable is that—within its own cultural, social, political, or religious expectations—it is the "good" people who fail to help and one of the "bad" people who does. That is what challenges the given normalcy of audience expectations, hierarchical prejudices, and ethnic presuppositions.

In summary, therefore, Jesus's story of the Good Samaritan in 10:30–35 must be read apart from those Lukan frames added before it (10:25–29) and after it (10:36–37). That is my first step. Then, having removed it from its literary context in the gospel of Luke, the second and equally important step is to replace it in its social context in the world of Jesus.

First, in the Jewish homeland, the priest and the Levite—think of them as first-level and second-level clergy—represent the culturally given "good guys." Priest and Levite versus Samaritan represent the positive and negative cultural polarities of first-century Jewish tradition. Similarly, gentry inside the coach and carriage workers outside the coach represent the social and cultural polarities of Fielding's world. But the stories are turned on their head when the "good guys" act badly and the "bad guys" act well.

Second, had Jesus intended an example parable about helping somebody in distress, he could easily have done so by telling his story with *unspecified* characters, such as: "A man was going down, . . . a first traveler, . . . a second traveler, . . . a third traveler." Had he wanted to insist that such help applied even to enemies in distress, he could have done it: "A Samaritan was going down, . . . a first traveler, . . . a second traveler, . . . a third traveler." Those would have been classic example parables, but as soon as Jesus specified the reputable clergy as nonhelpers and the disreputable Samaritan as helper, we have—as he intended—a classic challenge parable.

Finally, one wonders why this was not clearly obvious throughout almost two millennia of Christian tradition—or even for Luke himself. It is because "good Samaritan" is—for us by now—a redundant cliché. It is simply a standard term for somebody who helps another in distress. It has long ago lost any hint of oxymoron—like, say, a square circle. We do not hear it as so many first-century Jewish ears would have—as a cultural paradox, a social contradiction in terms. For centuries before the time of Jesus, there had been tension between Jews and Samaritans, and a "good Samaritan" was more paradox than cliché.

That tension started when Israel split into separate northern and southern kingdoms in the late 900s BCE. It intensified when the Assyrian Empire captured the northern kingdom in the late 700s BCE and the Babylonian Empire captured the southern kingdom in the early 500s BCE. It was an estrangement between descendants of the same ancestors, but by the first century it had hardened into ethnic, political, and religious animosity within the land of Israel. Think, for example, of this story:

> Jesus sent messengers ahead of him. On their way they entered a village of the Samaritans to make ready for him; but they did not receive him, because his face was set toward Jerusalem. When his disciples James and John saw it, they said, "Lord, do you want us to command fire to come down from heaven and consume them?" But he turned and rebuked them. Then they went on to another village. (Luke 9:52–56)

Here, next, is an even more lethal incident from about twenty years after the time of Jesus. In his *Jewish War*, the historian Josephus tells how a fight started "between the Galileans and the Samaritans" when "a great number of Jews were going up to Jerusalem to the Feast of Tabernacles and a certain Galilean was slain" as the pilgrims passed through Samaria on their way south to Judea (2.232). When the story reached Jerusalem, "it put the multitude into disorder, and they left the feast; and without any generals to conduct them, they marched with great violence to Samaria; nor would they be ruled by any of the magistrates that were set over them" (2.234).

The situation became so serious that the Syrian governor had to intervene with his legionary troops. He started with crucifixions and beheadings, but finished by sending the most eminent Jewish and Samaritan leaders as well as the highest local Roman officials for trial before Caesar. "Jews," says John 4:9, "do not share things in common with Samaritans." Except, maybe, fighting? Think, therefore, of "good Samaritan" at the time of Jesus less as a cliché than as a challenge, a provocation, a paradox, an oxymoron, a contradiction in terms.

My conclusion is that the Good Samaritan was not intended by Jesus as a simple example story, a straightforward moral lesson, a positive paradigm for compassionate behavior. The story presumes that compassionate help is the proper response. But the story as an example of moral behavior does not seem the primary intention of the parable as told by Jesus. It becomes an example story only in Luke's context and interpretation. Rather, it is better understood as a challenge parable, a story that challenges listeners to think long and hard about their social prejudices, their cultural presumptions, and, yes, even their most sacred religious traditions.

THIS CHAPTER'S FINAL STEP questions whether this is all a waste of time. Maybe we should simply rejoice in that diversity of interpretation and accept the parables of Jesus as riddle and example and challenge all mixed up together. Indeed, to return one final time to Augustine, that is his own almost postmodern conclusion about Jesus's parables.

This time my text is from his *Confessions*, written in 397–398, that is, between his earlier interpretation of the Good Samaritan as an example parable in 397 and his later interpretation of it as a riddle parable or allegory in 399–400. He asks in his *Confessions*—maybe a little defensively?—"What harm would be done if I should interpret the meaning of the sacred writer differently from the way some other person interprets?" Especially, "since many different things may be understood from these words, all of which may be true." In other words:

> Since each person tries to understand in the Holy Scripture what the writer understood, what harm is done if one person understands what You, the Light of all truth-speaking minds, show that person to be true, although the author read did not understand this aspect of the truth even though he did understand the truth in a different meaning? (12.18)

Maybe, then, the Good Samaritan is both riddle *and* example? But, if so, it cannot be both riddle-for-incomprehension, as in Mark 4, *and* example-for-imitation, as in Luke 10, at the same time, because imitation requires comprehension.

There is also this fundamental question. Is the primary norm for the interpretation of the Good Samaritan or any of the parables "what the writer understood," as best one can interpret it, or is the primary norm "what Jesus intended," as best one can interpret that? We do, after all, call them the parables of Jesus, not the parables of Mark or Luke.

Even more basically, I myself prefer Alice's to Humpty Dumpty's views on "words" and find it equally applicable to "parables." Lewis Carroll's 1871 novel *Through the Looking Glass* gives us this very prophetic conversation on that subject:

> "When *I* use a word," Humpty Dumpty said, in rather a scornful tone, "it means just what I choose it to mean—neither more nor less."
>
> "The question is," said Alice, "whether you *can* make words mean so many different things."
>
> "The question is," said Humpty Dumpty, "which is to be master—that's all."

In the first part of this book, therefore, and especially in this chapter's parable of the Good Samaritan, I attempt to understand the purpose and intention of *Jesus* rather than the interpretation and understanding of *Luke*. Because, although an example parable may be good, a challenge parable is a far more importantly subversive operation. Why? Because challenge parables humble our prejudicial absolutes, but without proposing counterabsolutes in their place. They are tiny pins dangerously close to big balloons. They push or pull us into pondering whatever is taken totally for granted in our world—in its cultural customs, social relations, traditional politics, and religious traditions. Challenge parables remind us, as in the final words of Gide's parable, to "be careful on the steps."

I BEGAN THIS CHAPTER by showing what I mean by a challenge parable. For that demonstration I chose Gide's counterparable to the example parable of the Prodigal Son. It challenges us to think more deeply and radically about "departing from home" rather than about "returning to home."

After that case study, I turned to Jesus's most famous parable, that of the Good Samaritan. We saw it read as a riddle, an example, and a challenge parable. I proposed that, although example is certainly Luke's intention, that derives from his framing it within a literary context derived from Mark's double-commandment dialogue about loving God and neighbor. My preliminary conclusion, then, is that the Good Samaritan was intended by Jesus as a challenge parable, and that challenge parables are the most important of the three types of parables. What comes next?

You will recall from Chapters 1 and 2 that I gave instances of both riddle and example parables from the Christian Old Testament. In Chapter 4 I give instances of challenge parables from that same pre-Jesus biblical tradition. Those both demonstrate further the power of challenge and also indicate that Jesus was certainly not inventing challenge parables, but simply using an inherited option already present in the Old Testament itself.

Furthermore, in Chapter 2 we mentioned in passing three book-length *example* parables—Tobit, Judith, and Esther. The challenge parables to be seen next in Chapter 4 will also be book length, but now they are the *challenge* parables of Ruth, Jonah, and Job.

CHAPTER 4

Challenge Parables: Part II

THE WORD AGAINST THE WORD

WHEN I WAS IN HIGH SCHOOL, from 1945 to 1950, the standard English curriculum established by Ireland's Board of Education involved a different Shakespearean play for each year. My memory recalls *The Merchant of Venice, Richard II, Henry IV, Hamlet,* and *Macbeth*—but I am not totally secure on the order. We had to learn most of the major soliloquies of each year's play by heart, because questions in the government-set examinations presumed it and usually concluded with something about "quoting freely."

I was probably about thirteen years old when my class studied what Shakespeare called *The Life and Death of King Richard the Second,* the first in his four plays about the rise of the royal House of Lancaster. It was written around 1595, but focuses on Richard II, who became king of England at the age of ten in 1377. He was born in a monastery, died in a dungeon, and, during his twenty-two-year reign, managed to alienate alike both the peasantry and the aristocracy.

The play is set between 1398 and 1400, when, during Richard's absence at war in Ireland, his estranged cousin Henry Bolingbroke rallies both Commons and Lords to his cause and captures the returning Richard in Wales. Henry is crowned as Henry IV, and

Richard is eventually imprisoned far from London in Pontefract (or Pomfret) Castle near Leeds in West Yorkshire. (You may recall that castle if you have seen Showtime's series *The Tudors*.) He is dead within a year—his murder not directly ordered, but indirectly willed by Henry, because, as he would later admit, "Uneasy lies the head that wears a crown" (*Henry IV*, pt. 2, act 3, sc. 1, l. 31).

I learned much of that play by heart over sixty years ago, but my clearest memory is of the imprisoned Richard, who believed most fervently in the divine right of kings, pondering how he could be both king and not king at the same time. And how Henry could be not king and king at the same time. These are the lines I remember best—although I have now admittedly checked them against their source:

> For no thought is contented. The better sort,
> As thoughts of things divine, are intermix'd
> With scruples, and do set the word itself
> Against the word:
> As thus, "Come, little ones;" and then again,
> "It is as hard to come as for a camel
> To thread the postern of a needle's eye."
> (act 5, sc. 5, ll. 11–17)

That phrase about the biblical "word itself against the word" has stuck with me throughout the years, although I certainly make no claim that it directed my life into research and publication on the history and theology of the Christian Bible. It does, however, magnificently summarize what I have found there during half a century of study.

"The word against the word" is a perfect theme for this chapter, as the biblical tradition uses challenge parables to remind itself that God can never be *fully* trapped by our human imagination, not even—or especially—in Torah or prophecy, wisdom or *eschaton*, Old or New Testament, Jesus or gospel. A biblical challenge parable intends to remind us that, as with Moses in Exodus 3:5, it is quite acceptable to stand on holy ground and talk with God, as long as you remember first to remove your shoes. That too is a challenge parable.

IN THIS CHAPTER WE explore the books of Ruth, Jonah, and Job to show that book-length challenge parables existed in the Old Testament *before* the time of Jesus. In other words, his stories did not so much invent a new type of parable as choose an option already present in his biblical tradition. But before I begin any detailed exploration, two introductory questions are necessary. One is why I need three case studies—would one or two not suffice? The other is whether these three case studies share any common background.

First, why do I need *three* cases from the pre-Jesus biblical tradition? Do I think you will not get my point after one or at least two instances? After even a single case—say, Ruth—you will certainly understand my primary point about the existence of challenge parables long before Jesus. But I also have a secondary point, and this requires that we work our way through all three books—one after another and in the sequence: Ruth, then Jonah, and finally Job.

That secondary point is that, throughout those three parabolic books, the challenge drives deeper and deeper into the heart of the biblical tradition: Ruth challenges a part of the Bible, Jonah challenges the whole of the Bible, and Job challenges the God of the Bible. Furthermore, that threefold escalation from Ruth through Jonah to Job is repeated within that last book all by itself. Job challenges first a part, then the whole, and finally the God of the biblical tradition.

In summary, then, we will need all three books—and in that specific sequence—to see clearly that their challenge is not simply about *biblical words against biblical words*, but about *the biblical Word against the biblical Word*—as in the subtitle to this chapter.

My second question concerns the common historical background of these three books. There is one very important but also rather obvious distinction necessary to understand that background. Indeed, without that background they are not challenge parables, but merely short stories.

We all recognize the distinction between a story's *setting* and a story's *writing*, between the time in which a story is *located* and the time in which a story is *composed*. Margaret Mitchell's famous novel *Gone with the Wind,* for example, was set in the 1860s and 1870s, during and after the American Civil War, but written during the 1920s and 1930s. This is a crucial distinction to remember when reading our three biblical challenge parables because each is set in a very different time but all were written in the same historical matrix.

The book of Ruth is set during the time when Israel was still guided by charismatic leaders—the "judges"—rather than by the later royal and dynastic rulers. Imagine Ruth in the period of the book of Judges. The book of Jonah is set during the time of the Assyrian Empire and its great capital city of Nineveh. Imagine Jonah in the period of the book of Isaiah. The book of Job is set during the time of the most ancient ancestors of Israel. Imagine Job in the period of the book of Genesis. But it is not so much when the stories are *set* as when they are *written* that establishes their deliberate purpose as challenge parables. When is that common time period?

Here is what we must know about the historical matrix within which our three parables were composed. First, between 597 and 587 BCE, the Babylonians destroyed the southern half of Israel, including Jerusalem and its Temple, and took the Jewish aristocracy into "Babylonian Exile." Second, by the middle of that same century, however, the Persians, having conquered the Babylonians, sent those exiled Jews home to rebuild their Temple, city, and homeland as well as restore their laws, customs, and traditions—thereby enabling them to pay their taxes and establishing Israel as a buffer against Egypt. Think of it as the Persian version of the American Marshall Plan. Instead of simply looting their conquered—"liberated"—territories, the Persians restored the shattered peoples and economies in order to establish viable clients and allies rather than create future problems and rebellions.

It was a very, very dangerous time for Israel. Its separate existence and ethnic survival could have—precisely within that *supportive* imperial melting pot—slowly and steadily disappeared into the gene pool of the Middle East. It was a time to rebuild the defensive walls of Israel's capital city and the protective walls of Israel's ancient identity. It was a time to restore both religion and law, both Temple and Torah. It was a time for decision, not discussion; for resolution, not rebuttal; for proclamation, not provocation. It was, therefore, a time for resolute certainties and secure absolutes.

It was precisely in that general ferment of conservative certainties that the three parables of Ruth, Jonah, and Job proclaimed their challenges to the powerful principles, presuppositions, and prejudices of the "Persian Restoration." They did not so much propose paradigm shifts against that restoration as pose paradigm questions within it and to it. All of this introduction must be kept in mind as we turn now first to Ruth, then to Jonah, and finally and climactically to Job.

THE BOOK OF RUTH is my first case study of a challenge parable in the Old Testament. It is also the most beautiful tale in the entire biblical tradition. I begin with a summary of Ruth as a *story* before considering it as a *challenge*.

A famine forces a Bethlehem peasant family—Elimelech and Naomi along with their two sons, Mahlon and Chilion—to immigrate across the river Jordan to the non-Israelite land of Moab. Elimelech dies, and Mahlon and Chilion marry Moabite women named Orpah and Ruth. Then both husbands die. And so, with three male deaths in five verses, the story is ready to begin with only the three women left (1:1–5).

Having heard that the famine was over, Naomi determines to return home. What happens next negates all those folktales about tensions between mothers-in-law and daughters-in-law. Both Orpah and Ruth insist that they will leave their own country to be with her in Bethlehem. But Naomi tells them to stay in Moab and find new husbands. Orpah agrees to stay, but Ruth still refuses:

Do not press me to leave you
    or to turn back from following you!
Where you go, I will go;
    Where you lodge, I will lodge;
your people shall be my people,
    and your God my God.
Where you die, I will die—
    there will I be buried.
May the Lord do thus and so to me, and more as well,
    if even death parts me from you! (1:16–17)

After that most gracious declaration, the story records their return home: "Naomi returned together with Ruth the Moabite, her daughter-in-law, who came back with her from the country of Moab. They came to Bethlehem at the beginning of the barley harvest" (1:22). Notice that double emphasis on "Moabite" and "from the country of Moab."

Next I make a short story even shorter. Naomi has Ruth encounter—and delicately seduce—a "kinsman on her husband's side, a prominent rich man, of the family of Elimelech, whose name was Boaz" (2:1). Ruth and Boaz are married, and their firstborn child is a son. That is, of course, the expected happy ending to this beautiful tale of fidelity to family and loyalty to tradition. This story, told so fully from a female viewpoint, ends with these lines:

The women said to Naomi, "Blessed be the Lord, who has not left you this day without next-of-kin; and may his name be renowned in Israel! He shall be to you a restorer of life and a nourisher of your old age; for your daughter-in-law who loves you, who is more to you than seven sons, has borne him."

Then Naomi took the child and laid him in her bosom, and became his nurse. The women of the neighborhood gave him a name, saying, "A son has been born to Naomi." They named him Obed; he became the father of Jesse, the father of David. (4:14–17)

But that last line—indeed, that last word—is a very surprising conclusion to this pastoral idyll. We are suddenly and unexpectedly hurtled from private peasant story to public royal dynasty.

Finally, that story has two striking aspects. One is that the audience is never allowed to forget that Ruth is a *Moabite* and not an *Israelite* woman. The word "Moab" is emphasized heavily at the start and finish of the story (1:1, 2, 6, 7, 22; 4:3, 5, 10). Ruth herself is identified as "a Moabite wife" (1:4), as "the Moabite who came back with Naomi from the country of Moab" (2:6), or more simply and regularly as "Ruth the Moabite" (1:22; 2:2, 21; 4:5, 10).

Another is that there is a *double* emphasis on the descent of David, the once and future king of Israel, from Ruth and Boaz. Here is how the book concludes:

The women of the neighborhood gave him a name, saying, "A son has been born to Naomi." They named him Obed; he became the father of Jesse, the father of David.

Now these are the descendants of Perez: Perez became the father of Hezron, Hezron of Ram, Ram of Amminadab, Amminadab of Nahshon, Nahshon of Salmon, Salmon of Boaz, Boaz of Obed, Obed of Jesse, and Jesse of David. (4:17–22)

We are told twice about that lineage of Obed to Jesse to David. We are told twice, therefore, that the Moabite woman Ruth was the great-grandmother of Israel's ideal king. What has happened is that what we thought was an *example parable*—what happens if one is faithful to family and tradition?—has turned into a *challenge parable*—what happens if a Moabite woman is the ancestor of David?

I turn now to see how short story becomes challenge parable. Imagine hearing that story within the historical matrix of the Persian restoration in the 500s and 400s BCE. The Persian Empire had placed the Jewish leaders Ezra and Nehemiah in charge, with an imperial mandate to restore their ancestral laws—as part of its program for all its newly acquired ex-Babylonian territories. For Israel, that meant revival of the laws of the Torah and especially of the book of Deuteronomy, that final and climactic text of the "Five Books of Moses." Among those Deuteronomic laws is this one:

> No Ammonite or Moabite shall be admitted to the assembly of the Lord. Even to the tenth generation, none of their descendants shall be admitted to the assembly of the Lord, because they did not meet you with food and water on your journey out of Egypt. (Deut. 23:3–4a)

According to the tradition of the exodus, Israel escaped from Egyptian bondage and entered the promised land from the eastern desert just north of the Dead Sea. That meant traveling through the tribal territories of Moab and Ammon. Those peoples were naturally suspicious, unhelpful, and somewhat hostile to Israel in transit through their lands. Hence that *eternal* edict against any Ammonite or Moabite ever becoming a *convert* to the people of Israel.

I move next from general legal theory to specific historical practice. During that post-Babylonian Persian restoration, between, say, 550 and 450 BCE, Ezra and Nehemiah focused on one specific problem to preserve the ethnic identity of their people. *They demanded an immediate end to all Israelite marriages with foreign women.* Listen to this drumbeat of the term "foreign women or wives":

> We have broken faith with our God and have married foreign women from the peoples of the land, . . . trespassed and married foreign women, and so increased the guilt of Israel. . . . Separate yourselves from the foreign wives. . . . Let all in our

towns who have taken foreign wives come at appointed times,
. . . all the men who had married foreign women, . . . descendants of the priests who had married foreign women. . . . All
these had married foreign women, and they sent them away
with their children. (Ezra 10:2, 10, 11, 14, 17, 18, 44)

They separated from Israel all those of foreign descent. . . .
Foreign women made even him [Solomon] to sin. . . . Shall
we . . . do all this great evil and act treacherously against our
God by marrying foreign women? . . . I cleansed them from
everything foreign. (Neh. 13:3, 26, 27, 30)

The ethnic reforms of Nehemiah are even more precise than
those of Ezra. Before that last quotation comes this specification
based on that text of Deuteronomy 23:3–4a cited above:

On that day they read from the book of Moses in the hearing
of the people; and in it was found written that no Ammonite
or Moabite should ever enter the assembly of God, because
they did not meet the Israelites with bread and water [during
their desert exodus from Egypt]. . . . When the people heard
the law, they separated from Israel all those of foreign descent.
(Neh. 13:1–2)

Since this proscription was ethnic rather than religious, foreign
wives and their children could probably not have become "converts" to Israel. But even if some others could do so, Ammonites
and Moabites could not do so—ever. In other words, according to
Deuteronomic theology and postexilic dogmatism, Ruth could never
have said to Naomi, "Your people shall be my people, and your God
my God" (1:16).

The book of Ruth is gentle, delicate, and gracious. Familial loyalty and tribal tradition are deeply embedded in it. Yet it is only one
single story about one single individual. How can its tiny nonvio-

lent presence oppose or even subvert the absolute, massive, violent dicta of Ezra and Nehemiah? How can a specific story stand against general law? Maybe one could even dismiss it as the exception that proves the rule about—and against—Moabites? But that would not work, because this Moabite exception to the rule produced David, the once and future king of Israel.

Hear, then, the book of Ruth as a delicate but definite challenge proclaimed within the postexilic situation to those Deuteronomic commandments. What, it asks gently, if Boaz and Ruth had divorced? What if, as it were, Obed had been abandoned with his foreign mother? Think of the book of Ruth as an example parable with a scorpion sting in its tail that turned it into a challenge parable in the very last verses and then forced Israel to read it all as such. What would have happened to Israel's history, as it were, if Boaz had divorced Ruth and abandoned their son Obed?

The book of Ruth is a *challenge* to one specific point in the Deuteronomy-based reforms of Ezra and Nehemiah. In the biblical tradition, that decree against Moabites comes *before* the time of David and its implementation by Ezra and Nehemiah comes *after* his time. Right between them is the story of Ruth and David's Moabite-Israelite ancestry. But how can any of those laws be valid since David was God's destined ruler of Israel? This subversive challenge parable reminds us that general law proposes what a single story disposes.

I BEGAN THIS SERIES with the book of Ruth because its challenge touches only on one aspect of the biblical tradition during the Persian restoration, namely, that alien wives and children—especially Moabite or Ammonite ones—must be divorced and rejected from Israel. I turn next to the book of Jonah, which challenges not one, but two even more basic aspects of the general biblical tradition, namely, that prophets are good and obedient while Gentiles—and especially Assyrians—are bad and disobedient. It challenges, in other words, the whole biblical tradition of insiders and outsiders, of God's chosen ones and God's rejected ones. I follow the same pattern here as with Ruth, looking first at Jonah as a short story and then as a challenge parable.

Jonah receives a typical prophetic mission mandate from God: "The word of the Lord came to Jonah son of Amittai, saying, 'Go at once to Nineveh, that great city, and cry out against it; for their wickedness has come up before me'" (1:1–2). Jonah's response is to travel immediately in the opposite direction. He is ordered east by land and heads west by sea, away "from the presence of the Lord" (1:3).

Next, when God sends a storm that threatens to sink the ship, the non-Jewish sailors realize that it is due to Jonah, "for the men knew that he was fleeing from the presence of the Lord, because he had told them so" (1:10). Reluctantly they cast him overboard, and the sea immediately calmed. "Then the men feared the Lord even more, and they offered a sacrifice to the Lord and made vows" (1:16). The non-Jewish mariners respect God more than does the Jewish prophet.

The silliness of this recalcitrant prophet does not even merit divine anger. God simply sends alternative transportation—that famous "large fish"—to bring Jonah home. And so, after an appropriate psalm of thanksgiving for his deliverance (2:1–9), "the Lord spoke to the fish, and it spewed Jonah out upon the dry land" (2:10).

Then, Jonah's mission is repeated: "The word of the Lord came to Jonah a second time, saying, 'Get up, go to Nineveh, that great city, and proclaim to it the message that I tell you'" (3:1–2). This time Jonah heads obediently eastward.

What happens next is surely one of the strangest events in the entire prophetic tradition. Jonah proclaims the shortest sermon in the history of homiletics, the briefest threat in the history of prophecy: "Forty days more, and Nineveh shall be overthrown!" (3:4). And the Bible's smallest threat results in the Bible's greatest repentance:

The people of Nineveh believed God; they proclaimed a fast, and everyone, great and small, put on sackcloth. When the news reached the king of Nineveh, he rose from his throne, removed his robe, covered himself with sackcloth, and sat in ashes. Then he had a proclamation made in Nineveh: "By the decree of the king and his nobles: No human being or animal, no herd or flock, shall taste anything. They shall not feed, nor shall they drink water. Human beings and animals shall be covered with sackcloth, and they shall cry mightily to God. All shall turn from their evil ways and from the violence that is in their hands. Who knows? God may relent and change his mind; he may turn from his fierce anger, so that we do not perish." (3:5–9)

And the result of that instant, total, and massive repentance is that "when God saw what they did, how they turned from their evil ways, God changed his mind about the calamity that he had said he would bring upon them; and he did not do it" (3:10).

Finally, Nineveh's deliverance "was very displeasing to Jonah, and he became angry" (4:1). He retires outside the city, constructs a shelter from the sun, and waits to see what will happen. God grows a bush to shade him, immediately destroys it, and sends a hot desert wind in its place. Jonah, of course, complains: "It is better for me to die than to live" (4:10). Finally, and climactically, God gets the last word—as the first word—in this fascinating satire:

The Lord said, "You are concerned about the bush, for which you did not labor and which you did not grow; it came into being in a night and perished in a night. And should I not be concerned about Nineveh, that great city, in which there are more than a hundred and twenty thousand persons who do not know their right hand from their left, and also many animals?" (4:10–11)

What message does this story intend? It is surely, you might argue, an example parable, a story warning you that you cannot disobey God or avoid your vocation? Why, then, do I call it a challenge parable? Because of, on the one hand, what the standard biblical tradition *expects* of prophets and, on the other, what it *does not expect* of Gentiles.

How, next, does Jonah the short story become a challenge parable? First, the general expectation of biblical prophecy is both clear and consistent. It is forged in the dialectic between these two standard and reversed phrases:

The message of God	comes to	the prophet
The prophet	proclaims	the message of God

The prophetic destiny is a reciprocal and interactive loop between divinity and humanity, as the message received becomes the message delivered. That interaction is best expressed by the insistent mantra "Thus says the Lord," a phrase that appears in the prophetic books over 350 times.

The traditional biblical prophet is—need it be said?—obedient to God. The very term announces that fidelity, as it comes from two Greek words: *pro*, "for," and *phēmi*, "to speak." A prophet is one who *speaks for* God, whether the message is about past, present, or future matters. An *obedient prophet* is a redundancy. A *disobedient prophet* is an oxymoron, a contradiction in terms, a square circle. Furthermore, a biblical prophet is not just obedient, but often eager to deliver the divine message. A classical example is the call of Isaiah, who "heard the voice of the Lord saying, 'Whom shall I send, and who will go for us?" And Isaiah said, 'Here am I; send me!' (6:8). So much, then, for the biblical tradition's positive expectations of prophets. What about its negative expectations of Ninevites?

The traditional image of biblical Nineveh is equally clear and consistent. The ancient city was located on the east bank of the Tigris (near modern Iraqi Mosul) and became the magnificent capital of Sennacherib, who ruled the Assyrian Empire from 705 to 681 BCE. His father, Sargon II, who ruled from 722 to 705, had completed the devastation of the northern half of Israel in 721 BCE. Sennacherib then tried to do the same to the southern half in 701 BCE, but was ultimately unsuccessful.

In his own imperial *Annals*, recorded on a hexagonal prism, he says, "Hezekiah [King of Judah] himself I shut up in Jerusalem, his capital city, like a bird in a cage." But the prophet Isaiah taught the caged bird to sing:

> Thus says the Lord concerning the king of Assyria: "He shall not come into this city, shoot an arrow there, come before it with a shield, or cast up a siege ramp against it. . . . For I will defend this city to save it, for my own sake and for the sake of my servant David." (37:33, 35)

Samaria, capital of the north, was destroyed and its inhabitants deported—hence the "ten lost tribes of Israel"—and Jerusalem was besieged, but not conquered. So what do you think biblical tradition thought of the Assyrians and their great capital city of Nineveh?

The name "Assyria" is equated with other representative "supremely evil" places: "Woe to you, Assyria, who conceal the unrighteous within you! O wicked nation, remember what I did to Sodom and Gomorrah" (2 Esd. 2:8); "The pride of Assyria shall be laid low, and the scepter of Egypt shall depart" (Zech. 10:11). Indeed, Nineveh itself tended to be treated as a paradigm case for evil cities. A rather terrible example is in the book of the prophet Nahum, which is a long and bitter "oracle concerning Nineveh" (1:1). The text is focused gleefully on Nineveh's—impending or accomplished?—destruction, as the Medes and Babylonians conquered the Assyrians in 612 BCE. Here are two representative examples:

> Nineveh is like a pool
> > whose waters run away.
> "Halt! Halt!"—
> > but no one turns back.

"Plunder the silver,
    plunder the gold!
There is no end of treasure!
    An abundance of every precious thing!"
Devastation, desolation, and destruction!
    Hearts faint and knees tremble,
all loins quake,
    all faces grow pale! (2:8–10)

Ah! City of bloodshed,
    utterly deceitful, full of booty—
no end to the plunder!
    The crack of whip and rumble of wheel,
galloping horse and bounding chariot!
    Horsemen charging,
flashing sword and glittering spear,
    piles of dead,
heaps of corpses,
dead bodies without end—
    they stumble over the bodies! (3:1–3)

That is what the Old Testament actually thinks of Nineveh, for what the Assyrians had done to the northern Israelite capital of Samaria and attempted to do to the southern Israelite capital of Jerusalem.

In the book of Jonah, the prophet is childishly disobedient, and the Ninevites are unbelievably obedient. Hear that story against that general biblical vision of prophets and Assyrians. Basic presuppositions and fundamental expectations are reversed. What does that do to the security and certainty of the postexilic restoration? The parable of Jonah challenges the Bible even more deeply than did the parable of Ruth.

As always, in a challenge parable, popular expectations and communal traditions are serenely reversed—but only, of course, in one single story. It is particular story against general ideology, parable against myth, and pin against balloon.

MY THIRD AND FINAL case study of an Old Testament challenge parable is the book of Job. That story challenges biblical tradition not just on *one* aspect and at a surface level—as did Ruth—or on *two* aspects and on a deeper level—as did Jonah—but on *three* aspects and on the deepest possible level. Job is actually a multichallenge parable and, as such, it is the most powerful parable in the entire biblical tradition. The book of Job has always been considered—and justly so—among the masterpieces of world literature.

I begin, as usual, with the story before discussing its triple challenge. Our present book of Job is a carefully crafted interaction between prose and poetry as well as between narrative and debate. Even a cursory reading of the book makes its division into *story in prose* and *debate in poetry* strikingly obvious. Also clear is the fact that the *story in prose* at the beginning and end of the book frames the central section, the *debate in poetry*:

[A1] Story in prose: Opening scenes (1:1–2:13)
   [B1] Debate in poetry: Friends and Job (3:1–37:24)
   [B2] Debate in poetry: God and Job (38:1–42:6)
[A2] Story in prose: Closing scenes (42:7–17)

In other words, despite discussions about *possible* earlier versions of that story in prose, the present book must not be dismembered as if it were the work of an inadequate cut-and-paste author. I leave that aside for the moment, but will return to that distinction of story in prose and debate in poetry a little later.

Here, in brief, is the book's content. God claims that Job is the holiest person in the world. But "the Satan"—not Christianity's chief devil, but God's attorney general—responds that Job is holy only to obtain benefits from God. They agree on a test with Job as guinea pig. He is stripped of everything—children and possessions, wealth and health. But he still retains both his sanctity and his integrity.

Three friends—Eliphaz, Bildad, and Zophar—and then an added fourth friend—Elihu—try to console him by explaining his catastrophic situation: he is being punished for some sin and, if he repents, God will forgive him. But Job objects, wanting to know what sin he did to justify this suffering and how it could have been so great if he cannot remember it. Then God reduces Job to stuttering silence by overpowering him with the majesty of creation and Job's own inability to understand it.

Finally, God proclaims that the friends are wrong in their interpretation of Job's situation and "the Lord gave Job twice as much as he had before" (42:10). Furthermore, "Job lived one hundred and forty years, and saw his children, and his children's children, four generations" (42:10). End of story, start of parable. End of reading, start of thinking.

Job is, as mentioned above, a three-level challenge parable in which each level probes ever deeper into the heart of the biblical tradition. But even though those challenge levels can be distinguished, they cannot be ultimately separated, as each interacts with the others to form a single matrix.

The first level of Job as challenge parable is in the story in prose (1:1–2:13; 42:7–17). It involves *Israel* and especially its covenantal exclusivity and ethnicity. The second level of the challenge parable is in the first debate in poetry between the friends and Job (3:1–37:24). It involves *Torah* and especially its Deuteronomic formulation of divine rewards for virtue and divine punishments for vice (see, for example, Deuteronomy 28). The third level of the challenge parable is in the second debate in poetry, between God and Job (38:1–42:6). It involves *God* and especially the character of divinity at the core of the biblical tradition. I now take up each of those challenges, but again, remember, they can be distinguished, but not separated, in the overall thrust of this magnificent book.

The first and surface-level challenge parable in the book of Job appears in the book's framing prose sections (1:1–2:13; 42:7–17). It is in fact immediately announced in the book's opening verses:

There was once a man in the land of Uz whose name was Job. That man was blameless and upright, one who feared God and turned away from evil. There were born to him seven sons and three daughters. He had seven thousand sheep, three thousand camels, five hundred yoke of oxen, five hundred donkeys, and very many servants; so that this man was the greatest of all the people of the east. (1:1–3)

Job is not only the "greatest of all the people of the east," he is also the holiest man in the world for, as God proclaims, "there is no one like him on the earth, a blameless and upright man who fears God and turns away from evil" (1:8).

The holiest man on earth and the greatest man in the east is from the land of Uz? In other words, Job is not a Jew, but a Gentile. So where exactly is "the land of Uz" and what else does the biblical tradition say about it?

Jeremiah 25:15–26 gives a very complete list of kings, nations, and lands that are enemies of God. The prophet is told by God, "Take from my hand this cup of the wine of wrath, and make all the nations to whom I send you drink it. They shall drink and stagger and go out of their minds because of the sword that I am sending among them" (25:15–16). The list includes everyone surrounding Israel and, indeed, it even starts with "Jerusalem and the towns of Judah, its kings and officials" (25:18).

The list of divine enemies then continues from "Pharaoh king of Egypt, his servants, his officials, and all his people," through "all the mixed people; all the kings of the land of Uz; all the kings of the land of the Philistines—Ashkelon, Gaza, Ekron, and the remnant of Ashdod," and on to "Edom, Moab, and the Ammonites" (25:19–21).

That "land of Uz" must be somewhere toward the Negev desert and include those tribal Edomites immediately south of Judah.

That is confirmed by the biblical book of Lamentations, a dirge for the destruction of Jerusalem and its Temple by the Babylonians in 586 BCE. It warns Edom against rejoicing over Israel's devastation, for it may be next to fall, and calls it "daughter Edom, you that live in the land of Uz" (4:21). In other words, "the land of Uz" is an enemy of Israel that includes Edom, but apparently extends much farther south into the Negev.

What did the ancient Israelites actually think of the Edomites who lived in the land of Uz? Here is one prayer: "Remember, O Lord, against the Edomites the day of Jerusalem's fall, how they said, 'Tear it down! Tear it down! Down to its foundations!'" (Ps. 137:7). Edom had rejoiced over and participated in the destruction of Jerusalem and its Temple by the Babylonians. And here is one prophecy:

> Thus says the Lord God concerning Edom: . . . I will surely make you least among the nations; you shall be utterly despised. . . . I will bring you down. . . . I will destroy the wise out of Edom. . . . You should not have rejoiced over the people of Judah on the day of their ruin. . . . You should not have looted his goods on the day of his calamity. (Obad. 1, 2, 4, 8, 12, 13)

Edom is not just an adjacent territory or even a sometime enemy of Israel. It assisted in and rejoiced over the Babylonian devastation of Israel's capital city and sacred Temple. In summary, therefore, and immediately as the book of Job opens, Israel is challenged to imagine that the holiest—and richest—person on earth is one of its ancient ethnic enemies.

You can now see clearly how the story in prose is a challenge parable directed to Israel itself. The holiest—and richest—man on earth is not a covenanted Israelite, but a hated Edomite. Our three Old Testament book-length challenge parables have escalated from a single very good Moabite—in Ruth—through a city full of very, very good Assyrians—in Jonah—to the holiest and richest man as a very, very, very good Edomite. (No surprise, then, to find later Jesus's good Samaritan or, later still, Fielding's good postillion.)

The second and deeper-level challenge parable in the book of Job dominates the first of the book's two debates in poetry, the one between the friends and Job (3:1–37:24). Around and around they go, as they attempt to explain the reason for Job's sudden and terrible misfortune.

Among all those long, repetitive, and fruitless arguments between Job and his friends, I focus here on how the friends assert repeatedly that, since God is just and no mere mortal may question God, Job's sufferings must be God's punishments for his past sins and that, if he will only confess and beg for mercy, God will certainly forgive him. They are utterly sincere in their interpretation of why Job is suffering, but why are they so certain they have the right answer?

Their certainty comes from the Torah itself and, more specifically, from the book of Deuteronomy, the climactic law code in the Pentateuch. Deuteronomy 28, for instance, promises: "All these blessings shall come upon you and overtake you, if you obey the Lord your God" (28:2) and then lists twelve verses of very specific blessings including, for example: "Blessed shall be the fruit of your womb, the fruit of your ground, and the fruit of your livestock, both the increase of your cattle and the issue of your flock" (28:4).

That same chapter goes on to warn Israel: "If you will not obey the Lord your God by diligently observing all his commandments and decrees, which I am commanding you today, then all these curses shall come upon you and overtake you" (28:25). The list of curses is far longer than that of blessings. It goes on for fifty-three verses including, for example: "Cursed shall be the fruit of your womb, the fruit of your ground, the increase of your cattle and the issue of your flock" (28:18).

Job's four friends, or comforters, are imagined as Deuteronomic fundamentalists. They reason that when Job lost his large family, thousands of livestock, and "very many servants" (1:2–3), God must have been cursing him with punishment for disobedience. They are by-the-book Deuteronomists who believe—with the Torah—that God rewards virtue and punishes evil; those who suffer or flourish are being, respectively, punished or rewarded. All poor Job can respond—again and again—is that he does not know what sins he committed to deserve such ghastly punishments: "Teach me," he begs, "and I will be silent; make me understand how I have gone wrong" (6:24).

Ancient hearers or modern readers know, of course, that the friends are totally wrong in their analysis of Job's situation and are forced, therefore, to wonder whether, if they are so wrong, can Deuteronomy 28 be so right. God eventually tells the friends what the book's hearers or readers have always known, namely, that Job is totally and utterly innocent. As God finally tells Eliphaz: "My wrath is kindled against you and against your two friends; for you have not spoken of me what is right, as my servant Job has" (42:7). *Job's situation is about a divine wager on his integrity and not about a divine punishment for his sin.* But, still, if the prose parable challenges Israel, the poetic parable challenges Torah. The book's audience is forced for forty chapters to listen to bad theology encased in great poetry. We knew the friends were wrong *from the start,* and God certified them as wrong *at the end.* What, then, is left of Deuteronomy 28 and its theological certitudes as they stutter into silence?

We reach the third and deepest level of the multichallenge parable of the book of Job when we focus on the second of those two debates in poetry, the one between God and Job (38:1–42:6). There are only two rounds in this much shorter set of debates:

God (38:1–40:2) and Job (40:3–5)
God (40:6–41:34) and Job (42:1–6)

You will notice that God always speaks first, and that Job only gets a few verses of (non)response. God "answered Job out of the whirlwind" (38:1), but, considering the audience's prior knowledge and, of course, with all due respect, that divine voice is more wind than whirl.

Here is the problem that makes God more bully than mystery in this parable. *Why does God never tell Job the truth, the whole truth, and nothing but the truth?* The book's hearers or readers know the truth from the very beginning: it is simply about Job's integrity and God's wager against Satan's accusation. But Job is never told the truth, even at the very end. The book's multilevel parable escalates from challenging Israel's covenantal pride, to challenging Torah's Deuteronomic sanctions, and finally to challenging God's very character.

In Robert Frost's 1945 play *A Masque of Reason*, God admits to owing Job both divine thanks and divine apologies for a very long time. God presumes that by now Job has figured out "the part he played." To do what? Then comes this magnificent line with which—finally—God admits to Job what it was all about, namely, "to stultify the Deuteronomist." The book of Job rendered foolish (*stultus* in Latin) the absolute security of those Deuteronomic proclamations.

Job is told in Frost's play that Deuteronomic theology placed God in "moral bondage to the human race." Before Job, God was totally involved in rewarding virtue with prosperity and punishing vice with adversity, but Job "set God free to reign." The truth is, unfortunately, that the book of Job did not "change the tenor of religious thought," as suggested by God to Job in Frost's play. The book of Job became, at most, a minor speed bump on the Deuteronomic superhighway. The Deuteronomist is still alive and well when the disciples ask Jesus, "Who sinned, this man or his parents, that he was born blind?" (John 9:2). And is still there today when a disaster survivor asks, "What did I do to deserve this?"

Nonetheless, even if Job's challenge did not completely "stultify the Deuteronomist" or successfully "change the tenor of religious thought," the book of Job's deepest challenge is emphasized in Frost's play by how long it took God to tell Job the truth. "I've had you on my mind," says God, "a thousand years." That deepest level challenges us to think about the character of God because, from the very start, we know the full truth, but God never admits it to Job. God gives Job back double for all he had lost (42:10), everything twofold, but still not the truth.

THIS CHAPTER LOOKED AT three challenge parables from the Old Testament tradition and each is—in its final form—a protest against the inevitable absolutes of the Persian restoration. It was a dangerous period for Israel's tribal loyalty, ethnic identity, and covenantal fidelity, not because the Persians persecuted it lethally, but because Persia supported it imperially. It was a very dangerous moment for Israel's future when God, through the prophet Isaiah, called Cyrus "my Messiah" (45:1).

The book-length parables of Ruth, Jonah, and Job challenged ever more deeply the security of Israel's Persian-era absolutes and exclusivities. They were challenges to the Bible, from the Bible, by the Bible, in the Bible. Those parables escalated their protest from Ruth through Jonah to Job. I placed them in that order to emphasize the external threefold escalation through them. But Job itself contains an internal threefold escalation—a question posed critically to Israel's ethnicity, the Torah's sanctions, and God's veracity.

It is surely very strange, is it not, how Israel's ancient tribal and imperial enemies—Moabites, Ninevites, and Edomites—become ideals in these serenely fictional stories? After a good Moabite, good Ninevites, and a good Edomite, we should have been ready for—and should not have been surprised by—a good Samaritan from Jesus. We should have immediately acknowledged that challenge parable from Jesus and recognized how Luke had changed it into an example parable. In any case, it is clear that challenge parables, therefore, existed before the time of Jesus and probably influenced his own parables as well. In other words, that reading of the Good Samaritan as challenge parable in Chapter 3 has been rendered almost traditional—even if countertraditional—by those case studies in Chapter 4. What, then, comes next in Chapter 5?

The next question is probably clear by now. Is that Good Samaritan an exceptional challenge parable among the stories of Jesus? Is it, maybe, the only one? In the next chapter, therefore, I return to consider some more of Jesus's best-known parables. Furthermore, as we see other challenge parables in that chapter, we will have to imagine their original *oral* context as distinct from their present *written* condition. How do we imagine Jesus's challenges as actually working in practice?

All of that still leaves a climactic Chapter 6. The major questions there will be twofold. First, why did Jesus choose challenge parables as his special and distinctive style with which to proclaim the kingdom of God? Second, does that conjunction of the kingdom and challenge, of the kingdom as challenge, speak only to its earliest and most ancient Jewish hearers or also—and maybe even more so—to those of us who are today its latest and most modern Christian readers?

CHAPTER 5

Challenge Parables: Part III

LET ANYONE WITH EARS TO HEAR LISTEN!

IN 1973 I WAS AN associate professor at DePaul University in Chicago and had just published *In Parables: The Challenge of the Historical Jesus*, the first in a series of books that would culminate with *The Historical Jesus: The Life of a Mediterranean Jewish Peasant* in 1991. An editor from Argus Press asked me to write a more popular version of *In Parables* to be published in 1975. When finished, I called it *The Dark Interval: Towards a Theology of Story*, having borrowed part of that title from *The Book of Hours*, written by the Prague-born German-language poet Rainer Maria Rilke from 1899 to 1903. For Rilke, the "dark interval" was the musical interval between the notes of life and death, which are so hard to reconcile, because "death's note tends to dominate." I did not, however, use Rilke's phrase the same way in my title. I used it for the pause between hearing and understanding or reading and interpreting. I intended it as the holding moment between parable and interpretation or challenge and response.

That title, *The Dark Interval*, referred more to those who *heard* the original oral version of the parables and had to interpret for themselves than to those who *read* them in later written versions, where they were already interpreted for them—and us—by evangelists and tradition. Reread, for example, that written version of the Good Samaritan in the last chapter. Time your reading. It will probably take you less than one minute. But that is a written plot summary, not an oral performance. Had Jesus told it like that, a cough from the audience could have ruined the key word, "Samaritan." And, besides, an oral audience would have interrupted him with questions and objections, comments and disagreements. Give Jesus an hour, not just a minute, for that story.

I also remember another but later request from my editor at Argus. Among the parables I discussed in the book was that of the Pharisee and the Tax Collector. It opens like this: "Two men went up to the temple to pray, one a Pharisee and the other a tax collector" (Luke 18:10). Before Jesus's original audience even heard the rest of the parable, that opening juxtaposition would have made them immediately uneasy. I wanted my readers to sense that initial surprise. So I asked them to imagine a modern equivalent in which a Roman Catholic priest opens his Sunday sermon like this: "A pope and a pimp went into St. Peter's to pray." I asked them to think of representative "good" and "bad" characters in their own story world. I asked them to feel the shock of that opening, with its abrupt juxtaposition of pope and pimp at prayer in St. Peter's.

I was—and still am—rather proud of my line's elegant *p* alliteration. But when my editor read the manuscript, he asked me—and I agreed—to remove my modern rephrasing because, he said, it might offend Roman Catholic readers. That was, of course, exactly my intention. Well, not so much to offend *my* audience as to indicate with a modern instance how challenging, how offensive, how downright provocative Jesus's original juxtaposition would have been to *his* audience. Even before they heard the rest of the parable.

THAT MINOR MEMORY IS my overture for this chapter. Granted, from Chapter 3, that the Good Samaritan parable is neither riddle nor example, but rather challenge parable along the lines of those seen from the biblical tradition in Chapter 4, here are the questions for this present chapter.

Is Jesus's Good Samaritan parable an exceptional case or were challenge parables the regular type preferred by Jesus? Were more, most, or all of his parables such challenges? This chapter will answer that question in three steps.

The first step looks at two other parables by Jesus—the Pharisee and the Tax Collector as well as Lazarus and the Rich Man. These have exactly the same Good Samaritan structure of traditional "good guys" failing and traditional "bad guys" succeeding. In those cases the challenge to the audience—the lure to think, the enticement to debate—is fairly overt and clearly evident. They are clearly challenge parables.

The next step and the next two parables, the Vineyard Workers and the Master's Money, present challenges that are much more subtle, but still just as strongly present. They too attempt to raise consciousness in an oral situation of audience interaction.

The third and final step, before this chapter's concluding summary, is to glance more widely across the parables of Jesus. After all, we will have by then only looked at two parables in Chapter 3 and another four in this present chapter. But how do I plan to widen the sweep within the limited space available in part of one chapter? That will require a special strategy, namely, an emphasis on the clash between the *normalcy of format* and the *radicality of content* within Jesus's parabolic repertoire—within the general *anthropological* expectations of popular storytelling.

AFTER THAT AUTOBIOGRAPHICAL SNIPPET in my overture, the Pharisee and Tax Collector is the obvious parable with which to start the discussion. Watch, once again, how Luke—who is our only source for this parable—frames it with interpretation at start and finish:

[A1] *Opening frame from Luke:* He also told this parable to some who trusted in themselves that they were righteous and regarded others with contempt. (18:9)

[B] *Parable from Jesus:* Two men went up to the temple to pray, one a Pharisee and the other a tax collector. The Pharisee, standing by himself, was praying thus, "God, I thank you that I am not like other people: thieves, rogues, adulterers, or even like this tax collector. I fast twice a week; I give a tenth of all my income." But the tax collector, standing far off, would not even look up to heaven, but was beating his breast and saying, "God, be merciful to me, a sinner!" (18:10–13)

[A2] *Closing frame from Luke:* I tell you, this man went down to his home justified rather than the other; for all who exalt themselves will be humbled, but all who humble themselves will be exalted. (18:14)

For Luke that is an example parable of how—and how not—to pray. But, indeed, it would work well as such if any precise job descriptions were omitted and it simply said, "Two men went up to the temple to pray. The one, standing by himself, was praying thus: . . . The other one, standing far off, . . ." If, however, it is an example parable as interpreted by Luke, was it a challenge parable as intended by Jesus?

On the one hand, the Pharisees were—despite that insistent and inaccurate libel of them in the New Testament—close to and revered by the ordinary people. What was wrong, such people might have asked, with thanking God one was not a sinner? The Pharisee does not congratulate himself for his own sanctity, but thanks God for his grace—so what is wrong with that?

On the other hand, tax collectors had such a bad reputation that they were often combined—fairly or unfairly—in the cliché expression "tax collectors and sinners," as in Luke 5:30; 7:34; 15:1–2. How repentant was that tax collector, those same people might have asked? Was he like that Zacchaeus in Luke's very next chapter? He "was a chief tax collector and was rich," and he did not simply pray for mercy. When he met Jesus he said: "Look, half of my possessions, Lord, I will give to the poor; and if I have defrauded anyone of anything, I will pay back four times as much" (19:8).

But, once again, it is the traditional "good guy"—the Pharisee—who does badly and the traditional "bad guy"—the tax collector—who does well. That is a challenge to the normal expectations and presuppositions of Jesus's contemporary fellow Jews—just as in the Good Samaritan challenge parable.

That very same process of having traditional cultural expectations turned upside down—so that "many who are first will be last, and the last will be first" (Mark 20:31; Matt. 19:30) and "all who exalt themselves will be humbled, and all who humble themselves will be exalted" (Matt. 23:12; Luke 14:11)—reappears in the parable of Lazarus and the Rich Man.

It is provocative, by the way, that Jesus gave the poor man a name, Lazarus, and the rich man none. The opposite might have been culturally expected—either both should have been anonymous or, if one was named, then it should have been the rich man. In fact, later tradition, in an attempt to solve this inequality, takes the term in the Latin translation of the New Testament, *dives*, which simply means "rich man," and turns it into a proper noun, "Dives." But here is what the parable actually says:

> There was a rich man who was dressed in purple and fine linen and who feasted sumptuously every day. And at his gate lay a poor man named Lazarus, covered with sores, who longed to satisfy his hunger with what fell from the rich man's table; even the dogs would come and lick his sores. (Luke 16:19–21)

I pause for a moment at that point in the parable. Notice that neither the rich man nor the poor man has done anything particularly moral or immoral. *They are simply described economically rather than appraised morally.* The parable continues:

The poor man died and was carried away by the angels to be with Abraham. The rich man also died and was buried. In Hades, where he was being tormented, he looked up and saw Abraham far away with Lazarus by his side. He called out, "Father Abraham, have mercy on me, and send Lazarus to dip the tip of his finger in water and cool my tongue; for I am in agony in these flames." But Abraham said, "Child, remember that during your lifetime you received your good things, and Lazarus in like manner evil things; but now he is comforted here, and you are in agony." (Luke 16:22–25)

The parable then continues with a request from the rich man that Lazarus be sent to warn his five brothers, but he is told: "If they do not listen to Moses and the prophets, neither will they be convinced even if someone rises from the dead" (16:31). I bracket all of 16:27–31 as a Lukan addition based on postresurrection Christian experience in which it took *both* the interpretation of "Moses and the prophets" (24:27) *and* the recognized presence of Jesus himself (24:28–30) for "eyes to be opened" (24:31–32). Its presence does not, in any case, change my reading of the parable as a challenge.

That story is actually an extremely surprising reversal of audience expectations. As I mentioned above, we are not told that the rich man did anything wrong or the poor man did anything right. Yet their roles in this world are reversed in the next world. Does that not challenge any world's standard presumptions about the fortunate rich and the unfortunate poor? *Is heaven and hell about rewards merited and punishments deserved or about simple reversals of earthly status?* What if, in the next life, this life's nonsuffering *haves* will become suffering *have-nots* and this life's suffering *have-nots* will become nonsuffering *haves.* A simple reversal of fortune? Think about that for a moment!

THINK, IN FACT, MORE widely about all the reversals of cultural normalcy and audience expectations in the parables of Jesus seen so far. Imagine them especially in the face-to-face situation of an oral interaction. Try to imagine it as it would have originally happened. Would there have been an absolute and respectful silence for, say, an hour-plus as Jesus performed his story? Or would there have been interruptions and pushbacks, agreements and disagreements, not only between speaker and hearers, but among the hearers themselves?

It is precisely in such audience interaction that orally delivered challenges attempt to raise the consciousness of listeners by luring and leading them into thinking for themselves. In other words, challenge parables are a participatory pedagogy, a collaborative education. (In Latin *docere* means "to teach" and *ducare* means "to lead." Our word "e-ducation" means "to lead thought out" rather than "to push thought in.")

If an audience kept complete silence during a challenge parable from Jesus and if an audience filed past him afterward saying, "Lovely parable, this morning, Rabbi," Jesus would have failed utterly. Move on, Master, to a different parable or a different audience.

Before continuing, I return once more to those two preceding parables. As in the paradigmatic Good Samaritan story, there was a clear reversal of traditional expectations within Jesus's own culture as its positive poles, or "good guys"—cleric, scholar, and aristocrat—were negated, and its negative poles, or "bad guys"—Samaritan, tax collector, and pauper—were exalted. In my next two cases, there are similar polar dialectics, but they are less obvious, more subtle, and would have demanded—and probably received—greater oral interaction. In all challenge parables, however, the audience is lured, led, and provoked into reaction, response, and reflection. Challenge parables are participatory—because provocative—pedagogy.

THE PARABLE OF THE Vineyard Workers is found only in Matthew 20:1–16. It concerns "a landowner who went out early in the morning to hire laborers for his vineyard. After agreeing with the laborers for the usual daily wage, he sent them into his vineyard" (20:1–2). After that opening, the parable's central section is framed by the theme of "standing idle" like this:

> [9 A.M.] When he went out about nine o'clock, he saw *others standing idle* in the marketplace; and he said to them, "You also go into the vineyard, and I will pay you whatever is right." So they went.
> [12 P.M.] When he went out again about noon
> [3 P.M.] and about three o'clock, he did the same.
> [5 P.M.] And about five o'clock he went out and found *others standing around;* and he said to them, "Why are you *standing here idle* all day?" They said to him, "Because no one has hired us." He said to them, "You also go into the vineyard." (20:3–7).

For the moment, just notice those emphasized frames; the opening single mention of "others standing idle" (20:3) and the closing double mention of "others standing around" and "standing here idle all day" (20:7). I will return to them later. But, for now, you probably remember what happened at 6 P.M.:

> When evening came, the owner of the vineyard said to his manager, "Call the laborers and give them their pay, beginning with the last and then going to the first." When those hired about five o'clock came, each of them received the usual daily wage. Now when the first came, they thought they would receive more; but each of them also received the usual daily wage. And when they received it, they grumbled against the landowner, "These last worked only one hour, and you have made them equal to us who have borne the burden of the day and the scorching heat." But he replied to one of them, "Friend, I am doing you no wrong; did you not agree with me for the usual daily wage? Take what belongs to you and go; I choose to give to this last the same as I give to you. Am I not allowed to

do what I choose with what belongs to me? Or are you envious because I am generous?" (20:8–15)

How is the parable of the Vineyard Workers to be interpreted? In other words, how do we imagine the oral audience of Jesus in the first-century Roman-controlled Jewish homeland would have responded to it?

It is possible, of course, that his first hearers would have immediately and exclusively focused on that 6 P.M. moment and argued for or against the vineyard owner's fairness. They might all have debated about the personal and individual justice of that distribution of pay. But I am not convinced that a Galilean peasant audience's free-for-all reaction would allow interpretation to remain exclusively there—for three reasons.

One reason is that the protagonist is a "vineyard owner." Such an occupation demanded major capital investment with labor-intensive preparation and maintenance—maybe even starting with a terraced hillside—several years before a first harvest produced any results. The average peasant might not have been endeared to that "capitalist" from the very start of the story.

Another reason is that Jesus relentlessly depicts the owner as a cheapskate. He keeps trying to have as *few* workers to pay as possible. He goes out again and again—even as late as 5 P.M.—rather than hire all that were available at 6 A.M. that morning. Jesus's story emphasizes that the owner went out those extra four times. Jesus could have had—if he had wanted—the workers arrive by themselves at those various times throughout the day.

A final and conclusive reason is that deliberate emphasis on "idleness" at 9 A.M. and 5 P.M. Would the workers have agreed with that snide comment? Above all, there is that outrageously provocative comment by the owner at 5 P.M.: "Why are you *standing here idle* all day?" And we can imagine their reply (through gritted teeth?): "Because no one has hired us." (Then—as now—one blames the *unhired* worker for laziness!) Would nobody have picked up, protested, and then debated that particular aspect of the parable?

I propose—for those three reasons—that at least some, most, or all of Jesus's audience would have raised questions not just about the *owner's* generosity, but about the *system's* perversity. How is it that at high harvest in the vineyards, when, with time pressing, labor should have been at an absolute premium and paying top denarius, there were so many day laborers still looking for work when it was almost sunset? Strange, is it not, how all that turned out for the owner's and not the workers' advantage?

The intention and purpose of that challenge parable were to raise the audience's consciousness about the distinction between personal or individual justice and injustice, on the one hand, and structural or systemic justice and injustice, on the other. If everyone talked only about the *owner* and not the *system*, Jesus's challenge would have failed. Move on Jesus, try it again somewhere else, or remove it from your repertoire forever.

Look, one final time, at those accusatory words about "idleness." They are not actually necessary if the story is about the master's generosity. But they are vitally necessary to provoke the audience—or at least day laborers in it—to protest against them and, thereby, raise the issue of—in my words—the distinction between personal and individual justice or injustice (the master) and structural and systemic injustice (the economy). That is a challenge parable hard—and very successfully—at work. I turn next to another parable about money—from a challenge about paying out money to one about lending out money.

IN CHAPTERS 4 AND 5 I discussed several parables of Jesus for which we have only one extant version. I look finally at a parable that has three versions, two inside and one outside the New Testament. This is the parable of the Master's Money.

One version, in Matthew 25:14–30, has three characters to whom a man, departing on a journey, entrusts valuable resources for investment:

> It is as if a man, going on a journey, summoned his slaves and entrusted his property to them; to one he gave five talents, to another two, to another one, to each according to his ability. Then he went away.
>
> The one who had received the five talents went off at once and traded with them, and made five more talents. In the same way, the one who had the two talents made two more talents. But the one who had received the one talent went off and dug a hole in the ground and hid his master's money. (25:14–18)

A talent of gold weighed about 30 pounds and was worth about 6,000 denarii—with a single denarius representing a laborer's daily pay. In ancient terms, the revenues from Antipas's domains in Galilee and Perea were about 200 talents. In modern terms, that first slave had just received $2 million. In other words, Jesus is capturing his audience's attention with a "fairy-tale" amount of money:

> After a long time the master of those slaves came and settled accounts with them. Then the one who had received the five talents came forward, bringing five more talents, saying, "Master, you handed over to me five talents; see, I have made five more talents."
>
> His master said to him, "Well done, good and trustworthy slave; you have been trustworthy in a few things, I will put you in charge of many things; enter into the joy of your master."
>
> And the one with the two talents also came forward, saying, "Master, you handed over to me two talents; see, I have made two more talents."
>
> His master said to him, 'Well done, good and trustworthy

slave; you have been trustworthy in a few things, I will put you in charge of many things; enter into the joy of your master." (25:19–23)

The first two slaves converse with the master using the same language verbatim. Recall that, in the Good Samaritan parable, the priest and Levite were also described identically: "A priest was going down that road; and when he saw him, he passed by on the other side. So likewise a Levite, when he came to the place and saw him, passed by on the other side" (10:31–32). Those first two similar descriptions raise expectations for a very different third one:

Then the one who had received the one talent also came forward, saying, "Master, I knew that you were a harsh man, reaping where you did not sow, and gathering where you did not scatter seed; so I was afraid, and I went and hid your talent in the ground. Here you have what is yours."

But his master replied, "You wicked and lazy slave! You knew, did you, that I reap where I did not sow, and gather where I did not scatter? Then you ought to have invested my money with the bankers, and on my return I would have received what was my own with *interest* (Greek *tokos*). So take the talent from him, and give it to the one with the ten talents." (25:24–28; italics added)

Notice, for future consideration, that description of the master's unfair and greedy character and how even the master himself agrees with it.

There is a second and strikingly different version of this parable in Luke 19:12–26. First of all, it is combined and framed within another story about a would-be ruler who went abroad to obtain— successfully—a kingdom (19:12, 14, 27). Next, the money involved is pounds instead of talents—with a pound worth about 100 denarii, while, as you recall, a talent was about 6,000. Furthermore, the number of slaves and the amounts of money are also different: "He summoned ten of his slaves, and gave them ten pounds, and said to them, 'Do business with these until I come back'" (19:13). Finally, the amounts accrued are also different:

> When he returned, having received royal power, he ordered these slaves, to whom he had given the money, to be summoned so that he might find out what they had gained by trading.
>
> The first came forward and said, "Lord, your pound has made ten more pounds."
>
> He said to him, "Well done, good slave! Because you have been trustworthy in a very small thing, take charge of ten cities."
>
> Then the second came, saying, "Lord, your pound has made five pounds."
>
> He said to him, "And you, rule over five cities." (19:15–19)

Still, despite there being ten slaves in Luke, only three receive any attention in the final review. After those two, comes this third and final one:

> Then the other came, saying, "Lord, here is your pound. I wrapped it up in a piece of cloth, for I was afraid of you, because you are a harsh man; you take what you did not deposit, and reap what you did not sow."
>
> He said to him, "I will judge you by your own words, you wicked slave! You knew, did you, that I was a harsh man, taking what I did not deposit and reaping what I did not sow? Why then did you not put my money into the bank? Then when I returned, I could have collected it with interest."
>
> He said to the bystanders, "Take the pound from him and give it to the one who has ten pounds." (19:20–24)

But all those differences we noted between Matthew and Luke only draw forceful attention to how almost verbatim is that climactic interchange between the master and the third slave. There is the same description of the master as greedy, his own acceptance of that assessment, and the final mention of "interest." Hold all of that in mind as we look at the third version.

The parable of the Master's Money is among those parables of Jesus present in gospels both inside and outside the New Testament. There is another and even more different version of it in the *Gospel of the Nazarenes*, an expansion of Matthew's Greek text used by Christian Jews from western Syria in the first half of the second century. There is no extant manuscript of that gospel, and its scattered fragments are found only in quotations by early Christian theologians.

The fourth-century bishop Eusebius of Caesarea, for example, gives us this version of the Master's Money in his *Theophany* (4.12):

> [The master] had three servants: one who squandered his master's substance with harlots and flute-girls, one who multiplied the gain, and one who hid the talent; and accordingly one was accepted (with joy), another merely rebuked, and another cast into prison.

But how are those three reactions to be distributed among the three servants? If you take it as a *simple parallel sequence*, the three different actions get these three judgments:

> [A1] one who squandered his master's substance with harlots
> and flute-girls,
>> [B1] one who multiplied the gain,
>>> [C1] and one who hid the talent;
> [A2] one was accepted (with joy),
>> [B2] another merely rebuked,
>>> [C2] and another cast into prison.

But that makes no sense because, despite what happens to the latter two servants, the multiplier and the hider, the first one, the squanderer, could hardly have been "accepted (with joy)." Instead, of course, the story must be read as a *reversed parallel sequence*, with this overall structure:

[A1] one who squandered his master's substance with harlots and flute-girls,
> [B1] one who multiplied the gain,
>> [C1] and one who hid the talent;
>> [C2] one was accepted (with joy),
> [B2] another merely rebuked,
[A2] and another cast into prison.

This version of the Master's Money was presented in elegant reversed parallelism—a poetic device we saw in Chapter 1 as Mark 4:11–13 cited Isaiah 6:10. But that structure means that, of the three servants, the squanderer is "imprisoned" [A1, A2], the multiplier is "rebuked" [B1, B2], and the hider [C1, C2] is "accepted." The hider is, in other words, the ideal servant.

So what about the interpretation of this multiversion parable? Where exactly is its challenge? That question must be answered—once again and always—by trying to imagine the reaction of a first-century Jewish audience. Jesus would have welcomed discussion and debate. Would some, many, most, or all agree or disagree with the first two servants and denigrate or praise the third one in the versions of Matthew and Luke? Or, again, what would they think of that third version? If they generally agreed with what happened to the squanderer, would they agree or disagree that the hider was better than the multiplier and was, in fact, the ideal investor?

In any case, what exactly was at stake on either side of that debate in the time and place of Jesus? Here is a clue. On the one hand, those two versions of the Master's Money in Matthew and Luke contain the only mention of "interest" in the entire New Testament

(Matt. 25:27; Luke 19:23). On the other, there are several mentions of it in the Old Testament—*and every single one of them is negative.* It is surely strange, then, to presume that the first two slaves are a positive and the final one a negative example—for a first-century Jewish audience faithful to covenant and tradition. In other words, is the audience being provoked to agree *or* disagree with the master's actions? To agree or disagree with *which* slave's actions? And thereby to think for or against that *multiplication* of money known as *interest?*

What does the Torah think about taking interest from one's fellow Jews? The answer is very clear in all three of the oldest law codes—in Exodus 22–23, Deuteronomy 12–26, and Leviticus 17–26—within the five books of the present Torah:

> If you lend money to my people, to the poor among you, you shall not deal with them as a creditor; you shall not exact interest from them. (Exod. 22:25)

> You shall not charge interest on loans to another Israelite, interest on money, interest on provisions, interest on anything that is lent. (Deut. 23:19)

> Do not take interest in advance or otherwise make a profit from them, but fear your God; let them live with you. You shall not lend them your money at interest taken in advance, or provide them food at a profit. (Lev. 25:36–37)

Advance interest means that, if you require a loan of 100 denarii at 10 percent, I give you 90 and you owe me a 100 back. *Accrued interest* means that I give you 100 and you owe me 110 back.

As you will recall from Chapter 4, the Babylonians, having destroyed the Temple, took Jerusalem's lay and priestly aristocracy into exile at the start of the 500s BCE. During the exile, the priest-prophet Ezekiel placed both those types of interest taking alongside many other forms of injustice and violence:

[If one] does not take advance or accrued interest [but] withholds his hand from iniquity, executes true justice between contending parties . . . he shall surely live. . . . [If one] takes advance or accrued interest; shall he then live? He shall not. He has done all these abominable things; he shall surely die; his blood shall be upon himself. . . . [If one] withholds his hand from iniquity, takes no advance or accrued interest, observes my ordinances, and follows my statutes . . . he shall surely live. (18:8–9, 13, 17)

Imagine how serious those accusations were in the context of the Babylonian exile, judged as divine punishment for infidelity to the Torah. Again: "You . . . take bribes to shed blood; you take both advance interest and accrued interest, and make gain of your neighbors by extortion; and you have forgotten me, says the Lord God" (22:12).

Finally, 4 Maccabees, written at the start of the 40s CE, insists on fidelity to Torah with regard to interest taking:

As soon as one adopts a way of life in accordance with the law, even though a lover of money, one is forced to act contrary to natural ways and to lend without interest to the needy and to cancel the debt when the seventh year arrives. (2:8)

We must, in other words, hear that parable of Jesus with ancient Jewish ears attuned to Torah and not with modern American ears attuned to Wall Street.

I suggest, therefore, that, on the immediate level, the intention of Jesus was to create audience debate between the Roman pro-interest tradition within the empire and the Jewish anti-interest tradition within the Torah. If there were those in his audience, for example, "who do not lend money at interest, and do not take a bribe against the innocent" (Ps. 15:5), that parable would have created an intensely religio-political argument with others who might have disagreed with that ideal.

The parable is not simply about *interest*, but about *world*. Or, better, it is about world as embodied here in interest, as incarnated here in profit. The parable challenges you to think about these questions. What about interest and gain? Whose law do you follow? Do you live by the Torah or the practices of Rome? Do you live in a Jewish or a Gentile world? Do you live under God or under Rome? Do you accept God's laws or Rome's customs? Who is in charge of Israel—is it God or Rome? Are you Roman or Jewish? How can you be both? Questions would necessarily move from the taking of interest to the imagining of one's world.

For Jesus—as indeed for all of his legal and prophetic ancestors—it was never simply a question of two divergent responses to interest. It was always a question of two divergent visions of the world as incarnated in two divergent visions of interest. It was always about whether or not—as Moses warned Pharaoh—"The earth is the Lord's" (Exod. 9:29). It was always about whether or not—as the psalm confesses—"The earth is the Lord's and all that is in it, the world, and those who live in it" (24:1). It was about, of course, how the earth was to be fairly distributed as a world for all God's people.

Finally, it is incorrect to focus on Matthew's term "talents" and take Jesus's story as an example parable advising full use of our God-given physical or spiritual "talents." That may be very wise advice, but it is not the thrust of this challenge parable. First, it would make God admit to being "harsh," would have God say, "I reap where I did not sow, and gather where I did not scatter" (25:24, 26). Second, it would make the New Testament God of Jesus support interest taking against the Old Testament God of Torah. That interpretation simply avoids the pointed challenge of Jesus, which is, to put it bluntly: Do you stand with the greedy or the needy?

I TURN NEXT TO the third step in this chapter's sequence. But first, as mentioned at its start, there is this difficulty. How do I, in the short space still available, look more widely across the parabolic repertoire of Jesus to suggest that challenges—rather than riddles or examples—were his characteristic parabolic style?

My plan is to contrast, for the parables of Jesus, the traditional normalcy of his general *format* with the radical novelty of his specific *content* within the *anthropological* expectations of popular storytelling—both in its general folklore tradition and in its specific Jewish tradition.

On the one hand, Jesus's parable *format* is very consistent with standard folklore storytelling customs. On the other hand, his parable *content* is emphatically not what general—or Jewish—storytelling would lead you to expect. That is precisely the power of its challenge, and, of course, what I mean by the "power of parable" in this book's title.

The *format* reassures you that all is culturally normal, but the *content* resolutely subverts that traditional normalcy. Think about that clash of format and content, that discrepancy between style and substance, because that is precisely where you can see challenge parables at work. I look first at format and then at content—but with the wide reach of anthropology as my guide for both aspects of Jesus's parables.

For over forty years Alan Dundes was a brilliantly controversial professor of folklore studies at the University of California, Berkeley. He assembled a collection of articles on folklore, and among them was a very famous one from 1909, "Epic Laws of Folk Narrative," by the Danish scholar Axel Olrik, first given at an interdisciplinary congress at Berlin in 1908. By *laws* Olrik meant standard narrative traditions, customs, and expectations in popular storytelling throughout folktale, legend, and myth. Olrik's classic essay enumerated thirteen such principles and called them *laws*, "because they limit the freedom of composition of oral literature in a much different and more rigid way than in our written literature."* Granted the brevity of

---

* Alan Dundes, ed., *The Study of Folklore* (Englewood Cliffs, NJ: Prentice-Hall, 1965), p. 131.

even Jesus's longest parables, their style fits well within Olrik's general "laws." Here are a few examples, with emphasis on the number of protagonists in Jesus's stories.

Olrik mentions the "law of concentration on a leading character," and Jesus will very often do even better with only one character on whom to concentrate the narrative of a parable. Think, for example, of the rich fool in Luke 12:16–21, the treasure finder or the pearl buyer in Matthew 13:44–46, the tower builder or the warring king in Luke 14:28–32, the sower, seen in Chapter 1, and the shepherd or the housewife finding lost things, seen in Chapter 2. Watch, for yourself, and see how often that happens in other parables.

Olrik also notes the "law of twins," that is, of two characters in a story. This is often combined with the "law of two to a scene." Examples would be the master and steward in Luke 16:1–12, the widow and judge in Luke 18:1–8, the sleeper and knocker in Luke 11:5–8, and, of course, the Pharisee and the tax collector or Lazarus and the rich man just seen in this chapter. Once again, think of other cases for yourself.

With regard to Olrik's "law of three characters," we have already seen the father with two sons in the Prodigal Son; the priest, Levite, and Samaritan in the Good Samaritan; and the three servants in the Master's Money. Another example is the three guests who are too busy to come in the parable of the Great Dinner in Luke 14:16–24.

Notice, also, how Olrik's "law of repetition" appears in those three-character stories. In the Good Samaritan, priest and Levite are described repetitively and verbatim: ". . . going down that road, . . . saw him, . . . passed by on the other side" (Luke 10:31–32). Similarly with the first two servants in the Master's Money: "Well done, good and trustworthy slave; . . . I will put you in charge of . . ." (Matt. 25:20–23).

The "law of three" dictates that, when you have three characters or tests or trials, the first two will often be repetitively unsuccessful, but the third one will be successful, final, and climactic. That worked from priest to Levite to Samaritan, and it also worked—at least in Jesus's challenge—from first to second to third servant in the Master's Money. First two failures and finally a success.

That also exemplifies the "law of patterning"—keeping similar scenes as repetitive as possible. So, then, after the priest and the Levite had passed by, Jesus's audience would know—before anything else was said—that the third character would be the positive one to watch at the story's climax. So also with those first two and then that final slave in the Master's Money.

Finally, again and again throughout Jesus's parables, we find Olrik's "law of contrast," the tendency toward polarization, especially of "good" versus "bad," "ins" versus "outs," "haves" versus "have-nots," and those who fail versus those who succeed. Think, for example, of the Two Sons in Matthew 21:28–32 or of the Wise and Foolish Virgins in Matthew 25:1–13.

But all of that common and traditional *format*, all of those standard aspects of popular oral storytelling, make the difference in Jesus's *content* even more dramatic. I turn, then, from expected *format* to unexpected *contrast*.

In Dundes's collection, there are also two articles by the anthropologist William Bascom. In the first one, "Folklore and Anthropology," he notes, "Folklore serves to sanction the established beliefs, attitudes, and institutions, both sacred and secular, and it plays a vital role in education in non-literate societies."* In the second one, "Four Functions of Folklore," he asks rhetorically whether there are any instances in folklore "which suggest that the individual destroy or even disregard the institutions and conventions of his society."† Since those comments are correct, the unconventional challenge parable and the conventional folklore story are set on a collision course. And that can be made even more specific with regard to Jewish storytelling.

---

* Dundes, ed., *Study of Folklore*, p. 33.

† Dundes, ed., *Study of Folklore*, p. 297.

The Belgrade-born anthropologist Heddy Jason wrote a doctoral dissertation at Indiana University on a database of stories collected from Near Eastern Jews who had emigrated from Muslim countries to live in Israel. This is her conclusion on those stories:

> The religious leader is implicitly the representative of the supreme values of the society and a questioning of his personal qualities or his right to leadership detracts from the validity of those values. For this reason there is not a single story in the whole Jewish Near Eastern material at our disposal which portrays the rabbi in a negative light or ridicules him as, on the contrary, the priest is frequently ridiculed in the Christian European tradition, or as, occasionally, is the rabbi in Jewish European society.*

In other words, Jesus's challenge parables seduced his audience by the expectedness of their *format*, while they subverted them with the unexpectedness of their *content*.

Do not, then, ever hear any of the specific names or classes or acts or episodes in the parables of Jesus with modern Christian ears; try to use ancient Jewish ears. And imagine the reactions among those first hearers in his original oral audiences. The probably unthought and possibly unseen foundations of their traditional world were being projected, probed, and pondered by those parables.

IN THIS PRESENT CHAPTER, I looked in some depth at four more challenge parables apart from that paradigmatic story of the Good Samaritan, and here are some conclusions from those cases.

Challenge parables submit their destiny to their audiences. Jesus can hope and intend, to be sure, but ultimately he cedes control to

---

* Heddy Jason, *Conflict and Resolution in Jewish Sacred Tales* (Ann Arbor, MI: University Microfilms, 1968), p. 90.

his hearers. He can only trust that the provocation of the challenge's content will raise consciousness about some aspect of the normalcy his people take for granted. And so it was, of course, with Ruth, Jonah, and Job before him.

Challenge parables *mean*—that is, intend—to make us probe and question, ponder and wonder, discuss and debate, and, above all else, practice that gift of the human spirit known as thinking. About what? About the absolutes of our religious faith, the certainties of our theological vision, the presuppositions, presumptions, and prejudices of our social, political, and economic traditions.

Challenge parables are not about replacing certitude with doubt, because certitude and doubt are but opposite ends of the same spectrum. Challenge parables foster not periodic doubting, but permanent questioning. Their hope is—from the poet Rainer Maria Rilke—to help us "love the questions" and "live the questions." Their purpose is—from the poet Gerard Manley Hopkins—to "Jolt / Shake and unset your morticed metaphors." Their intention is—from the prophet Micah—to make us "walk *humbly* with our God."

Jesus was, of course, an oral teacher with an interactive audience. Parables that we can read in a minute or two would have taken an hour or two to tell, would have been regularly interrupted by agreement and disagreement, and would have been intended to provoke—yes, provoke—discussion, debate, and thought. But always understand that such challenges intend to shake the foundations of one's world. Socrates did it with challenge *questions*, and Jesus with challenge *parables*. And in the long run, both processes proved lethal to the speaker—and immortal for the speaker.

By now you have guessed the subject of the next and final chapter in this book's first part. Matthew, for example, began the parable of the Vineyard Workers by saying, "The kingdom of heaven is like a landowner who went out early in the morning to hire laborers for his vineyard" (20:1). And that correlation of the *kingdom of God* and the *parables of Jesus* comes up repeatedly in the gospel texts.

In fact, there is a massive consensus in modern biblical scholarship on these three conclusions: first, that the fundamental message of Jesus was about the kingdom of God; second, that Jesus spoke very often in parables; and third, that he often made a correlation between kingdom and parable. That gives us the generative questions for the next chapter. *Why* did Jesus use such challenge parables? Is there some intrinsic connection between Jesus's *medium* of parabolic challenge and his *message* of God's kingdom? And, if so, what is it?

CHAPTER 6

The Kingdom of God

THE CHALLENGE OF COLLABORATION

ALTHOUGH HE HIMSELF DID NOT coin the term "paradigm shift," it was *The Structure of Scientific Revolutions*,[*] by Thomas S. Kuhn, then professor of the history of science at the University of California, Berkeley, that made it famous. He used the term to argue that progress in the *physical* sciences was not a smoothly linear development, but rather a series of disruptive innovations.

At any given stage there is, Kuhn proposed, a *normal paradigm* taken for granted and taught simply as the way it is, as science or even as reality. Then, with anomalies and misfits accumulating, normal science moves into a *crisis mode*. Finally, a radically alternative vision or revolutionary new model is proposed, and there occurs—often through a younger generation—a *paradigm shift* from the old model to the newer one, from, say, Ptolemy to Copernicus, Newton to Einstein, or biblical literalism to Darwinian evolution. ("Paradigm shifters" are much like "outliers" in Malcolm Gladwell's 2008 book of that same name.[†] They are individuals who by the interaction of

---

[*] Thomas S. Kuhn, *The Structure of Scientific Revolutions*, 3rd ed. (Chicago: Univ. of Chicago Press, 1996).

[†] Malcolm Gladwell, *Outliers* (New York: Little, Brown, 2008).

chance or luck and work or study successfully challenge general tradition with a specific vision and change the world one way or another.)

Although the term "paradigm shift" has been massively used, abused, and confused outside its original meaning, it is still a very useful explanatory concept not just for the physical sciences, but for many social and even human "sciences" as well. I use it in this chapter as an equivalent term for a revolutionary change, a basic tradition swerve, or a fundamentally disruptive innovation.

Just think, for example, of the first century CE as a crisis of multiple religio-political paradigm shifts. By the start of that century, after twenty years of savage civil war, the Roman Empire had shifted its paradigm from a republic ruled by two aristocrats in office for only a year to a monarchy ruled by one dynasty in control for as long as possible. That is *political* paradigm shift writ large. By the end of that same century, after eight years of class warfare and colonial revolt, the Jewish homeland was devastated, Jerusalem and its great Temple were destroyed, and leadership had shifted its paradigm from Temple, priest, and sacrifice to Torah, rabbi, and study. That is *religious* paradigm shift writ large.

In between those Roman and Judean revolutions came the Galilean revolution inaugurated by Jesus of Nazareth. Compared to those social earthquakes, his seemed at first but a minor surface tremor. But that is often how seismic disturbances start. In the religio-political world, Jesus was a master paradigm shifter, a supreme tradition troubler, and, for some, a divine outlier.

Think, to begin with, of the following example of Jesus's visionary challenge to his contemporary Judaism. In 1995, John J. Collins, then professor of Hebrew Bible at the University of Chicago Divinity School, published *The Scepter and the Star: The Messiahs of the Dead Sea Scrolls and Other Ancient Literature*. Apart from minor, special, or even sectarian visions of God's messianic agent, there was, he proposed, this standard common expectation:

This concept of the Davidic messiah as the warrior king who would destroy the enemies of Israel and institute an era of unending peace constitutes the common core of Jewish messianism around the turn of the era.

There was a dominant notion of a Davidic messiah, as the king who would restore the kingdom of Israel, which was part of the common Judaism around the turn of the era.*

But, since much of the New Testament was part of the "other ancient [Jewish] literature" in his book title, how does it see Jesus as God's messianic agent? In an early comment, as striking as it is passing, Collins notes:

Although the claim that he [Jesus of Nazareth] is the Davidic messiah is ubiquitous in the New Testament, he does not fit the typical profile of the Davidic messiah. This messiah was, first of all, a warrior prince, who was to defeat the enemies of Israel.†

In summary, therefore, the interpretation of Jesus as the Davidic Messiah within the "Christian," that is, "messianic," New Testament is *atypical* with the common consensus on that figure in its contemporary environment. That is a *paradigm shift*, a revolutionary change, a swerve within the Jewish popular consensus of its time and place.

THIS OVERTURE SERVES TO introduce the four governing questions for this chapter. First, what was the general biblical tradition of God's kingdom *before* the time of Jesus? Next, why is that tradition

---

* John J. Collins, *The Scepter and the Star* (New York: Doubleday, Anchor Bible Reference Library, 1995), pp. 68, 209.

† Collins, *Scepter and the Star*, p. 13.

described by scholars as *eschatological* and *apocalyptic*? What, in other words, is meant by an *apocalyptically eschatological* kingdom of God? Then, what has Jesus to say about such a divine kingdom and, if he represents a paradigm shift within the contemporary understanding of it, what exactly is his innovation? Finally, granted all of that, how is the *medium* of Jesus's challenge parables particularly or especially appropriate to that *message* of God's kingdom?

THE BEST PLACE TO begin an answer to the first question about the pre-Jesus tradition of God's kingdom is in the Old Testament book of Daniel, written in the mid-160s BCE. The Jewish people were then under severe persecution from the tottering Syrian Empire of Antiochus IV Epiphanes—who was not exactly the divine *epiphany* Israel had expected. In response to his attacks, Daniel 7 asserted an absolute confrontation between, on the one hand, earthly and imperial kingdoms and, on the other, a heavenly and transcendental kingdom. That clash is revealed to Daniel in a dream vision with two separate acts.

The *first act* concerns earth's empires. An *empire* is one people or nation using other peoples or nations for its own use, benefit, and advantage. Daniel 7 identifies four such major empires prior to its time of writing.

The first three are the Babylonian, Median, and Persian Empires. They are not *personified*, made to be "like" human persons, but rather *animalified*, said to be "like a lion, . . . like a bear, . . . like a leopard." Those empires are like wild beasts attacking the earth or like roaring ocean waves assaulting the shore (7:2–6). For the fourth, the Greek Empire of Alexander the Great, there was no feral beast adequate for comparison with its dreadful war machine. It is terrifyingly "different . . . different . . . different" (7:7, 19, 23). And, the Syrian Empire is but a broken remnant of that great world empire. It is only to be counted as a tiny horn on the Greek beast's head (7:8, 11, 20, 21).

In heaven, however, God, the eternally "Ancient One," convened

a great court of justice, a great tribunal of judgment. "Their dominion was taken away" from those feral beasts (7:12). It was taken from
all of them, or, in other words, imperialism itself was solemnly condemned by God.

The *second act* concerns God's kingdom. A mysterious figure, *not*
one like a beast, but "one like a human being" is presented before
God. (As English male chauvinism once used "mankind" for "humanity," so, in Daniel 7, Semitic male chauvinism originally used
"one like a son of man" for "one like a human being.") This transcendental figure receives, personifies, and brings down to earth the
kingdom of God as the ultimate replacement for those condemned
empires. This is proclaimed three times, but with three very deliberate stages or steps:

> *Stage 1: To him* was given dominion and glory and kingship,
> that all peoples, nations, and languages should serve him. His
> dominion is an everlasting dominion that shall not pass away,
> and his kingship is one that shall never be destroyed. (7:14)

> *Stage 2:* But *the holy ones* of the Most High shall receive the
> kingdom and possess the kingdom forever—forever and ever.
> (7:18)

> *Stage 3:* The kingship and dominion and the greatness of the
> kingdoms under the whole heaven shall be given *to the people
> of the holy ones* of the Most High; their kingdom shall be an
> everlasting kingdom, and all dominions shall serve and obey
> them. (7:27)

That sequence imagines the kingdom of God as created and pre-
pared in heaven—like a model city in an architect's office. But, pre-
pared there (Stage 1) and conserved there (Stage 2), it is to come
down eventually to this earth (Stage 3).

First, it is given into the care and protection of that mysterious "one like a human being"—probably the archangel Michael. Next, he, along with "the holy ones"—probably the angels—must guard it in heaven. Finally, it comes down to earth for "the people of the holy ones of the Most High"—certainly and definitely the people of Israel.

You will notice, however, that we are not told *how* and *when* that will happen. Neither are we told how exactly the kingdom of God comes down to earth and *differs* from those great empires. Externally, they were temporary and passing, they came and went, but the kingdom of God is permanent and everlasting. But how precisely does it differ from them internally? How—*internally*—is its rule or dominion different from theirs?

MY SECOND QUESTION CONSIDERS the two official words that scholarship uses to discuss that kingdom of God in its advent from heaven to earth. They call it an *eschatological* and/or an *apocalyptic* kingdom.

The Greek noun *eschaton*—and its derivatives "eschatology" and "eschatological"—have been mystified beyond all human comprehension in recent scholarship, but they are actually very simple concepts. In itself, *eschaton* means the "last" or "end" of something, so its meaning depends completely on what that something is. It could be, for example, simply the end of a ticket line at any airport in Greece. What, then, did *eschaton* mean in the biblical tradition? End of what?

Israel's *covenantal faith* was that a God of "justice and righteousness" had created the earth and chosen Israel to be a witness to a lifestyle of distributive justice. But Israel's *colonial experience* was that the earth was thoroughly unjust and that Israel had received far more than its fair share of imperial injustice. Israel reconciled its faith and its experience by insisting that God would some day—"in days to come"—make an "end" to the evil, injustice, oppression, war, and violence here below upon a transformed earth. *Eschaton* was not, repeat not, about the destruction of the earth, but about the transfiguration of this earth. The direction of *eschaton* was not from earth to heaven, but rather from heaven to earth. My own translation of that biblical eschatology is: *the Great Divine Cleanup of the World*.

Next, what does the Greek noun *apocalypsis*—and its English derivatives "apocalypse" and "apocalyptic"—mean? An apocalypse is simply a revelation (Latin *revelatio*), a divine or prophetic message about something. So, once again, everything depends on what that something is. In the biblical tradition, *apocalyptic eschatology* meant—in my terms—some *Special Divine Revelation about the Great Divine Cleanup of the World*. In itself, that message could be about *any* aspect of that cleanup. But, at the time of Jesus, it had come to focus on one very special aspect of it. What was that?

Think of that first century CE in the Jewish homeland. Those four and a bit empires of Daniel were all gone, and in their place was the Roman Empire, the greatest empire the world had ever known—or maybe would ever know. Imperial dominion was getting stronger, not weaker. So any credible apocalyptic eschatology had to be a revelation that persuasively answered these questions: If not now, why? If not now, when? Will God act soon? In our lifetime? Is the Great Cleanup imminent? If your apocalypse or revelation was that it was all decades distant, you would probably be an instant ex-apocalyptic eschatologist and had better keep your day job. If your apocalypse or revelation was that it would all happen soon, that was easy to say, but something more than mere assertion was needed to be persuasive.

One final point. To speak of God's "kingdom" is to use a word that is both archaic and patriarchal. What that word focuses on in its original languages is best translated as "style of rule" or "ruling style." It ponders how this world would be if God were actually seated down here ruling—as it were—from a human throne. How would the "ruling style" of God differ from that of a human emperor? That is what is at stake in the phrase "kingdom of God."

MY THIRD QUESTION IS about Jesus's vision as a paradigm shift within that contemporary expectation of Jewish apocalyptic eschatology. It concerns his own creative innovation within that biblical tradition about the kingdom of God. But what is the best way to explain and emphasize Jesus's tradition swerve in the short space of this chapter?

My strategy is to compare and contrast John the Baptist, as representing Israel's *paradigm* for the advent of God's kingdom, with Jesus, as representing a *paradigm shift* in that tradition about that same divine transformation of the world. But, before proceeding, I need to utter a word of caution.

In comparing and contrasting them, I do not intend any cheap exaltation of Jesus over John. I am convinced that Jesus learned tremendously from John—learned both what to say and do, but also what not to say and not to do. Furthermore, the execution of John probably saved Jesus from a like fate under a tetrarch who was smart enough (he ruled for forty-three years) not to kill two popular prophets in close proximity to one another. Still, with all due respect, Jesus differed profoundly from John by proclaiming a paradigm shift within the standard expectations of their contemporary apocalyptic eschatology. I will proceed with three steps.

I look first at the Baptist's vision of God's advent under three basic aspects. It is *imminent*; that is, it will happen very, very soon. It is *interventionist*; that is, it will involve transcendental divine power— alone. It is *violent*—not of course with human violence, but with the divine violence of an avenging God who comes punitively against any opposition, whether Jewish or Roman.

Next, I note the various stories about the difference between John and Jesus in the gospel texts. In other words, similarities and differences, comparisons and contrasts between John and Jesus are not just my invention, but already there in the gospel tradition.

Finally, I compare Jesus's message with John's under those same three aspects of the proclamation about God's kingdom on earth. But with Jesus, as distinct from John, that divine advent will be *present* rather than *imminent*, *collaborative* rather than *interventionist*, and *nonviolent* rather than *violent*. I begin with John's own message.

What, asked John, was delaying God? Why did God not act imme-diately? Why not now? Because of the people's sins, said John, in a not very original response—you will recall Deuteronomy 28 from Chap-ter 4. What, you can imagine those accused people asking, can we do?

This is where John got very, very original by inventing a great symbolic or sacramental reenactment of the exodus from Egypt. Here is his program. First, they would go out into the desert east of the Jordan. Next, they would pass through the river, and as its waters washed their bodies, repentance would wash their souls. Finally, they would emerge into the promised land as a newly purified people and, then, surely then, God would act to clean up the mess of the world, because then, surely then, God would have no reason to delay any longer. God's advent was *imminent*, an any-day-now affair.

God's imminent advent was also, of course, *interventionist* in that a purified and holy people could certainly prepare for it and maybe even hasten its coming, but it would still be an act of transcendental intervention by God alone. No wonder, therefore, that when "John the baptizer appeared in the wilderness, proclaiming a baptism of repentance for the forgiveness of sins, . . . people from the whole Judean countryside and all the people of Jerusalem were going out to him, and were baptized by him in the river Jordan, confessing their sins" (Mark 1:4–5). John's vision was interactive, operational, and very, very persuasive.

Furthermore, John's apocalypse/revelation was about the *immi-nent intervention* of the *avenging* God. Just listen to his invective:

When he saw many Pharisees and Sadducees coming for bap-tism, he said to them, "You brood of vipers! Who warned you to flee from the wrath to come? Bear fruit worthy of repen-tance. Do not presume to say to yourselves, 'We have Abraham as our ancestor'; for I tell you, God is able from these stones to raise up children to Abraham. Even now the ax is lying at the root of the trees; every tree therefore that does not bear good fruit is cut down and thrown into the fire." (Matt. 3:7–10)

Luke, for example, had two serious problems with that account of John's message. First of all, he found it so negative that he added his own more positive message after it:

> The crowds asked him, "What then should we do?" In reply he said to them, "Whoever has two coats must share with anyone who has none; and whoever has food must do likewise." Even tax collectors came to be baptized, and they asked him, "Teacher, what should we do?" He said to them, "Collect no more than the amount prescribed for you." Soldiers also asked him, "And we, what should we do?" He said to them, "Do not extort money from anyone by threats or false accusation, and be satisfied with your wages." (3:10–14)

But that was only Luke's first problem. His second problem was even more serious.

In our present New Testament, John's message about the advent of God was turned into one about the advent of Christ. But Christ did not act like an avenging presence, did not look like the wrath to come. Metaphors of cutting down trees and burning chaff with fire did not seem appropriate for him. So, once again, Luke created a conversation to remedy the discrepancy. John's disciples reported to him in prison that Jesus had just healed the Capernaum centurion's slave and raised the Nain widow's son (7:1–18). So John sent them to Jesus with this question: "Are you the one who is to come, or are we to wait for another?" (7:19). Jesus tells them: "Go and tell John what you have seen and heard: the blind receive their sight, the lame walk, the lepers are cleansed, the deaf hear, the dead are raised, the poor have good news brought to them. And blessed is anyone who takes no offense at me" (7:22–23).

John was an apocalyptic eschatologist, that is, a prophet with a revelation of the imminence of God's avenging advent, God's punitive intervention to transform a world grown old in evil. I emphasize once more that John did not advocate human violence or armed rebellion. Any eschatological violence was the prerogative of God. John's own nonviolent resistance is certified by Herod Antipas, who both executed John—because he was rebellious—and refrained from rounding up his followers—because he was nonviolent. That was how Romans or Romanizers handled *nonviolent resistance* to imperial law and order.

We must, however, start with—and always remember—this: *John's prophetic vision was as incorrect as it was persuasive.* For what intervened was not an avenging God, but an avenging tetrarch; what came was not the kingdom of God, but the cavalry of Antipas. John died in lonely isolation at Machaerus, the southernmost fortress in Antipas's territories. And God did nothing to stop it. That was something—for Jesus—to think about.

Next, we must see the *general* contrast between John and Jesus even within the gospel tradition before attempting to specify the *precise* contrast that I see between them.

Those who opposed both John and Jesus agreed that, although they were both strange, they were strange in opposite directions: "John came neither eating nor drinking, and they say, 'He has a demon'; the Son of Man came eating and drinking, and they say, 'Look, a glutton and a drunkard, a friend of tax collectors and sinners!'" (Matt. 11:18–19). We can bracket those name-calling interpretations—John as demon-possessed and Jesus as a drunken glutton—and still conclude that John and Jesus struck their opponents as being somehow opposites. One can, after all, abstain from food because of committed asceticism or demand food because of distributive justice. But the differences between John and Jesus are more complicated than that simple summary by their adversaries.

On the one hand, since Jesus was definitely baptized by John in the Jordan, he must have accepted his message of apocalyptic eschatology, his vision of God's imminent and avenging intervention for the Great Divine Cleanup of the World. We can be sure about John's baptism of Jesus, because of the gathering embarrassment about it as the tradition developed: Mark accepted it (1:9); Matthew protested it

(3:13–15), Luke hurried it (3:21a), and John omitted it entirely (1:29–34). Furthermore, the Spirit's descent on Jesus and God's address to Jesus render somewhat irrelevant anything that happened between John and Jesus—as all four evangelists attest (Mark 1:10–11; Matt. 3:16–17; Luke 3:21b–22; John 1:32–34).

On the other hand, when we hear Jesus speaking with his own voice and out of his own vision, he speaks and acts very differently from John. *Jesus neither denigrates nor agrees with John.* Think, for example, of this comment by Jesus about John:

> Truly I tell you, among those born of women no one has arisen greater than John the Baptist; yet the least in the kingdom of heaven is greater than he. (Matt. 11:11)

> I tell you, among those born of women no one is greater than John; yet the least in the kingdom of God is greater than he. (Luke 7:28)

The supreme accolade in the first half of each of those verses yields to a supreme indifference in the second half.

Another caution. The phrase "kingdom of heaven" is not about heaven, but about earth or, better, it is about God's kingdom coming down from heaven to earth. Notice, in that citation, that Matthew's "kingdom of heaven" is the same as Luke's "kingdom of God." The former politely uses the "dwelling" for the "dweller," as we today use "the White House says" for "the President says."

Matthew himself can even use both phrases in the same unit: "Truly I tell you, it will be hard for a rich person to enter the kingdom of heaven. Again I tell you, it is easier for a camel to go through the eye of a needle than for someone who is rich to enter the kingdom of God" (19:23–24). And, of course, the Lord's Prayer insists—in the Greek word sequence—that God's kingdom is "as in heaven so also on earth" (Matt. 6:10). It comes down here below and is, therefore, always about God's earth itself.

The opponents of John agree that they are opposites of each other. Yet Jesus began his public presence in agreement with and submission to John's vision. But then—carefully, respectfully, and quite definitely—Jesus distanced his own message from that of the Baptist. How is that to be explained? The answer is in the next and third step in contrasting John and Jesus.

My interpretation is that Jesus watched, Jesus learned, and *Jesus changed, because of what happened to John*. The Baptist had announced the imminent advent of God, but God did not come. John was executed, and God did not intervene to prevent his martyrdom. In response, Jesus radically reinterpreted *eschaton*—what was it to be?—*apocalypse*—when was it to be?—and *messiah*—who was it to be? He changed his understanding not only about the kingdom of God, but about the God of the kingdom. When he finally spoke with his own vision and his own voice, Jesus differed profoundly from John by proclaiming *a paradigm shift within their contemporary Jewish apocalyptic eschatology*. You can see Jesus's innovation most clearly by contrasting it with John's vision focused on those three points of divine imminence, divine intervention, and divine vengeance.

In the first major difference, Jesus proclaimed God's *presence* rather than God's imminence. John announced, as we just saw, that God's Great Cleanup of the World was *imminent*, was an any-day-now event. Jesus proclaimed, on the contrary, that God's transformative advent was *present*, was already here and now on earth. God's kingdom was imminent, in the future, for John, but already present for Jesus. Here are several examples of Jesus's stunning paradigm shift:

> The kingdom of God is not coming with things that can be observed; nor will they say, "Look, here it is!" or "There it is!" For, in fact, the kingdom of God is among you. (Luke 17:20–21)

> The law and the prophets were in effect until John came; since then the good news of the kingdom of God is pro-

claimed, and everyone tries to enter it by force. (Luke 16:16; Matt. 11:12–13)

If it is by the finger of God that I cast out the demons, then the kingdom of God has come to you. (Luke 11:20; Matt. 12:28)

Blessed are the eyes that see what you see! For I tell you that many prophets and kings desired to see what you see, but did not see it, and to hear what you hear, but did not hear it. (Luke 10:23b–24; Matt. 13:16–17)

The wedding guests cannot fast while the bridegroom is with them, can they? As long as they have the bridegroom with them, they cannot fast. The days will come when the bridegroom is taken away from them, and then they will fast on that day. (Mark 2:19–20; Matt. 9:15–16; Luke 5:34–35)

Jesus came to Galilee, proclaiming the good news of God, and saying, "The time is fulfilled, and the kingdom of God has come near; repent, and believe in the good news." (Mark 1:14b–15; Matt. 4:17)

Notice that final example. Every part of it points not to the *future soon*, but the *present now* of the kingdom of God.

Furthermore, recall, from the start of this chapter, that the "one like a human being" (literally, "one like a son of man") was assigned in the book of Daniel to bring God's kingdom down to earth for the "people of the holy ones of the Most High" (7:27). But Mark insists repeatedly that Jesus is that "Son of Man," that he is already present on earth (2:10, 28), that he will die and rise from the dead (8:31; 9:9, 12, 31; 10:33, 45; 14:21, 41), and that he will finally return in glory (8:38; 13:26; 14:26). But, of course, if Jesus the Son of Man, that is to say, Jesus as the truly Human One, is already on earth, then the kingdom of God is already in the world.

The second major difference between Jesus and John concerns

collaboration rather than intervention. Imagine, for a moment, a first-century audience's reaction to the—well, yes, absurdity—of Jesus's proclamation about the presence of God's kingdom here below. Look around you, hearers would have told Jesus, nothing has changed—the tetrarch Antipas is still there, the governor Pilate is still there, and, above all else, the emperor Tiberius is still there. Where, they would have asked, is God's Great Cleanup actively operational? You have simply replaced, they would have told Jesus, a "when" we cannot know with a "where" we cannot see. What would, what could, Jesus have answered to those powerful objections to his vision of the kingdom of God?

In answer Jesus proclaimed another—and, indeed, necessarily concomitant—aspect of his paradigm shift within contemporary eschatological expectation. You have been waiting for God, he said, while God has been waiting for you. No wonder nothing is happening. You want God's intervention, he said, while God wants your collaboration. *God's kingdom is here, but only insofar as you accept it, enter it, live it, and thereby establish it.* That is the only possible interpretation that does not render Jesus's claim of the kingdom's presence a bad and cruel joke. He is announcing, in other words, not a realized, but a realizable *eschaton* or, better, a *collaborative eschaton.* The Great Divine Cleanup will not happen without God, but neither will it happen without us. It is about a divine-and-human collaboration and not about a divine-only intervention.

John is the tradition's paradigm, and this is his message: "The kingdom's train is entering the station. Be on it or be under it." Jesus is the tradition's paradigm shift, and this is his countermessage: "You yourselves are the kingdom's train. God is the tracks. And what good are tracks without train or train without tracks?

The third major difference between Jesus and John concerns the mode of the kingdom's advent: it is *non-violent* rather than violent. By claiming the kingdom's presence, Jesus was invoking a bilateral divine-human collaboration, not a unilateral divine intervention.

("Covenant," by the way, was always a bilateral term.) But was that collaboration to be nonviolent or violent? Was Jesus demanding nonviolent or violent resistance to Rome as the contemporary incarnation of Daniel's "beastly" imperialism?

My answer will be that Jesus proclaimed nonviolent resistance to the injustice of Roman imperialism in a world that belonged to a just and nonviolent God. But I am certainly not claiming that Jesus—let alone Christianity—invented nonviolent resistance as distinct from the violent resistance of his contemporary homeland Judaism. My argument advances, therefore, in two steps—first, the Jewish experience of violent and nonviolent resistance to Rome, before, during, and after the time of Jesus; and second, how Jesus's program for God's kingdom fits within those contemporary options.

First, the Jewish experience of violent and nonviolent resistance to imperialism: In the first two hundred years of Rome's control over the Jewish homeland there were four major movements of armed rebellion, but also four major movements of unarmed resistance. Jesus lived, most likely, from about 4 BCE to about 30 CE. Watch, then, the dates of these violent and nonviolent revolts against Rome:*

Violent Resistance	Nonviolent Resistance
Under Augustus (4 BCE)	Under Augustus (6 CE)
Under Nero (66–74 CE)	Under Tiberius (26–36)
Under Trajan (115–17)	Under Tiberius (26–36)
Under Hadrian (132–35)	Under Caligula (40)

---

* Most of the sources are in Josephus, *Jewish War* and/or *Jewish Antiquities*. *Four violent revolts:* (1) 4 BCE, in *JW* 2.39–79; *JA* 17.250–99a; (2) 66–74 CE, in *JW* 2.277–7.455; (3) 115–17 CE, in Cassius Dio, *Roman History* 68.32.1–3; (4) 132–135 CE, in Cassius Dio, *Roman History* 69.12:1–14:3; 15:1. *Four nonviolent revolts:* (1) 6 CE, in *JW* 2.118, 433, 7.253; *JA* 18.1–10, 23–25; 20.102; (2) 26–36 CE over Pilate's standards, in *JW* 2.169–174; *JA* 18.55–59; (3) 26–36 CE over Pilate's aqueduct, in *JW* 175–177; *JA* 60–62; (4) 40 CE, in *JW* 2.184–203; *JA* 18.261–309; Philo, *On the Embassy to Gaius* 184–260. If you wish to read those texts, they are almost all available online.

You will notice immediately—from the left column—that Jesus grew to adulthood in the long lull between the first two armed rebellions against Rome, in 4 BCE and 66–74 CE. But you will also notice—from the right column—that he grew up during three and before a fourth act of massive, well-organized, unarmed, nonviolent resistance against Rome.

In speaking of Jesus's vision of nonviolent resistance within the collaborative kingdom of God, I emphatically do not mean that Jesus invented nonviolent resistance. It was—even more proximately than violent resistance—among the options in his immediately contemporary Jewish world. It is wise, by the way, not to presume that our modern world invented nonviolent resistance.

Second, how did Jesus fit within that Jewish matrix, which contained nonviolent as well as violent resistance to Rome? I consider that his message and program were based on nonviolent resistance for the following four main reasons.

The first reason concerns *Jesus and God:* his nonviolent resistance to the injustice of imperialism was proclaimed in collaboration with a nonviolent God. For Jesus, collaboration with God's kingdom now present on earth meant: "Love your enemies and pray for those who persecute you, so that you may be children of your Father in heaven; for he makes his sun rise on the evil and on the good, and sends rain on the righteous and on the unrighteous" (Matt. 5:44–45); or again: "Love your enemies, do good to those who hate you, bless those who curse you, pray for those who abuse you. . . . Love your enemies, do good, and lend, expecting nothing in return. Your reward will be great, and you will be children of the Most High; for he is kind to the ungrateful and the wicked" (Luke 6:27–28, 35). In other words, the model for human nonviolence is divine nonviolence, God as "your Father" (Matt. 5:48; Luke 6:36).

The second reason to see Jesus as a nonviolent resister concerns *Jesus and Weapons.* Jesus's companions struggled with the outward symbolism of nonviolence, which he had demanded from them.

Could you not carry at least a *defensive* weapon for your journey—a staff for a peasant or a sword for an aristocrat? Look at these no-and-yes, yes-and-no responses that indicate ongoing debate on that question within the tradition after Jesus:

Weapon	Do Not Use	Use	Do Not Use
Staff	Matthew 10:10; Luke 9:3	Mark 6:8	
Sword		Luke 22:35-36	Luke 22:37-38, 49-52

You can read over those texts and imagine the debates behind them about the use or nonuse of even a defensive weapon. For example, that earlier source for the "staff" material in Matthew and Luke—called the Q Gospel by scholars—explicitly forbids it, while the later text of Mark explicitly commands it! Both, of course, in the name of Jesus.

The third reason for classing Jesus as a nonviolent resister is Mark's story of *Jesus and Barabbas*, even though it is fictional parable rather than factual history. Mark wrote his version of the gospel after the Jewish revolt of 66–74 had left Jerusalem devastated and its Temple destroyed forever. His parable imagines Pilate confronted with two revolutionary figures, both publicly opposing Roman law and order. One is called Barabbas (whose name means "son of the father") and is violent. The other is Jesus (Son of the Father) and is nonviolent. Pilate arrests Barabbas along with his followers: "A man called Barabbas was in prison with the rebels who had committed murder during the insurrection" (15:7). Jesus is in prison alone—his companions are not arrested. The point of Mark's parable is that, in 66–74 CE, Jerusalem chose the wrong savior—the violent rather the nonviolent one.

The fourth reason for concluding that Jesus's resistance was nonviolent concerns *Jesus and Pilate*. This is another parable, again before Pilate, but this time in John 18:33–38. John imagines an interchange between Pilate and Jesus in which Pilate asks Jesus what he has done to be handed over to him (18:35). In Jesus's response (18:36), notice how the key phrase is repeated twice to frame his claim:

My kingdom is not from this world.

If my kingdom were from this world,

my followers would be fighting to keep me from being handed

over. . . .

But as it is, my kingdom is not from here.

Focus on that accurate contrast between the kingdom of God and the kingdom of Rome. Rome's kingdom is obtained and maintained, preserved and protected by violence, but God's kingdom will not allow violence even to free Jesus.

In other words, and I cannot emphasize this enough, Pilate got it precisely right (as did Antipas with John earlier). With *violent rebels*, Roman officials executed the leader and as many followers as they could capture. With *nonviolent rebels*, Roman officials executed the leader and ignored the followers. On the level of this most secure historicity, Pilate certifies for all time that Jesus was both a revolutionary—hence a need for public, legal, official crucifixion—but also nonviolent—hence no need to round up his companions. For Jesus and for many other Jews both before and after him in that dangerous first century, nonviolent resistance rather than violent rebellion was the preferred strategy against Roman imperial control.

I CONCLUDE THIS CHAPTER's third section, on Jesus's innovative, paradigm-shifting vision of God's kingdom, with two codicils.

The first is that, granted the shock of that interpretation, we should not be surprised that those who accepted it tried to mitigate its disruptive challenge. (That happens amid *every* paradigm shift. Augustus, for example, assured everyone—sincerely or insincerely?—that he was simply restoring the republic.) They said it would be over soon. The *eschaton*—the advent of God's kingdom on earth—had morphed from an *instant* of divine intervention to a *period* of human-divine collaboration. But, they said, *eschaton* as that period would be a short one. From Paul through Mark to Revelation, the earliest Christians certainly agreed that it would all be over soon—within, say, their own lifetime. The "soon" of the kingdom's *start* in the contemporary Jewish paradigm became the "soon" of the kingdom's *end* in the paradigm shift of Jesus. It is possible—but not certain—that Jesus himself imagined an imminent consummation of the kingdom's presence. But, if he did, then he—like all those others who certainly so imagined—were flatly wrong; they were off by two thousand years and still counting.

The second codicil is that, in discussing how a normal or standard paradigm is finally displaced by a new or revolutionary one, Kuhn concludes that "the transfer of allegiance from paradigm to paradigm is a conversion experience that cannot be forced." He quotes both Charles Darwin and Max Planck in his support. Darwin in his *On the Origin of Species* confessed, "I by no means expect to convince experienced naturalists. . . . I look with confidence to the future—to young and rising naturalists." Planck in his *Scientific Autobiography* admits that "a new scientific truth does not triumph by convincing its opponents and making them see the light, but rather because its opponents eventually die, and a new generation grows up that is familiar with it."* Even if a revolutionary shift commences within an older generation, it is often consummated only within the following one.

That a successful paradigm shift often requires a generational transition helps to explain the saying of Jesus: "I have come to set a man against his father, and a daughter against her mother, and a daughter-in-law against her mother-in-law; and one's foes will be members of one's own household" (Matt. 10:35–36). Notice that there is nothing in that aphorism about tension between husbands and wives or between brothers and sisters. Those in each of the three opposing pairs are from different generations. That is how, finally, the paradigm shifts—along with the generational shift.

---

* Kuhn, *Structure of Scientific Revolutions*, p. 151.

MY FOURTH AND FINAL question in this chapter concerns the cor-relation between Jesus's parables as *medium* and God's kingdom as *message*. How does all we have seen in the earlier chapters on Jesus's challenge parables connect with what we have seen in this chapter on Jesus's kingdom vision? My answer is that challenge parables are a profoundly appropriate rhetoric—even, indeed, an absolutely nec-essary one—for the two aspects of Jesus's vision of that kingdom, namely, its collaborative and nonviolent characteristics. I take up those correlations in that order—first, challenge parable and a col-laborative divine kingdom; second, challenge parable and a nonvio-lent divine kingdom.

I mentioned earlier that challenge parables concede ultimate authority and responsibility to the audience. All parables are inter-active, but challenge parables are especially so. Their purpose is to make you think about the fundamental presuppositions of your world, and the parabler must trust that the audience will respond creatively. We today are in much the same position in commenting on Jesus's parables. We can certainly use anthropology, sociology, history, and archaeology to *imagine* how first-century Jewish audi-ences *might* have responded. But we can never tell how they did in any specific case.

Imagine, for example, that Jesus told his Good Samaritan par-able, and the ongoing response from the audience was that all its pro-tagonists were idiots. Nobody, an audience might argue, would go down that dangerous road alone. Sensible people would have waited to form small caravans. Well, maybe the Samaritan would have had to travel alone. But all the others should have traveled together in safety. And then the Samaritan would have had no person to help. Stupid people, stupid story! If that had happened, there was little Jesus could do with that audience—they had, as it were, hijacked his story and taken it in a very different direction.

Think about that parable of the Unjust Steward, who, under threat of dismissal by his master, reduces the debts of his tenants

(Luke 16:1–7). It should have raised the audience's consciousness about the relationship between a "rich man," his "manager" (a slave?), and his debtors (tenant farmers?). How would they have responded? Would the audience have only focused on the individual actions of the "manager," or would they have been forced to discuss the structural constraints of the system?

Or, again, think about that parable of the Wicked Tenants, who murder the son of their absentee master to acquire the vineyard for themselves (Mark 12:1–8). Leave aside its present riddle aspect as an allegory of Jesus in 12:9–12, and imagine a first-century Galilean audience hearing that story. Would some find that murder acceptable—even by divine law? Would they agree the tenants were, as we say, "wicked"? Would others find it understandable, but not prudent—the authorities would surely exact vengeance? Would some, many, or even most find it unacceptable on moral grounds? Jesus could not have known their reactions beforehand and neither can we afterward.

Why, then, did Jesus trust so much in his audience and grant so much to their reaction? Why not just tell them what he wanted to say openly and literally—like a modern church sermon? Because *a challenge-parable medium is perfect for a paradigm-shift message*. Because *a collaborative* eschaton *requires a participatory pedagogy*.

Jesus is not just announcing to his audience that God's kingdom is now present. He is announcing that is *only* present *if and when* it is accepted, entered into, and taken upon oneself. If discussion and debate, agreement and disagreement, argument and contradiction do not arise from and because of his challenges, then no change in consciousness can take place, no paradigm shift can occur, and no kingdom of God can be present. Because, first, *challenge parables are paradigm shifters*, and because, second, *the kingdom of God is itself a transcendental challenge parable* sent, as Daniel 7 said, from heaven to earth.

You can even think of certain parables from Jesus as precisely and exactly parables of that paradigm shift itself. Think, for example, of the parables of the Treasure and of the Pearl:

> The kingdom of heaven is like treasure hidden in a field, which someone found and hid; then in his joy he goes and *sells all that he has* and buys that field. (Matt. 13:44)

> Again, the kingdom of heaven is like a merchant in search of fine pearls; on finding one pearl of great value, he went and *sold all that he had* and bought it. (Matt. 13:45)

Even completely apart from Jesus's usage of them, those are perfect metaphors for a paradigm shift, for a tradition swerve, for a fundamental disruptive innovation. But, of course, Jesus correlates them with the kingdom of heaven—that is, with God's kingdom "as in heaven, so on earth" (Matt. 6:10 in the Greek word order). For him, those twin stories imagine the Great Divine Cleanup of the World as here and now present. But it is present only by a divine-human participation and a divine-human collaboration. It is a treasure and a pearl demanding a transformation of the old and known past into a new and unknown future.

Nobody has ever summarized Jesus's challenge better than two African bishops who lived about five thousand miles and fifteen hundred years apart. "God made you without you," said Augustine of Hippo in 416. "He doesn't justify you without you." That was magnificently misquoted by Desmond Tutu of Cape Town in 1999: "St. Augustine says, 'God, without us, will not; as we, without God, cannot.'"

That preceding section indicates the first correlation between challenge parables and a *collaborative* kingdom of God. This next one indicates that correlation with a *nonviolent* kingdom of God. It is quite possible to proclaim a paradigm shift with language—or even parables—that are ideologically and rhetorically violent and might even directly or indirectly, deliberately or accidentally, provoke physical violence. But it is the definition of challenge parables to be delicately provocative and gently subversive rather than violently angry and aggressively hostile. Challenge parables are not attack parables.

Think again of Ruth or Jonah or Job from Chapter 4. Each story lured rather than forced its hearers to reconsider their cultural certainties and traditional absolutes. What could be more gentle, for instance, than that lovely pastoral idyll of Ruth with loyalty to both family and tradition ideally rewarded—happy ending!—with a first-born *son!* There is no explicit attack on the laws of Deuteronomy or the decrees of Ezra and Nehemiah. All it asks is this: What does it mean that the great-grandmother of David, the once and future king of Israel, was a Moabite woman?

In summary, therefore, Jesus's challenge parables are not only profoundly appropriate, but even rhetorically necessary as a collaborative invitation for a collaborative *eschaton* and as a participatory pedagogy for a participatory kingdom of God. They are equally necessary as a nonviolent medium for a nonviolent message. They are short stories that delicately subvert the great story of the Bible. They do not deny it or even destroy it. But, as "word against the word," their quiet voices remind us that the Bible is still our story about God rather than God's story about us.

IN PART I OF this book, I proposed a simple *threefold typology of parables* involving stories that point metaphorically beyond themselves to some external referent that has to be discovered by their recipients. That typology includes *riddle parables* or allegories, *example parables* or moral stories, and *challenge parables* or provocations.

Focus, for a moment, on those cases already seen from the Christian Old Testament. Recall the riddle parable about the lion told by Samson to the Philistines, the example parables about the trees told by Jotham to the Shechemites and the lamb told by Nathan to David. Recall also the challenge parables about the loving Moabite, the repentant Ninevites, and the holiest Edomite from the books of Ruth, Jonah, and Job addressed to the absolutes of postexilic Israel.

The first two types—*riddle* and *example*—all have a somewhat adversarial edge, but the third type—*challenge*—is extremely gentle in its provocative content. Those three challenge books are *pedagogical*, or instructive, rather than *polemical*, or aggressive. They want to seduce you into thought rather than beat you into silence and batter you into subjection. That is also the mode used by the challenge parables of Jesus just seen in those same preceding chapters. Even if ironic, they are always irenic.

We will have to watch that spectrum from the pedagogical to the polemical in Part II, because if the parables *by* Jesus were primarily pedagogical challenges, those *about* Jesus will usually move beyond pedagogy to polemic and beyond challenge to attack. Throughout Part II the fundamental question is whether Jesus is—for Christians—the incarnate *challenge* parable of God to the world or rather the incarnate *attack* parable of God against the world.

Before moving directly to Part II, however, I insert a short Interlude. My purpose is to prepare for the transition from Part I to Part II, which is a transition from total fiction to a mixture of fact and fiction. The parables *told by* Jesus were fictional stories about fictional characters. The parables *told about* Jesus show a fascinating spectrum from fictional to factual stories about historical characters. If, by the way, we dislike fiction in our gospels, we should take the matter up not just with the gospel writers, but with Jesus. They picked up that rhetorical strategy from his own lips. The only difference is that his parables were about fictional characters and their parables are about historical characters.

The following Interlude leaves all of that aside for a moment and looks at a Roman case study in which you can see a historical fact and a historical figure being morphed into parable or, better, into diverse and even contradictory parables. You can call it a case of historical parable or parabolic history or history fictionalized as parable. By whatever name, it should prepare us for Part II, where we move finally from challenge parables *by* to challenge parables *about* Jesus and, indeed, to Jesus as the Christian God's great challenge parable to the world.

Interlude

The Lure of Parabolic History

CAESAR AT THE RUBICON

WE NO LONGER KNOW THE exact course of the ancient Rubicon, let alone the exact spot where Julius Caesar crossed it. Yet, from then to now, "crossing the Rubicon" has been a cliché for passing the point of no return in an endeavor. In Caesar's time, that river of destiny, flowing from the Apennines to the Adriatic, marked the physical boundary between Cisalpine Gaul, to its north, and Italy proper, to its south. It also marked the legal boundary across which a general could not bring his army without becoming, *ipso facto*, a criminal, a traitor, and an enemy of the state.

On that January day in 49 BCE, the death throes of the Roman republic escalated from their previous level, eighty years of savage civil discord, to a new level, twenty years of savage civil war. You could go back and date the start of it all from that moment in 133 BCE when Tiberius Gracchus, tribune of the people, made this famous accusation—you will remember another version from elsewhere:

> The wild beasts that roam over Italy have their dens, each has
> a place of repose and refuge. But the men who fight and die
> for Italy enjoy nothing but the air and light; without house or

home they wander about with their wives and children. (Plutarch, *Life of Tiberius Gracchus* 9.4)

That started a class war that was not simply the *haves* against the *have-nots*. Rather, on one side were the *populares*, or "popular ones," the have-nots led by some of the haves; on the other were the *optimates*, or "best ones," the haves led by some others of the haves. It was, as civil strife became civil war, Caesar and military might for the *populares* against Pompey and legal right for the *optimates*.

Athens had invented democracy and learned that, although you could have democracy and empire, you could not have them both at the same time for long. Rome had invented republic and was about to learn that, although you could have republic and empire, you could not have them both at the same time for long.

I intend this Interlude as a very deliberate connection and a very specific transition from challenge parables *by* Jesus in Part I to challenge parables *about* Jesus in Part II. Indeed, when challenge parables *about* Jesus get big enough, we call them gospels. This move from the first to the second part is, in other words, the move from parable as parable to history as parable.

In Part I those challenge parables *told by* Jesus involve *fictional characters in fictional stories*. In my paradigmatic case study of the Good Samaritan, for example, Jerusalem, Jericho, and the steep descent between were—then as now—factual geography. But, still, all else is fiction, even if set in that factual location. The victim, priest, Levite, and Samaritan were all fictional. So also were the bandits, donkey, innkeeper, and those two denarii. (But, of course, even fictional stories can reveal much about general history—that there were bandits along that desert road, for example, or that the local currency was denarii rather than dollars.) But, apart from those generalities and the actuality of that precise location, parables *by* Jesus involve *fictional characters in fictional stories*.

In Part II the challenge parables *about* Jesus will involve a much more unnerving mix of fact and fiction, history and parable. We will be looking not at *fictional* characters in fictional stories, but at *factual* characters in fictional stories or, if you prefer, *historical characters in parabolic stories*. For example, I consider it a historical fact that Jesus was executed by Pilate on a Roman cross (and more on that in the Epilogue). But Mark records that Jesus's death occurred on the *day after* the Passover meal (Mark 14:12–16), while John records it on the *day of* the Passover meal (John 18:28). Only one of those is history, the other is parable—and probably both are parable: Last Supper *as* Passover meal for Mark, and Jesus *as* Pascal Lamb for John. All history might be able to tell us is that Jesus died sometime in the week-long preparation for Passover.

This Interlude brackets Jesus Christ for a moment to concentrate on Julius Caesar and his now proverbial "crossing of the Rubicon." I proceed in two steps. I look first at our best reconstruction of what happened historically at that fateful river. Is it a historical event? Then, second, I look at how different accounts turned that history into parable and left us with parabolic history or historical parable.

Throughout those two steps, we must always be aware that we are absolutely dependent for any final judgment on the existence of multiple sources and, indeed, on several independent ones. If there were only one version or if we had many exact copies from a single version, think how hard it would be to separate fact from fiction and history from parable. I will return to those two final points about *multiplicity* and *independence* of sources at the end of the Interlude.

I begin with *history as history*, with our best reconstruction of the Rubicon event. Three ancient authors give us the basic story of how the Roman civil war started without, however, expanding history into parable. In fact, two of them do not even name the fateful river.

Gaius Julius Caesar (100–44 BCE). Caesar both conquered Gaul in the 50s BCE and recorded the event himself in his *Commentaries on the Gallic War*. (I started Latin at age eleven in 1945 with that book. It begins: "All Gaul is divided into three parts." We translated it more accurately—outside class—as: "I divided each Gaul into three parts.") Just as Caesar did with that conquest in the 50s, he both acted in and recorded what happened afterward in the early 40s in his *Commentaries on the Civil War.*

In that account Caesar crossed the Rubicon without ever mentioning it. First, he tells us that "he was then at Ravenna, awaiting an answer to his moderate demands" from the Senate (1.5). Next, "he harangued his soldiers," defending himself against Pompey and the Senate, who were demanding his unprotected return and subsequent trial at Rome. The legionaries cried out that they were "ready to defend their general, and the tribunes of the commons, from all injuries" (1.7). Finally, then and only then, "having made himself acquainted with the disposition of his soldiers, Caesar set off with that legion to Ariminum" (1.8). But, of course, as he marched southward from Ravenna to Ariminum—today's Rimini—he crossed the Rubicon and did not even bother to mention it.

That omission was not from conscious embarrassment about the legality of his armed invasion of Italy. Such was unlikely from Caesar in any case. It was also quite unnecessary when he was writing after 48 BCE with Pompey already defeated on a Greek battlefield at Pharsalus and then assassinated on an Egyptian beach at Alexandria. In the great scheme of his glorious destiny, small rivers did not count for much with Caesar. Besides, the crime for a general was not simply to cross the Rubicon, but to do so *at the head of his army.* What was most important for Caesar was to make sure that army was with him. His address to the legionaries and their positive response was and should have been foremost in Caesar's mind then and also in his account later. But, of course, five years after that crossing of the unmentioned Rubicon, Caesar—like Pompey before him—would be dead by assassination.

Marcus Velleius Paterculus (19 BCE–ca. 37 CE). It is the start of the 30s CE before we get the next story about that opening event of Rome's civil war, but now the Rubicon is named. Velleius turned to writing history after a career spent in military operations and public affairs under the emperor Tiberius. His two-book *Compendium of Roman History* gives this succinct and accurate description of Pompey against Caesar in Rome's civil war:

> The one leader seemed to have the better cause, the other the stronger; on the one was the appearance, on the other the reality of power; Pompey was armed with the authority of the senate, Caesar with the devotion of the soldiers; . . . on the one side greater prestige, the other was more formidable. (2.49:1–2)

His account of how "the civil war burst into flame" is equally brief. "Caesar concluded that war was inevitable and crossed the Rubicon with his army. Gnaeus Pompeius, the consuls, and the majority of the senate abandoned first the city, then Italy, and crossed the sea to Dyrrachium" (2.49.4).

It is interesting to notice that in all three rounds of that civil war—first Caesar against Pompey, next Octavian and Antony against Brutus and Cassius, and finally Octavian against Antony—whichever side abandoned Italy to fight in Greece was always the loser. Antony should have taken notice.

Lucius Cassius Dio Cocceianus (ca. 155–ca. 229). Cassius Dio or Dio Cassius was a Roman consul writing in Greek. His eighty-book *Roman History* was a mountain to Velleius's molehill. Published between 211 and 233 CE, it is geographically even more terse than Caesar's account. He does not mention the Rubicon by name. But he does note the *implications* of Caesar's march to Ariminum:

> The senators . . . voted that Caesar should surrender his office to his successors and dismiss his legions by a given day, or else be considered an enemy, because acting contrary to the interests of the country. When Caesar was informed of this, he came to Ariminum, *then for the first time overstepping the confines*

of his own province. . . . Next he set out and marched straight
upon Rome itself, winning over all the cities on the way without any conflict. (41.3.4–4.2)

Even there, however, "overstepping" is a rather mild term for what
was constitutionally and legally considered to be a treasonous invasion of Italy.

I turn next to *history as parable*, to accounts that deliberately shroud
fact in fiction by clothing history in parable. Here are four other
Roman historians who, in the years between Velleius and Cassius
Dio, turn Caesar's crossing of the Rubicon from history into parable,
that is, into parabolic history or historical parable. All four of them
explicitly mention the river Rubicon and the last three introduce a
comment by Caesar that has become a proverbial cliché all by itself.

Marcus Annaeus Lucanus (39–65). Lucan, who came from Roman
Spain, was indicted for conspiracy against Nero and condemned to
suicide. His epic poem *Pharsalia*, or *Civil War*—written around 60
CE—survived despite its prorepublican and antimonarchical empha-
ses. Lucan summarized that war's two sides in this justly famous line:
"The conquering cause pleased the gods, but the conquered cause
pleased Cato" (1.128). Cato the Younger lived from 95 to 46 BCE and
sided with the *optimates*. He was a great conservative traditionalist
whose fateful mistake was to think you could become an empire and
still remain a republic.

Lucan's account is sternly negative and disapproving. It has
Caesar's "mighty soul pondering tumults and the coming shock," as
he arrives at the northern bank of the "little Rubicon." A dreadful
vision appears before him:

In face most sorrowful and ghostly guise,
His trembling country's image; huge it seemed
Through mists of night obscure; and hoary hair
Streamed from the lofty front with turrets crowned:
Torn were her locks and naked were her arms.

Then thus, with broken sighs the Vision spoke:
"What seek you, men of Rome? and whither hence
Bear you my standards? If by right you come,
My citizens, stay here, these are the bounds.
No further dare." But Caesar's hair was stiff
With horror as he gazed, and ghastly dread
Restrained his footsteps on the further bank. (1.212–223)

Caesar responds to that vision by appealing to the god Jupiter and the goddess Roma. He tells them: "[I am] your Caesar, conqueror by land and sea, . . . your soldier here and wherever you wish." Furthermore, if the Roman gods have an enemy, it is not Caesar but Pompey: "His only be the guilt whose acts make me your foe." And, without more ado, Caesar "gives the word and bids his standards cross the swollen stream." (1.224–235). You will notice that, in the meanwhile, the "little Rubicon" has become a "swollen stream."

Lucan cannot change history—Caesar crosses the Rubicon and heads for Rome. But by that vision Lucan turns history into very negative parable. Caesar is allowed to justify himself but, afterward, the vision is not recorded as withdrawing its warning, excusing his crossing, or accepting his explanation. But, of course, besides being negative and threatening, parabolic history can also be positive and accommodating—and that came next.

Gaius Suetonius Tranquillus (ca. 69/75–ca. 130). Suetonius, born in Roman North Africa, became an archivist under Trajan and then secretary to Hadrian. Those imperial patrons meant ample access to official records, and from those he wrote his *Lives of the Twelve Caesars*—from Julius Caesar, first of the Julio-Claudians, to Domitian, last of the Flavians. As you might expect, his parabolic interpretation of Caesar's Rubicon crossing in *The Deified Julius* section of the *Lives* flatly contradicts Lucan's version.

Suetonius's account is strictly positive and approving. With Suetonius, as with Lucan before him, when Caesar reaches the northern bank of "the river Rubicon, which was the boundary of his province, he paused for a while, and realizing what a step he was taking, he turned to those about him and said: 'Even yet we may draw back; but once you cross that little bridge, the whole issue is with the sword'" (31). But, then, instead of that negative "vision" in Lucan, we get this positive "sign" in Suetonius:

> All of a sudden there appeared hard by a being of wondrous stature and beauty, who sat and played upon a reed; and when not only the shepherds flocked to hear him, but many of the soldiers left their posts, and among them some of the trumpeters, the apparition snatched a trumpet from one of them, rushed to the river, and sounding the war-note with mighty blast, strode to the *opposite* bank. Then Caesar cried: "Take we the course which the signs of the gods and the false dealing of our foes point out. The die is cast." (32, my italics)

We now get that famous aphorism from Caesar, *iacta alea est*, "The die is cast" (literally, "Cast the die is").

Compare those two visions from Lucan and Suetonius. Lucan's personification of Rome is "sorrowful, ghostly, trembling, torn, and naked." Suetonius's is "a being of wondrous stature and beauty." Lucan's apparition forbids and threatens Caesar's advance, but Suetonius's leads and guides him across the Rubicon: "Accordingly, crossing with his army, and welcoming the tribunes of the plebeians, who had come to him after being driven from Rome, he [Caesar] harangued the soldiers with tears" (33). You will recall that the "harangue" to his soldiers took place, according to Caesar, *before*—as was appropriate and necessary—not *after* he marched southward with them to invade Italy.

Lucius Mestrius Plutarchus (ca. 46–120). Plutarch was born in Roman Greece and, as a biographical moralist, his most famous work was the *Parallel Lives of Noble Greeks and Romans*. He tells about Caesar at the Rubicon twice, once in comparing the successes of

Alexander the Great and Julius Caesar and then in comparing the failures of Agiselaus and Pompey.

Plutarch's version is less negative or positive than ambiguous. As in Lucan's and Suetonius's versions, Plutarch's *Life of Caesar* has Caesar stop on the northern bank of the Rubicon. But moral reflection replaces any sort of apparition:

> When he came to the river which separates Cisalpine Gaul from the rest of Italy (it is called the Rubicon), and began to reflect, now that he drew nearer to the fearful step and was agitated by the magnitude of his ventures, he checked his speed. Then, halting in his course, he communed with himself a long time in silence as his resolution wavered back and forth, and his purpose then suffered change after change. For a long time, too, he discussed his perplexities with his friends who were present, among whom was Asinius Pollio, estimating the great evils for all mankind which would follow their passage of the river, and the wide fame of it which they would leave to posterity. (32.5–7)

Plutarch also has that aphorism about the die being cast, but this Greek records it: "Let the die be cast, . . . [he said] with a sort of passion, as if abandoning calculation and casting himself upon the future, and uttering the phrase with which men usually prelude their plunge into desperate and daring fortunes" (32.8).

Finally, having omitted those apparitions in Lucan and Suetonius, Plutarch concludes his account with this devastatingly casual postscript: "It is said, moreover, that on the night before he crossed the river he had an unnatural dream; he thought, namely, that he was having incestuous intercourse with his own mother" (32.9).

Come back for a moment to Suetonius's *The Deified Caesar*. He too records that same dream, but dates it to 63 BCE, when Caesar was a military treasurer in Spain. He says Caesar was dismayed by a dream in which "he thought that he had offered violence to his mother." But, despite any Oedipal negativity, "the soothsayers inspired him with high hopes by their interpretation, which was: that he was destined to rule the world, since the mother whom he had seen in his power was none other than the earth, which is regarded as the common parent of all mankind" (7). When, therefore, that dream is transposed by Plutarch from 63 to 49 BCE and from Spain to Italy, is it—with Lucan—a warning against invasion or—with Suetonius—an invitation to world conquest? If, at the Rubicon, the "vision" of Lucan is negative and the "sign" of Suetonius is positive, the "dream" of Plutarch is profoundly ambiguous.

Appian of Alexandria (ca. 95–ca. 165). Appian was from Roman Egypt. He wrote his twenty-four-book *Roman History* around 160 CE, while a legal advocate before the imperial courts in Rome. Within it is a five-book section on the civil wars, and here is his Rubicon scene:

> When his course brought him to the river Rubicon, which forms the boundary line of Italy, he stopped and, while gazing at the stream, revolved in his mind the evils that would result, should he cross the river in arms. Recovering himself, he said to those who were present, "My friends, to leave this stream uncrossed will breed manifold distress for me; to cross it, for all mankind." Thereupon, he crossed with a rush like one inspired, uttering the familiar phrase, "The die is cast: so let it be!" (2.35)

Appian's version of the Rubicon crossing is the shortest of the four parabolic histories. Compared to Lucan's *negative* "vision," Suetonius's *positive* "sign," and Plutarch's *ambiguous* "dream," Appian's "stop" is a *neutral* description.

Those last three authors all have the "die is cast" aphorism. Furthermore, Caesar's comments are very similar in Plutarch—"great evils for all mankind which would follow their passage of the river, and the wide fame of it which they would leave to posterity"—and, reversed, in Appian—"to leave this stream uncrossed will breed manifold distress for me; to cross it, for all mankind."

Classical scholars have wondered whether Asinius Pollio, who was with Caesar at the Rubicon, might have been the source for that "die is cast" aphorism and that his account might be the common source for Suetonius, Plutarch, and Appian. That is not my present concern but, still, even if they have a common basis, it is even more interesting to see how each changes it in his own way. Only Plutarch, for instance, has Caesar's incestuous dream before his Rubicon crossing. Divergent sources are interesting, but so also are divergent adaptations of a common source. Both help us separate—if at all possible— history from parable within a historical parable or parabolic history.

WE HAVE JUST SEEN seven ancient accounts of Caesar's crossing of the Rubicon. The first three—Caesar, Velleius, and Dio—give us the basic history, factual characters in factual stories. The last four—Lucan, Suetonius, Plutarch, and Appian—all develop history into parables and, indeed, into four quite diverse ones. They give us factual characters in fictional—or at least fictionalized—stories. In summary, it is equally possible to tell factual-historical stories and fictional-parabolic stories about exactly the same historical incident. In other words, on January 10, 49 BCE, Caesar crossed the Rubicon, and the rest is—parable.

Imagine, for a moment, that we only had those former three authors recording the first overt act of Rome's twenty-year civil war. None of them has Caesar's famous "die is cast" aphorism. Only Velleius mentions the river Rubicon, but without any emphasis or explanation of its importance. Only Cassius Dio mentions its import, but does not mention the river by name. If that were all we had, would "crossing the Rubicon" have become a proverbial expression for passing the point of no return, for acting resolutely and irreversibly? No, it was not history as history, but history as parable that created that cliché we still use today. Could it even be that we always remember history best—or only—when it is seen through the lens of parable?

Finally, do not think those multiple parabolic interpretations of Caesar's Italian invasion represent some spectacular exception to the rest of his life. "Julius Caesar took his place in Western political discourse and action," writes Maria Wyke in her superb book *Caesar: A Life in Western Culture*, "as a call to revolution, an instrument of monarchic or dictatorial legitimation, a justification of repression, a precedent for assassination."* The entire earthly life, death by assassination, and heavenly ascension of Julius Caesar were rampant with parabolic history and historical parable. So were the earthly life, death by execution, and heavenly ascension of Jesus Christ.

THIS INTERLUDE HAS ESTABLISHED three factors about the parabolic history of the Rubicon crossing that prepare us for Part II. First and foremost, fictional-parabolic stories may not only contain fictional characters, they may also contain factual-historical characters. Second, we have multiple versions of that Rubicon incident. Third, with divergent versions of the same story or even divergent adaptations of the same version, we are sure that fact and fiction are both involved in a story. With only one account we are reduced to conjecture at best and prejudice at worst in making any such distinction.

Keeping those three factors in mind, I turn from the gospel of Caesar to the gospel of Christ and from seven versions of the Rubicon crossing in Roman history to four versions of the Incarnation in the New Testament. The four chapters of Part II will focus, respectively, on the gospels according Mark, Matthew, Luke-Acts, and John. And, as I start into those sections of the book, I have two challenges—one of format and the other of content.

---

* Maria Wyke, *Caesar: A Life in Western Culture* (Chicago: Univ. of Chicago Press, 2008), p. 145.

With regard to *format*, how can I adequately look at all four gospels in the space left in Part II? Each chapter would require a full commentary to show adequately that a gospel is a challenge parable not *by* but *about* Jesus—not a short parable, but parable writ large. My solution is, first, to focus each chapter on some specific theme or section in a given gospel that opens up dramatically the particular visionary emphasis of that author; then, second, I will scan the whole of that particular gospel and indicate shorter sections that most clearly reveal the intention and purpose of that writer's vision of Jesus.

With regard to *content*, I have an even more difficult challenge, and it picks up something mentioned already at the end of Part I. My general proposal is that parables *by* Jesus during his life begot parables *about* Jesus after his death; and, furthermore, that the four gospels not only contain *parables about* Jesus, but are best understood as four discrete *megaparables about* Jesus. But are those gospels, acting as megaparables, to be interpreted primarily as *challenge* parables?

That question arises because the challenge parables seen so far—either from the Old Testament or from the historical Jesus—are pedagogical rather than polemical. Even though the book of Ruth challenges ethnic absolutes, and even though the story of Jesus challenges ethnic attitudes, they do so gently and delicately. There is no character assassination or even nasty name-calling of what is being questioned or challenged. In Part II, we will have to assess whether each gospel moves beyond challenging what it opposes to attacking it bitterly or even dismissing it altogether. As parables *by* Jesus begot parables *about* Jesus, that increase in animosity from challenge through attack to dismissal may be the most striking development. To be blunt: Do the gospels as parables about Jesus push steadily beyond parable as challenge toward challenge as attack?

PART II

Parables Told about Jesus

CHAPTER 7

A Hymn for the Nameless

THE PARABLE GOSPEL ACCORDING TO MARK

BY THE LATE AFTERNOON OF September 2, 31 BCE, Queen Cleopatra VII of Egypt had escaped the surrounding squadrons of Octavian and Agrippa, picked up Mark Antony from his abandoned flagship, and fled with him to Alexandria and double suicide. Off Cape Actium on the northwestern coast of Greece, Octavian, son of the god Apollo by conception and son of the divine Julius Caesar by adoption, soon to be acclaimed *Augustus* in Latin, *Sebastos* in Greek—the "One to Be Worshiped"—had emerged victorious and triumphant from Rome's twenty-year civil war.

At Ephesus, capital of the Roman province of Asia Minor, the governor, Paulus Fabius Maximus, wondered what could be done to offer due thanks and appropriate honors to Augustus for saving the republic-become-empire from its orgy of self-destruction:

> The birthday of the most divine Caesar [Augustus] . . . we might justly equate with the beginning of everything—at least in practical terms—since he restored order when everything was disintegrating and falling into chaos and gave a new look to *the whole world*, a world which would have met destruction with the utmost pleasure if Caesar had not been born as a common

blessing to all. For that reason one might justly take this to be the start of life and living, the end of regret for having been born.

Augustus had saved not just Rome, Italy, or the Mediterranean, but—note my italics—"the whole world." The governor "proposed, therefore, that the birthday of Augustus should become New Year's Day for all the cities of Asia Minor" (modern western Turkey).

The League of Asian Cities accepted that suggestion enthusiastically. Both proposal and acceptance were carved on stone to be preserved in sacred precincts dedicated to the goddess Roma and the god Augustus, the divine couple at the center of the new world order. Our most complete inscription comes from Priene, just south of Ephesus, dates from 9 BCE, and legislates the governor's calendar change after this effusive preamble:

Since the Providence that divinely orders our existence applied her energy and zeal to bring to life the most perfect good in Augustus, whom she filled with virtues for the benefit of mankind, bestowing him upon us and our descendants as a saviour—he who put an end to war and will order peace, Caesar, who by his epiphany exceeded the hopes of those who prophesied good news (*euaggelia*), not only outdoing benefactors of the past, but also allowing no hope of greater benefactions in the future; and since the birthday of the god first brought to the world the good news (*euaggelia*) residing in him.

Many of those terms for Caesar Augustus in Roman imperial theology were used—in opposition and confrontation to them—for Jesus Christ in later Christian theology. Think, for example, of such terms as God (incarnate), Savior of the World, New Creation, Bringer of Peace, and—especially for this chapter and all of Part II—that twice-repeated term "good news." I will start with that expression, but first give you the sequence for this chapter.

THIS CHAPTER WILL DEVELOP over five stages. First, I look at the calculated challenge by the Christian "good news" about Jesus Christ (with the singular case, *euaggelion*, in Greek) to that "good news" about the first Caesar Augustus and all the subsequent Roman emperors with that same title (with the plural case, *euaggelia*, in Greek)

Second, I focus on how Mark announces his parable gospel as: "The beginning of the good news (*euaggelion*) of Jesus Christ, the Son of God" (1:1). That certainly challenges Roman imperial theology—but here is the key question: Is that challenge more presumption and presupposition than emphasis and focus for Mark?

Third, I choose a section of Mark's gospel as a paradigmatic answer to that preceding question. This will have two points: the first negative, the second positive. Surprisingly—and counterintuitively—Mark's challenge parable about Jesus is not primarily directed *externally* against Roman authority and leadership, but rather *internally* against Christian authority and leadership—especially against the revered Twelve disciples themselves. But, then, what is the positive counterpoint to the Twelve for Mark? Is it some other authority group or some other authority style?

Fourth, with that chosen section as basis, I suggest the overall purpose and intention of Mark's gospel and why it proclaims Jesus as a living parable. In other words, what is Mark's location in time and place, situation and community, and how does that explain what was just seen in response to those preceding questions.

Fifth, after all of that, I ask the final questions, which will be repeated for each chapter of Part II. Is the Jesus of this gospel a challenge parable or has he already been morphed into an attack parable? What is the distinction between that familiar type, the challenge, and this new type, the attack? And what is at stake in their difference?

MY FIRST POINT CONCERNS that word "good news" for Caesar and for Christ. In English we say that the "news *is* good or bad," so although the noun is plural, it is always used as singular in construction.

In Greek both the singular and plural forms, *euaggelion* and *euaggelia*, are used. How best to retain that distinction in English? Maybe, by distinguishing between the "Good News" or the "Gospel" (uppercase and singular) and "good news" or "gospels" (lowercase and plural)? Why is that distinction—so clear in the Greek original, but now lost in our English translations—so important?

We talk easily of "the four *gospels*" or of "the *gospels* of the New Testament," as if that plural term were not a problem. But the earliest followers of Jesus thought that there was only one single Gospel. Paul said so emphatically and rather sharply to the Galatians:

> I am astonished that you are so quickly deserting the one who called you in the grace of Christ and are turning to a different Gospel—not that there is another Gospel, but there are some who are confusing you and want to pervert the Gospel of Christ. But even if we or an angel from heaven should proclaim to you a Gospel contrary to what we proclaimed to you, let that one be accursed! As we have said before, so now I repeat, if anyone proclaims to you a Gospel contrary to what you received, let that one be accursed! (1:6–9)

Apart from the simple, unqualified, and emphatic term "the Gospel," Paul mentions "the Gospel of God" (Rom. 1:1), "the Gospel of his Son" (Rom. 1:9), "the Gospel of Christ" (Phil. 1:27), and climactically, "the Gospel the glory of Christ who is the image of God" (2 Cor. 4:4). But it is, always and ever, in the singular. It is "*the* Gospel," as if to say, there is only one Good News for the whole world. And it is not "the gospels" of Caesar, but "the Gospel" of Christ.

Turn now from Paul's letters, written in the 50s, to what we call "the four gospels," written from the 70s onward. After Paul's warning, we should think of them as four "gospel versions"—or "gospels" for short—of the One Gospel. That understanding held well into the second century. When, even at that later date, authors were officially designated for our "four gospels," the titles did not read "The Gospel *of*," but "The Gospel *according to*" Matthew, Mark, Luke, and John. In other words, there is still—and always—only one Gospel, but it is in four versions, four "according to"s. Although Roman theology would have "good news" (Greek plural) about each new Caesar Augustus, each new Savior of the World, each new Son of God, Christian theology would proclaim only one "good news" (Greek singular), namely, Jesus Christ, once and for all forever.

I TURN, IN MY second point, to focus the preceding discussion of "good news" on Mark. After the opening in which Mark announces John the Baptist as "the beginning of the Good News" (1:1), he immediately and programmatically underlines the importance of "*the* Gospel" with this summary about Jesus:

> After John was arrested, Jesus came to Galilee, proclaiming the Good News of God, and saying, "The time is fulfilled, and the kingdom of God has come near; repent, and believe in the Good News." (1:14–15)

In all those cases, of course, "Good News" or "the Gospel" is the Greek singular case (*euaggelion*). That summary announcement in 1:14–15 is clear enough on two fundamental points.

First, the kingdom of God is already present—those verbs "fulfilled" and "come near" are not in the future tense ("will be"), but in the perfect tense ("has been"). Second, that advent itself is *the* Gospel, *the* Good News—in the singular (*euaggelion*)—once and for all forever. It is opposed to the gospels, the good news—in the plural (*euaggelia*)—of the advent of a new emperor. It is even or especially opposed to that inscription from Priene that announced the cosmic good news (*euaggelia*) of Augustus's birth as renewed creation, as restarting the world all over again in peace and order.

By the end of that overture or prologue, we expect Mark's story will have the Good News (singular) of God in Christ confronting—

as a *challenge* parable—the good news (plural) of Rome in Caesar. And it does that, of course. Just think, for example, of the Gerasene demoniac incident in Mark 5:1–13.

First, his is the most impure or life-in-death form of demonic possession: "He lived among the tombs . . . night and day among the tombs." Next, his is also the strongest possession imaginable: "No one could restrain him any more, even with a chain; for he had often been restrained with shackles and chains, but the chains he wrenched apart, and the shackles he broke in pieces; and no one had the strength to subdue him" (15:3–4). Then, in a not so subtle comment, when the demon is asked his name, he replies, "Legion, for we are many." Finally, ordered by Jesus to leave the possessed man, Legion requests to be transferred to a nearby herd of swine "numbering about two thousand. The herd promptly rushed down the steep bank into the sea, and were drowned in the sea" (15:15). No further comment is necessary on that "Romans Go Home" manifesto.

But the anti-Roman theme is more general presupposition than specific project, more secondary presumption than primary purpose in Mark's gospel. The primary purpose seems focused more internally on the disciples than externally on Rome. Consider, for example, this admonition from Jesus:

> You know that among the Gentiles those whom they recognize as their rulers lord it over them, and their great ones are tyrants over them. But it is not so among you; but whoever wishes to become great among you must be your servant, and whoever wishes to be first among you must be slave of all. (10:42–44)

On the one hand, Mark's leadership model flatly contradicts Roman imperial normalcy—and most of human normalcy as well. But, on the other, it is specifically directed to the Twelve disciples, who are angry at two of their members for asking Jesus: "Grant us to sit, one at your right hand and one at your left, in your glory"

(10:37). Mark's gospel is much more directly and immediately about the use—and abuse—of power and authority by the twelve disciples rather than by the twelve Caesars. Its challenge is more internal than external. That is, by the way, the strangest aspect of this first gospel, and it will be my central focus for understanding Mark's gospel as parable.

IN THIS, MY THIRD point, I focus on that challenge to—and criticism of—the Twelve as leaders of the Christian community. I use that as my chosen focus to understand the entire parable gospel of Mark. But, before we begin, wonder for a moment why Mark is challenging leaders almost all of whom were dead by his time of writing in the early 70s—and many of whom had died as martyrs. Is he actually challenging something past, something present, or something permanent about Christianity? I will have two points in what follows, the first more negative, the second more positive.

The negative aspect of Mark's challenge to the Twelve appears most clearly in the long section 8:22–10:52. It is framed by twin stories about Jesus healing blindness, and both incidents open in similar fashion: "They came to Bethsaida," and a blind person is healed (8:22–26); "They came to Jericho," and a blind person is healed (10:46–52). Those healings are, of course, successful, and the second one concludes like this: "Jesus said to him, 'Go; your faith has made you well.' Immediately he regained his sight and followed him on the way" (10:52). For Mark, that does not simply mean "on the road" (of Galilee), but "on the Way" (of Jesus). So, then, how are the Twelve doing "on the Way"?

Within those twin frames of healed blindness Mark inserts three cases of unhealed—or, better, *unhealable*—blindness. If Jesus successfully heals blind outsiders in 8:22–26 and 10:46–52, he fails disastrously to heal blind insiders—the Twelve—in 8:31–10:45. Notice this triple construction:

	First Test	Second Test	Third Test
Prophecy by Jesus	8:31–32a	9:31	10:33–34
Reaction by the Twelve	8:32b	9:32–34	10:35–41
Response by Jesus	8:33–9:1	9:35–37	10:42–45

First, as they travel southward "on the way" to Jerusalem, Jesus prophesies his impending death and resurrection three times. Next, the Twelve respond with incredible obtuseness by focusing on their own power and authority in each case. Finally, Jesus attempts to heal their blindness by teaching them how power and authority operate within the now present kingdom of God.

In each prophecy, Jesus refers to himself as the "Son of Man," that is, as the "Human One" (8:31; 9:31; 10:33). You will recall those terms from Chapter 6 and its discussion of Daniel 7. There the earth's imperial kingdoms are *animalified* as feral beasts and only heaven's eschatological kingdom is *personified* as "a human being" or (literally) "a son of man." Since the Son of Man or the Human One is already present on earth in Jesus, then, of course, the kingdom of God is already present. But not, apparently, for the Twelve. Watch, now, what happens with them across three tests with each test moving from *prophecy* through *reaction* to *response*.

The *first test* is in 8:31–9:1. The *prophecy* is that "the Son of Man must undergo great suffering, and be rejected by the elders, the chief priests, and the scribes, and be killed, and after three days rise again."

The immediate *reaction* comes from Peter, who "began to rebuke him." Peter has just proclaimed to Jesus: "You are the Messiah" (8:29). But his meaning for that "Messiah" title is not that of Jesus. Maybe it is the standard contemporary expectation of a military and/ or transcendental warrior as God's eschatological plenipotentiary?

In his *response* Jesus "rebuked Peter and said, 'Get behind me, Satan! For you are setting your mind not on divine things but on human things.'" The word "rebuke" is a very strong verb for Mark. Jesus uses it, for example, in expelling demons during exorcisms (1:25; 3:12; 9:25), and here also Peter is treated as demonic, as "Satan."

Finally, Jesus expands that *response* to all who are present: "the crowd with his disciples." The kingdom's collaborative eschatology depends on others accepting their participation in the destiny of Jesus. "If any want to become my followers, let them deny themselves and take up their cross and follow me." It is not about Jesus *substituting for* them, but of them *participating with* Jesus. Have the Twelve finally gotten that message?

The *second test* is in 9:31–37. Once again, Jesus is "teaching his disciples. . . . But they did not understand." Need I emphasize the utterly parabolic, fictional, and artificial way in which Mark is creating this triple sequence? It is, by the way, another example of Olrik's law of three from Chapter 5, but Mark gives it—as we shall see below—a special final twist.

The *prophecy* is: "The Son of Man is to be betrayed into human hands, and they will kill him, and three days after being killed, he will rise again." No new information is given beyond the former version in 8:31–32a.

What is the *reaction* of the disciples? "They were afraid to ask Jesus," but when "they came to Capernaum; and when he was in the house he asked them, 'What were you arguing about *on the way*?' But they were silent, for *on the way* they had argued with one another who was the greatest." Markan irony again: they were "on the way," but not "on the Way."

Jesus's *response* is that he "sat down, called the twelve, and said to them, 'Whoever wants to be first must be last of all and servant of all.' Then he took a little child and put it among them; and taking it in his arms, he said to them, 'Whoever welcomes one such child in my name welcomes me, and whoever welcomes me welcomes not me but the one who sent me.'"

I emphasize that correlation of "servant" with "child." Do not wrap that "child" in sentimental modernity as sweet or simple, pure or innocent, or even necessarily precious and important. Put it back in its ancient status as a social nobody, as somebody who must first be accepted into the family to be even guaranteed its life. Think of that terrible letter from Hilarion to his wife, Alia, who is pregnant with their child: "If by chance you bear a child, if it is a boy, let it be, if it is a girl, cast it out [to die]." That letter, dated June 18, 1 BCE, was sent from Alexandria up the Nile to distant Oxyrhynchus and was found in that city's rubbish dumps, where also that child—if a girl—would have ended her life.

The *third test* is in 10:33–45. In every possible way, this third test is the climax of Mark's triple sequence. It is, as just mentioned, an example of Olrik's law of three, but here the third time is not success after two failures, but a final and climactic failure. (It is also, in a baseball metaphor, the third strike for the Twelve.)

In 10:33–34 the *prophecy* by Jesus is by far the most detailed and foretells step-by-step what Mark will later describe in detail:

We are going up to Jerusalem, and the Son of Man will be handed over to the chief priests and the scribes [14:10–11], and they will condemn him to death [14:63–64]; then they will hand him over to the Gentiles [15:1]; they will mock him [15:20], and spit upon him [15:19], and flog him [15:15], and kill him [15:24]; and after three days he will rise again [16:6].

Surely, you think, the Twelve will ask about those specific details—if not about execution and resurrection, then certainly about mocking, spitting, flogging. But, once again and climactically, they respond obtusely.

This time the *reaction* comes from James and John, the sons of Zebedee, in 10:35–37. Mark's sequence of reactions is: Peter in 8:32b, then the Twelve in 9:32–34, and finally James and John in 10:35–37. That is very deliberate. We first met Simon (Peter) in 1:16, James and John in 1:19, and the Twelve in 3:16–19. But even as the Twelve are appointed, the Leading Threesome all receive new names from Jesus in 3:16–17: "He appointed the twelve: Simon (to whom he gave the name Peter); James son of Zebedee and John the brother of James (to whom he gave the name Boanerges, that is, Sons of Thunder)."

In other words, those three disciples are emphasized as a Leadership Threesome within the Twelve—and always in that order of Peter, James, John. Those three are the chosen ones taken by Jesus to the Mount of Transfiguration in 9:2 and the Garden of Gethsemane in 14:33. But, says Mark, they failed Jesus there as well—they wanted to stay on the Mount, and they wanted to sleep in the Garden. Across the three *tests* under present discussion Mark intends to criticize Peter, the first of the Leading Threesome, in 8:33, then the Twelve as a whole in 9:32–34, and last the other two of that Leading Threesome in 10:35–40.

What, then, is the *reaction* of James and John to that detailed prophecy? It extends across a threefold dialogue with Jesus (10:35–36, 37–38, 39–40) and contains this incredibly insensitive reaction to his prophecy about execution and resurrection: "Grant us to sit," they ask Jesus, "one at your right hand and one at your left, in your glory" (10:37). And, worse still, their *reaction* begets this further and widening *reaction:* "When the ten heard this, they began to be angry with James and John" (10:41). By now, we know that what must follow is a severely corrective *response* from Jesus.

Here, once again, is Jesus's *response:*

> So Jesus called them and said to them, "You know that among the Gentiles those whom they recognize as their rulers lord it over them, and their great ones are tyrants over them. But it is *not so among you; but whoever wishes to become great among you* must be your servant, and whoever wishes to be first among you must be slave of all. For the Son of Man came not to be served but to serve, and to give his life a ransom for many." (10:42–45)

First, there is that explicit contrast between Gentile-style leadership and this radical revision of Jewish-style leadership. Next, that "not so" is directed specifically to the Twelve. It is their view and style of leadership that are opposed by Jesus. And the unconventional leadership style they are to exhibit is to be modeled on that of Jesus himself. Jesus is not just talking about humility, but about humility-in-power, not just about being a servant, but being a servant-as-leader. Finally, in the ancient world, it was especially those enslaved who were "ransomed," so that a leader who ransoms you is about liberation and not domination.

Think about this for a moment. The Twelve—and all others—were challenged to take up their cross and follow Jesus (8:34). That sounded like an invitation—not to *substitution by Jesus for them*, but to *participation with Jesus by them*. That sounded initially like a challenge to come to Jerusalem and get crucified alongside Jesus. But, by the end of Mark's triple sequence, that fellowship in the horror of Roman crucifixion was reinterpreted for the Twelve as a fellowship in the paradox of servant-style leadership. There were, for Mark, other ways of dying to imperial normalcy than by execution.

No doubt "taking the cross" might still mean martyrdom for them as leaders of the kingdom movement. But what Jesus emphasized now was less about how they were to die as criminal leaders than how they were to live as servant leaders. In its two-thousand-year history, by the way, Christianity has always had more of the former than the latter among its leadership. Jesus's challenge still holds true for us today.

I turn now to the second point in this chapter's third section. It concerns Mark's positive challenge, set over against that preceding sequence of three negatives. If those named "apostles" or "disciples" all fail seriously, are there any ideal or even successful Christians—and Christian leaders—in Mark's story? If all the named leaders—Peter, James, and John—fail dismally, is the author of the gospel the only proper, correct, adequate leader? In what follows, watch the dialectic between the named and the nameless, between failure and success, between rejection and reception, and, evenhandedly, between female and male. Also remember, of course, that "Mark" is the name tradition gave to the anonymous author of the first gospel. That author is also nameless.

The last major section in Mark's gospel is framed by deliberately similar, but very surprising language. Each frame starts with Jesus "going ahead" of the disciples and ends with "they were afraid":

Galilee to Jerusalem: They were on the road, going up to Jerusalem, and Jesus was *walking ahead* of them; they were amazed, and those who followed *were afraid*. (10:32a)

Jerusalem to Galilee: "Go, tell his disciples and Peter that he is *going ahead* of you to Galilee; there you will see him, just as he told you." They went out and fled from the tomb, for terror and amazement had seized them; and they said nothing to anyone, for they *were afraid*. (16:7–8)

The opening frame involves *twelve named males*, while the closing frame involves *three named females*. The latter are specified like this:

There were also women looking on from a distance; among them were Mary Magdalene, and Mary the mother of James the younger and of Joses, and Salome. These used to follow him and provided for him when he was in Galilee; and there were many other women who had come up with him to Jerusalem. (15:40–41)

In that group there are both unnamed women and that named threesome, which is then repeated twice: "Mary Magdalene and Mary the mother of Joses saw where the body was laid" (15:47) and "Mary Magdalene, and Mary the mother of James, and Salome bought spices, so that they might go and anoint him" (16:1). In other words, just as Mark has a primary, named, male threesome—Peter, James, and John—so also does he have a primary, named, female threesome—Mary, Mary, and Salome.

In what follows—and as always with Mark—we must pay special attention to the sequence and structure of his story in order to understand his purpose and intention:

Opening negative example: twelve named males do not believe Jesus (10:32a–45)

First positive example: one unnamed female believes Jesus (14:3–9)

Second positive example: one unnamed male believes Jesus (15:39)

Closing negative example: three named females do not believe Jesus (16:1–8)

In the structure of 10:32–16:8 Mark interweaves and contrasts three different aspects of discipleship, *name, gender,* and *belief,* but, for him, *name* dominates the other two aspects. He does so by framing two positive examples with two negative examples. In all of this, we must continually remember that we are reading historical parable or parabolic history; that is, we are reading the history of Jesus around the year 30 CE made into parable by Mark around the year 70.

We have already seen Mark's *opening negative example,* how those twelve named male disciples paid no attention to Jesus's triple prophecy of his death and resurrection in 8:31–9:1; 9:31–37; and 10:33–45. We also saw how their obtuse indifference reached a climax in 10:33–45, which both concludes that section and opens the final one in Mark's narrative.

Next comes Mark's *first positive example.* In 14:3–9 an unnamed woman anoints Jesus with "costly ointment" at a banquet in Bethany. That is certainly a beautiful gesture, but why does it get this amazing accolade from Jesus: "Truly I tell you, wherever the good news is proclaimed in the whole world, what she has done will be told in remembrance of her" (14:9). What exactly has that unnamed woman done to achieve such a special status and receive such a unique promise?

She has, quite simply, believed Jesus. If you are going to die and rise, she thinks, I better anoint you now, because there may not be another chance. "You will not always have me," says Jesus. "She has done what she could; she has anointed my body beforehand for its burial" (14:7–8). She is, as it were, *the first Christian*, and she believed before any empty tomb was found or risen vision was granted. For her, Easter was the word of Jesus, and she believed it.

Mark might be imagining her among those unnamed women mentioned, as seen above, in 15:40–41. Recall that Mark began his story by recording how "Jesus came to Galilee, *proclaiming the Gospel of God*" (1:14). That comes to consummation here with this unnamed woman and, therefore, her story must always be told wherever "*the Gospel is proclaimed*" (14:9). She believes that, as Jesus foretold three times, he will be executed by Rome and resurrected by God in Jerusalem.

What follows next is a *second positive example*. Mark pairs the unnamed anointing woman with the unnamed confessing centurion as positive models of belief:

> Then Jesus gave a loud cry and *breathed his last*. And the curtain of the temple was torn in two, from top to bottom. Now when the centurion, who stood facing him, saw that in this way he *breathed his last*, he said, "Truly this man was God's Son!" (15:37–39)

That is, for Mark, a fully Christian confession. As Luke retells that Markan incident, he finds such an immediate conversion unlikely. So, instead, he simply says, "When the centurion saw what had taken place, he praised God and said, 'Certainly this man was innocent'" (23:47). But Mark, turning history (the execution of Jesus) into parable (the conversion of a centurion) knows exactly what he is doing. Once again, the unnamed one believes where the named ones fail.

Finally, Mark gives us his *closing negative example*. The text of 16:1–8 is a very, very strange way for Mark to end his story. Everywhere else—from 1 Corinthians 15 to John 20–21—the resurrection involves visions of the risen Jesus. And, indeed, such visions were later appended in what we call Mark 16:9–20. But Mark himself has only an empty tomb and an angelic explanation that "Jesus of Nazareth, who was crucified . . . has been raised; he is not here. Look, there is the place they laid him" (16:6).

Next, the three women are given a message for "his disciples and Peter," a command to leave Jerusalem and "see" Jesus in Galilee (16:7). But—as we saw above—that message is never delivered, because the women "went out and fled from the tomb, for terror and amazement had seized them; and they said nothing to anyone, for they were afraid" (16:8). In other words, Mark thinks that the Twelve stayed in Jerusalem after the death and resurrection of Jesus—against that undelivered angelic directive.

Compare that unnamed woman of 14:3–9 with the three named women of 16:1–8. I am speaking—I repeat—within the viewpoint of Mark's parable. Within it, a predeath anointing meant faith, but a postdeath anointing meant disbelief. For Mark, those named women "bought spices, so that they might go and anoint him. And very early on the first day of the week, when the sun had risen, they went to the tomb" (16:1–2). In other words, they expected to find and anoint the dead body of Jesus. They did not—from Mark's viewpoint—believe in what Jesus had said, and yet they had followed and assisted him from Galilee to Jerusalem.

In all of that—from Mark 10 through Mark 16—the named ones fail where the unnamed ones succeed. But gender is evenly balanced. The twelve named males and the three named females fail. But the unnamed female and the unnamed male succeed. The issue is not gender, but name. Mark's parabolic challenge *to* and *within* Christianity is an exaltation of leaders who liberate over leaders who dominate, a transcendence of charismatic over institutional leadership, and a hymn for the nameless over the named.

That reversed positive and negative are, of course, characteristic of challenge parables. Think, for example, of the "good" priest and Levite who do "wrong," and the "bad" Samaritan who does "right." So also in Mark's challenge gospel. The "good" named ones are counterpointed with the "bad" nameless ones. The challenge is to consider, ponder, meditate on the possibility of reversed status between the named and nameless Christians—before God and with Jesus.

WHAT, THEN, MY FOURTH question asks, is the location and situation of Mark's somewhat startling vision of Christian community. I imagine his gospel written among "the villages of Caesarea Philippi" (8:27) for refugees from the terrible destruction of Judea, Jerusalem, and its Temple in the great war of 66–74 CE. They had lost everything—their lands and possessions, their homes and their loves, their hope and maybe even their faith.

In his *Jewish War*, the historian Josephus claims that false prophecy led Jerusalem's Jews astray by promising them that the (first) coming of the Messiah would save them from the Roman onslaught (6.312–313). In his gospel, Mark claims that false prophecy led Jerusalem's Christian Jews astray by promising them that the (second) coming of the Messiah would save them from that same Roman destruction. And, says Mark—with parabolic hindsight and fictional creativity—Jesus had warned against that very delusion:

> Jesus began to say to them, "Beware that no one leads you astray. Many will come in my name and say, 'I am he!' and they will lead many astray. When you hear of wars and rumors of wars, do not be alarmed; this must take place, but the end is still to come. . . . And if anyone says to you at that time, 'Look! Here is the Messiah!' or 'Look! There he is!'—do not believe it. False messiahs and false prophets will appear and produce signs and omens, to lead astray, if possible, the elect." (13:5–7, 21–22)

Furthermore, Mark lays full responsibility for that mistaken conflation of the coming of Christ with the coming of Rome on the shoulders of the Twelve, that is, on their misunderstanding of Jesus and on the forty-year tradition that had derived from their incomprehension. He is not, in other words, talking about the Twelve in the 30s *with* Jesus, but the tradition of the Twelve *after* Jesus—the tradition that was operative from the late 30s to the 70s, when Mark was writing.

You should have understood, says Mark, that Jesus multiplied loaves and fishes for *both* Jews on the western side of the lake (6:35–43) *and* for Gentiles on the eastern side (8:1–9). You should have understood, says Mark, that the "only one loaf" was more than enough for all together in a common Christian Jewish-Gentile meal (8:14–17a). In other words, as Mark has Jesus say to them:

> "Do you still not perceive or understand? Are your hearts hardened? Do you have eyes, and fail to see? Do you have ears, and fail to hear? And do you not remember? When I broke the five loaves for the five thousand, how many baskets full of broken pieces did you collect?" They said to him, "Twelve" [6:35–43]. "And the seven for the four thousand, how many baskets full of broken pieces did you collect?" And they said to him, "Seven" [8:1–9]. Then he said to them, "Do you not yet understand?" (8:17b–21)

You should have led, says Mark, a *Christian Jewish and Gentile* community in Galilee and not a *Christian Jewish* community in Jerusalem. You never received, says Mark—in the climactic final words of his gospel—the last command of Jesus from the angel at his empty tomb. The women were told: "Go, tell his disciples and Peter that he is going ahead of you to Galilee; there you will see him, just as he told you," but they became too afraid to tell anyone (16:7–8).

Mark's gospel criticizes the Twelve—called and named to be "apostles" by Jesus in Mark 3:16–19—not only for failing to follow the vision of Jesus, but also for failing to follow his model of leadership. Indeed, it seems that, for Mark, the latter failure created or at least facilitated the former one. *It was because their style and mode of leadership were not like those of Jesus that its content and substance were not those of Jesus either.*

What do we think today when, after two thousand years, we read the challenge parable that is Mark's gospel? That exaltation of the nameless over the named is something Christianity should never forget. Its named leaders come and go, and much that they leave behind them is not to Christianity's credit. How few of them down through the centuries have exercised power, authority, and leadership as Jesus told the Twelve to: "Whoever wishes to become great among you must be your servant, and whoever wishes to be first among you must be slave of all" (10:43–44). That challenge still stands.

MY FIFTH AND FINAL question is whether Mark's presentation of Jesus is a *challenge* parable or whether it has already been morphed into an *attack* parable. Does Mark's Jesus challenge or attack the named Christian leadership of Peter, the Leading Threesome, and the Twelve in general. Be careful here, *for every attack is a challenge, but not every challenge is an attack.* One of the aspects I watch for in making that distinction is whether the story calls names, doubts honesty, impugns integrity, or even negates and dismisses what it challenges. If it does, the story has moved beyond nonviolent challenge to violent attack.

In Mark, the Twelve are accused not just of incomprehension, but of *culpable* incomprehension. That is the meaning of "hardened hearts" in 8:17. You will recall Pharaoh's "hardened heart" from Chapter 1. That is a very, very serious indictment. But, of course, as already mentioned, since most of the Twelve were long dead—and many as martyrs—it was their ongoing theological tradition, leadership style, and *named* importance that were Mark's ultimate target.

But even to be so repeatedly criticized *by Jesus* means that they had to have been *with Jesus* all the time "on the way," even if not "on the Way." Severe criticisms are given in that extremely hard-hitting section just cited from Mark, but notice how they are presented: "Do you . . . ? Are your hearts . . . ? Do you . . . ? Do you . . . ? And do you not . . . ? Do you not . . . ?" (8:17b–21). They are offered as *questions*, and the Twelve even get to answer twice amid that drumbeat of interrogation. They could, to the contrary, have been uttered as condemning statements: "You do . . . ! Your hearts are . . . ! You do . . . ! You do . . . ! You do not . . . ! You do not . . . !"

Taking everything into account, I think Mark's parable gospel of Jesus is still a challenge rather than attack. Indeed, if Mark were our only gospel version, that distinction might be picky and pedantic, might not be even worth raising. But I am already looking ahead to what will happen as we proceed through the next three gospel accounts, and what is sad there is how challenge escalates steadily into deeper and wider aspects of attack. As a first example of that unfortunate process, I turn next to the Parable Gospel according to Matthew.

CHAPTER 8

Rhetorical Violence

THE PARABLE GOSPEL
ACCORDING TO MATTHEW

IN 1959, I WAS SENT, as you will recall from the Prologue, to the Pontifical Biblical Institute in Rome for two years of postdoctoral specialization. The Biblicum—as it is known for short—is located just off the Corso, not far from the Trevi Fountain, somewhere in the heart of Rome.

By that fall I had been a monk in the thirteenth-century Roman Catholic Order of Servants of Mary since 1950 and a priest since 1957, and I had just obtained a Doctor of Divinity from Maynooth College, the national seminary of Ireland. I rather liked that European doctoral title, because later I received an honorary American Doctor of Humanities, and that combination of divinity and humanity keeps me in touch, *mutatis mutandis*, with Jesus.

I had to write a final thesis under the direction of Father Francis McCool S.J. to complete requirements for the Biblicum's degree of Licentiate in Sacred Scripture. But what was to be my topic?

As you will also recall from the Prologue, I saw Oberammergau's Passion play in 1960, and it started me thinking about anti-Semitism and the New Testament. But that was much too broad a subject for the time available. In seeking a more specific focus, however, I started reading the journal *Cahiers Sioniens*, a French periodical, issued between 1947 and 1955, which was very important in preparing the declaration on relations between Christianity and Judaism later promulgated by the Second Vatican Council.

In one of its final issues in 1954 was an article by Renée Bloch on the rabbinic traditions about Moses, which was continued into another article in *Recherches de Science Religieuse* in 1955. (Bloch died—much too soon—that same year.) Her articles studied the rabbinic *midrashim*, that is, those narrative expansions on biblical texts that emphasized moral elements and answered possible questions or objections about their content.

For example, did Moses just happen to be born after Pharaoh's command to kill all the newborn males of the Israelites? No, said the *midrashim*, Pharaoh had a dream, which his advisers interpreted as foretelling the advent of a predestined deliverer. Pharaoh's murderous net was cast, therefore, precisely to catch that coming savior. But why did all those Israelite parents—including, of course, those of the future Moses—not divorce one another to prevent the slaughter of newborn males? Because, said the *midrashim*, those special parents trusted in God or were commanded by God to conceive the predestined child.

Bloch also drew attention to the parallels between, on the one hand, Pharaoh and his advisers discussing Moses-to-be and, on the other, Herod and his advisers discussing Jesus-to-be. That gave me the topic for my licentiate paper. I proposed that the overall structure, specific sequences, and individual details of Matthew 1–2 were created on the precise model of those Mosaic *midrashim*. Matthew's infancy story about Jesus was derived from and modeled on those *midrashic* storytelling expansions of Exodus 1–2 about the infancy of Moses. That paper would be constitutive, by the way, for my understanding of biblical truth as parabolic history ever since.

Jesus, therefore, was immediately proclaimed by Matthew as the new Moses. Actually, even a cursory reading of Matthew 1–2 indicates that emphasis. Notice, for example, that the Magi—although led by their guiding star—stop off in Jerusalem to ask directions. Why was that necessary? Because *in this parabolic rather than historical overture*, Matthew is creating a parallel between the evil Pharaoh, who slaughters the infant males in Exodus 1–2, and the evil Herod, who does the same in Matthew 1–2. Herod is the new Pharaoh just as Jesus is the new Moses. Despite their guiding star, the Magi must ask for directions in Jerusalem, so that Herod can enter the story and become the new Pharaoh.

At the start of Matthew's gospel, the Magi ask Herod, "Where is the child who has been born king of the Jews?" (2:2). That title next appears at the end of his gospel, repeated three times, like a death knell, in 27:11–37. It appears, for instance, above the cross: "Over his head they put the charge against him, which read, 'This is Jesus, the King of the Jews'" (27:37). In other words, Matthew's gospel starts with a Rome-appointed king using lethal violence—unsuccessfully—against Jesus; it ends with a Rome-appointed governor doing the same—but successfully.

As with the preceding chapter on Mark, this present one will also have five main points. The first one picks up the theme of *violence* against Jesus as "king of the Jews" in Matthew (2:2; 27:11, 29, 37). Granted that violence *against* Jesus in Matthew, is there also violence *by* Jesus in that parable gospel? Furthermore, are there different types and dimensions of violence and, if so, are they linked and interconnected with one another?

The second point is to take a preliminary probe into Matthew's text—as earlier with Mark's—and thereby to establish a generative opening into his purpose and intention. I do this, however, in two steps—again, as in the last chapter—by looking first at an earlier text and then at a later one in Matthew and finally emphasizing their striking discrepancy. This will furnish my core insight into Matthew's mind.

The third point will also have two steps. The first one asks: Are the concluding results from that preceding stage merely a random element or do they indicate a dominant theme in Matthew? The second step asks: If so, is all of that of any lasting importance?

The fourth and fifth points will have the same questions as they did for Mark in Chapter 7. The fourth point explores how all of those preceding ones indicate the location and situation, concerns and communities of Matthew's focus. The fifth and final point asks: Is the Jesus of Matthew's gospel presented in a challenge parable or an attack parable?

MY FIRST POINT ASKS what must seem an absurd question: Granted the violence *against* Jesus, is there also violence *by* Jesus in Matthew? At first glance, that surely demands an emphatic negative response. Where, you may ask, is there violence *by* Jesus anywhere in Matthew? In fact, has Matthew 1–2 itself not inaugurally cauterized any such mistaken idea?

We saw at the start of Chapter 6 that, although the New Testament speaks of Jesus as the Davidic Messiah or new David, he is not depicted as the warrior prince who would save his people militarily from the Romans in the present, as David did from the Philistines in the past. Matthew 1–2 has also and immediately distanced Jesus from any such divine mandate.

On the one hand, in Matthew 1–2 Jesus is emphatically the Davidic Messiah or new David. Matthew opens his gospel with "the genealogy of Jesus the Messiah, the son of David, the son of Abraham" (1:1). And throughout his infancy story he calls Jesus "son of David" three times as often as Mark and Luke do—John never does. In his infancy story Joseph—as foster father—is also addressed as "son of David." Furthermore, Matthew 1–2 manages to cite "Bethlehem" as the birthplace of Jesus five times—compared with never in Mark, once in John, and twice in Luke. Jesus is, for Matthew, the new and messianic David.

On the other hand, as just seen, the entire structure and the component elements of Jesus's infancy are paralleled to that of Moses in the *midrashic* versions of Exodus 1–2. The theme of Jesus as the new Moses dominates and subsumes that of Jesus as the new David. But Moses is the giver of law, not the wager of war. In other words, for Matthew, the primacy of Moses over David is that of nonviolent law over violent war.

Furthermore, throughout Matthew's gospel Jesus is regularly conducting debates with various opponents. But he never uses any human—let alone transcendental—violence against them. He "wins" those arguments, presumably, since he always gets the last word. But although Matthew probably considers that, as the Davidic Messiah, Jesus has divine violence on call at any time, he never uses such force. Where, one repeats, is there ever violence *by* Jesus in Matthew?

But those two answers to my first step serve to raise the question of this second one: Are there various types, dimensions, and modes of violence? In this step I propose that human violence can move through three successive stages—from ideological through rhetorical to physical violence, as follows:

Ideological violence is *thinking* that persons, groups, or nations are inhuman, subhuman, or at least seriously lacking in the humanity one grants oneself.

Rhetorical violence is *speaking* on that presumption by dehumanizing those others with rude names, crude caricatures, and derogatory stereotypes or by calling them, say, political "traitors" or religious "heretics."

Physical—and even lethal—violence is *acting* on those presuppositions either by illegal attack or, if one has attained social power, by official, legal political action.

We say proverbially, "Sticks and stones will break my bones, but names (or words) will never hurt me." That is not true even in itself, but, more serious, it ignores our experience that *names and words* often escalate through *sticks and stones* to *ovens and crematoria*. Once ideology and rhetoric have dehumanized opponents, power will often consider it a duty—even a divine duty—to eliminate them. In other words, I propose to take ideologically based rhetorical violence very, very seriously.

Because of that escalatory danger, therefore, I repeat the basic, constitutive, and generative question for all of Chapter 8: Is there ideologically grounded rhetorical violence *by* Jesus in Matthew's parable gospel?

IN ANSWER TO THAT rephrased question about rhetorical violence *by* Jesus in Matthew, I move next into my second point. I take it in two steps: the first answer is that Jesus is not rhetorically violent; the second answer is that he is.

A first answer is that Jesus is *not rhetorically violent*. Start, on the one hand, with what we call the Sermon on the Mount in Matthew 5–7. Matthew, however, continuing his theme of Jesus as the new Moses would have called it: "The First Book of the New Torah by Jesus as the New Moses from on Top of the New Mount Sinai."

One preliminary point. For much of modern advertising, "old" is a pejorative term and "new" the accolade of excellence. It was not so in the ancient world. The "old" was the tried and true; the "new" was dangerous and suspicious. Augustus, for example, created a new dynastic monarchy while insisting he was restoring the old republic. The "new" was safest and best not as the "old" superseded and discarded, but rather as the "old" transformed and re*new*ed. So Matthew has Jesus say this:

> Do not think that I have come to abolish the law or the prophets; I have come not to abolish but to fulfill. For truly I tell you, until heaven and earth pass away, not one letter, not one stroke of a letter, will pass from the law until all is accomplished.

Therefore, whoever breaks one of the least of these commandments, and teaches others to do the same, will be called least
in the kingdom of heaven; but whoever does them and teaches
them will be called great in the kingdom of heaven. For I tell
you, unless your righteousness [*better:* justice] exceeds that of
the scribes and Pharisees, you will never enter the kingdom of
heaven. (5:17–20)

You will notice an internal challenge to "the least" inside the kingdom, but also an external one to the "scribes and Pharisees" outside
it. The clash is neither Jesus *versus* Moses, let alone "Christianity"
versus "Judaism," but rather Christian Judaism *versus* Pharisaic Judaism, or, in other words, Matthew's interpretation of the law *versus*
that of the scribes and Pharisees. How exactly, then—in Matthew's
inaugural challenge—is the "justice" of Christian Jews supposed to
exceed that of Pharisaic Jews?

Matthew follows that manifesto in 5:17–20 with a set of six legal
antitheses in which an older law is subsumed and transformed into
a newer one. Here is a summary of the six comments in Matthew's
vision of the justice of the law brought to its fulfillment in Jesus:

> *On murder* (5:21–26): "You have heard that it was said to
> those of ancient times, 'You shall not murder.'"
> "But I say to you": Do not even be angry, insult, or berate.

> *On adultery* (5:27–30): "You have heard that it was said,
> 'You shall not commit adultery.'"
> "But I say to you": Do not even have lustful thoughts.

> *On divorce* (5:31–32): "It was also said": Divorce is permitted.
> "But I say to you": Divorce is permitted only for "unchastity."

> *On false oaths* (5:33–37): "Again, you have heard that it was
> said to those of ancient times, 'You shall not swear falsely.'"
> "But I say to you, Do not swear at all."

On vengeance (5:38–42): "You have heard that it was said, 'An eye for an eye . . .'"

"But I say to you, Do not resist an evildoer. . . . Turn the other cheek."

On love (5:43–48): "You have heard that it was said, 'You shall love your neighbor and hate your enemy.'"

"But I say to you, Love your enemies and pray for those who persecute you."

You will notice two aspects of that set of antitheses. One is that the first clause may vary a little from long—"You have heard that it was said to those of ancient times"—to short—"You have heard that it was said"—to shortest—"It was also said." But the second clause is always the same, that emphatic and absolute, "But I say to you."

The more important aspect, however, is that all those items of Jesus's fulfilled or renewed law are so extreme that later Christianity has usually ignored them in general practice. That is not in any way to negate their power as hopes and ideals, but to recognize that their "justice" exceeded not only that of the "scribes and Pharisees" who lived then, but of most Christians who have ever lived since.

For my present question on Jesus's rhetorical violence in Matthew, I look in more detail at the first and last of those six antitheses. That first antithesis goes far beyond forbidding murder with this triple fulfillment:

I say to you that if you are angry with a brother or sister, you
    will be liable to judgment;
and if you insult a brother or sister, you will be liable to the
    council;
and if you say, "You fool," you will be liable to the hell of fire. (5:22)

Anger, insult, and name-calling are solemnly condemned with escalating divine judgments. In fact, the act of reconciliation takes precedence over the act of sacrifice: "Leave your gift there before the altar and go; first be reconciled to your brother or sister, and then come and offer your gift" (5:24).

The sixth and final antithesis consummates that opening vision by moving from negative to positive in its closing command:

> I say to you, Love your enemies and pray for those who per-secute you, so that you may be children of *your Father* in heaven; for he makes his sun rise on the evil and on the good, and sends rain on the righteous and on the unrighteous. . . .
> Be perfect, therefore, as your *heavenly Father* is perfect. (5:44–45, 48)

My italics emphasize that the reason and model for loving enemies is not political prudence or even ethical idealism. It is to be like, and thereby become children of, a God who acts in that way. In other words, for Jesus in Matthew's new law—the fulfilled and re*new*ed Torah—the positive nonviolence of loving enemies is derived from and modeled on the very character of God.

By now, my first question seems answered with an absolute nega-tive. Jesus solemnly forbids any *rhetorical* violence in the opening frame of those six moral escalations and any *ideological* violence in their closing frame. But, if the question of ideologically based rhetor-ical violence by Jesus starts—fortunately—with a negative answer, it later receives—unfortunately—an equally positive answer. That will be my second step in this second point.

The alternative answer—also in Matthew—is that Jesus is *rhe-torically violent*. On the other hand, then, watch what happens after those inaugural commands from Jesus at the start of the new Torah. Focus on just one word, a word that is, on the one hand, an insult by name-calling, and, on the other, rather far from prayer for per-secutors or love for enemies. That word is "hypocrites." As soon as Matthew finishes those six commands, these follow immediately:

Whenever you give alms, do not sound a trumpet before you, as *the hypocrites* do in the synagogues and in the streets, so that they may be praised by others. . . . Whenever you pray, do not be like *the hypocrites*; for they love to stand and pray in the synagogues and at the street corners, so that they may be seen by others. . . . Whenever you fast, do not look dismal, like *the hypocrites*, for they disfigure their faces so as to show others that they are fasting. (6:2, 5, 16)

Maybe that repeated use of "the hypocrites" *might* be excused its rhetorical violence despite a startling location right after those framing antitheses forbidding insulting names and demanding loving prayer. But Matthew later elevates that name-calling into a ghastly chapter-long chant—on the lips of Jesus:

Woe to you, scribes and Pharisees, hypocrites! (23:13)
Woe to you, scribes and Pharisees, hypocrites! (23:15)
Woe to you, blind guides (23:16)
You blind fools! . . . How blind you are! (23:17, 19)
Woe to you, scribes and Pharisees, hypocrites! (23:23)
You blind guides! (23:24)
Woe to you, scribes and Pharisees, hypocrites! . . . You blind
    Pharisees! (23:25, 26)
Woe to you, scribes and Pharisees, hypocrites! (23:27)
Woe to you, scribes and Pharisees, hypocrites! (23:29)
You snakes, you brood of vipers! How can you escape being
    sentenced to hell? (23:33)

My present emphasis is not just against nasty name-calling in general, but about the glaring discrepancy between this gospel parable's Jesus in Matthew 5 and the one in Matthew 23. Jesus opens by absolutely forbidding ideologically based rhetorical violence, but closes by doing himself precisely what he has earlier forbidden. Think, therefore, about this: *Does Jesus change his mind or does Matthew change his Jesus?*

MY THIRD POINT ALSO has two steps. The first one asks whether that contradiction between the Jesus of Matthew 5 and the Jesus of Matthew 23 is just some random exception or whether Matthew's Jesus is regularly presented as rhetorically violent. I answer that second option affirmatively and give you three case studies to prove it. They lead into my second step, which asks: Is that overall Matthean atmosphere of rhetorical violence a minor matter or of some ongoing importance for Christianity—and I answer that affirmatively with a fourth case study. I start, however, with some preliminary information to indicate how I will present those four cases.

There is a massive scholarly consensus that Matthew and Luke use Mark as their major source. There is also a strong—but not massive—consensus that Matthew and Luke use another major source besides Mark. It can be recognized when we see them with a parallel text not present in Mark. Scholars call that second source the Q Gospel or simply Q—the Q is short for the German word *Quelle*, meaning "source." Granted those two conclusions, if you compare Matthew's version of any incident with his sources, you can see most readily if and where he creates or intensifies any rhetorical violence by Jesus.

My first case study concerns *reaction to rejection*. The Markan Jesus tells his companions what to do if they are rejected while proclaiming the kingdom of God. Their reaction is to be minimal:

If any place will not welcome you and they refuse to hear you, as you leave, shake off the dust that is on your feet as a testimony against them. So they went out and proclaimed that all should repent. (Mark 6:11–12).

In Mark, that is, *at most*, a rather mild and implicit threat. Maybe not even a threat, more like a sort of physical "We're out of here" declaration. But Matthew adds to Mark a very explicit threat of his own in 10:15 and also another condemnation from the Q Gospel in 11:20–24:

"If anyone will not welcome you or listen to your words, shake off the dust from your feet as you leave that house or town." (Matt. 10:14; Luke 9:5; *from Mark 6:11*)

"Truly I tell you, it will be more tolerable for the land of Sodom and Gomorrah on the day of judgment than for that town." (Matt. 10:15; *from Matthew himself*)

Then he began to reproach the cities in which most of his deeds of power had been done, because they did not repent. "Woe to you, Chorazin! Woe to you, Bethsaida! For if the deeds of power done in you had been done in Tyre and Sidon, they would have repented long ago in sackcloth and ashes. But I tell you, on the day of judgment it will be more tolerable for Tyre and Sidon than for you. And you, Capernaum, will you be exalted to heaven? No, you will be brought down to Hades. For if the deeds of power done in you had been done in Sodom, it would have remained until this day. But I tell you that on the day of judgment it will be more tolerable for the land of Sodom than for you." (Matt. 11:20–24; Luke 10:12–15; *from Q*)

The language of Jesus escalates into violent invective in Q—and Matthew accepts it fully. Furthermore, it is no longer a question of "any place," but of very specific and named locations. Those small Jewish villages of Chorazin, Bethsaida, and Capernaum will fare worse on the day of judgment than the four Gentile cities of Tyre, Sidon, Sodom, and Gomorrah. That represents a huge increase in rhetorical violence, so that Mark is bracketed chronologically by that of the Q Gospel version before him and Matthew after him.

This second case study involves *refusal of any proof sign*. The pattern here is exactly the same as in the preceding case. Jesus is asked to give a sign from heaven proving his identity and validating his proclamation. He is challenged to justify himself by some heavenly manifestation from God. In Mark, the response from Jesus is both absolute and laconic:

> The Pharisees came and began to argue with him, asking him for a sign from heaven, to test him. And he sighed deeply in his spirit and said, "Why does *this generation* ask for a sign? Truly I tell you, no sign will be given to *this generation*." And he left them, and getting into the boat again, he went across to the other side. (Mark 8:11–13).

That is a simple but very emphatic refusal to give any proof—but without any name-calling.

Once again Matthew combines his two sources, Mark and the Q Gospel, so that the absolute refusal we just saw in Mark receives a single exception and—once again—condemnatory language overpowers Mark's simple statement:

> Then some of the scribes and Pharisees said to him, "Teacher, we wish to see a sign from you." But he answered them, "An evil and adulterous generation asks for a sign, but no sign will be given to it except the sign of the prophet Jonah. For just as Jonah was three days and three nights in the belly of the sea monster, so for three days and three nights the Son of Man will be in the heart of the earth. The people of Nineveh will rise up at the judgment with this generation and condemn it, because they repented at the proclamation of Jonah, and see, something greater than Jonah is here! The queen of the South

will rise up at the judgment with this generation and condemn it, because she came from the ends of the earth to listen to the wisdom of Solomon, and see, something greater than Solomon is here!" (Matt. 12:38–42; Luke 11:16, 29–32; *from Q*; see also Matt. 16:1–4).

The Jesus of the Q Gospel is much nastier than the one in Mark, but Matthew combines them so that Q's condemnatory language overcomes Mark's far milder rhetoric. You can see, for example, how Mark's "this generation" becomes "an evil and adulterous generation" in Matthew.

The third case study focuses on *the weeping and gnashing of teeth*. This case involves one of the nastiest threats ever placed on the lips of Jesus. Although it is not present in Mark, it appears once in the Q Gospel:

I tell you, many will come from east and west and will eat with Abraham and Isaac and Jacob in the kingdom of heaven, while the heirs of the kingdom will be thrown into the outer darkness, where there will be weeping and gnashing of teeth. (Matt. 8:11–12; Luke 13:28–29; *from Q*)

Matthew uses that single example from the Q Gospel not just once, but five times; it is escalated to a refrain that concludes five of the parables of Jesus:

[1] *Parable of the Weeds* (13:24–30, 36–43): They will throw them into the furnace of fire, where there will be weeping and gnashing of teeth. (13:42)

[2] *Parable of the Net* (13:47–50): Throw them into the furnace of fire, where there will be weeping and gnashing of teeth. (13:50)

[3] *Parable of the Great Dinner* (22:1–14): Bind him hand and

foot, and throw him into the outer darkness, where there will be weeping and gnashing of teeth. (22:13)

[4] *Parable of the Servants* (24:45–51): He will cut him in pieces and put him with the hypocrites, where there will be weeping and gnashing of teeth. (24:51)

[5] *Parable of the Master's Money* (25:14–30): Throw him into the outer darkness, where there will be weeping and gnashing of teeth. (25:30)

That turns those parables into warnings or negative examples of impending punishment. We already saw that Mark severely criticized the leadership of the Christian community and exalted the nameless over the named within it. Yet the challenge in his parable to the Twelve never quite escalated to the level of rhetorical violence in Matthew.

Those preceding three cases all concerned threatening invective and involved Matthew's acceptance of the Q Gospel's rhetorical violence on the lips of Jesus. I turn now to my third point's second step to assess the ongoing importance of that escalatory invective throughout Matthew. I use a fourth case study, but it is not just one of rhetorical violence by Jesus. It is created directly by Matthew himself and placed not on the lips of Jesus, but of his opponents themselves.

My fourth case study concerns the execution of Jesus. In recording what was *said by Jesus*, Matthew consistently escalates the level of verbal abuse. But something similar happens with things *done to Jesus*, especially in his trial and execution. I look here at only one example, but it is one that has had terrible results in subsequent history, results ranging from theological anti-Judaism to racial anti-Semitism. I begin with Mark's version to see what was there for Matthew to change:

[1] Now at the festival he used to release a prisoner for them, anyone for whom they asked. Now a man called Barab-

bas was in prison with the rebels who had committed murder during the insurrection.

[2] *The crowd* came and began to ask Pilate to do for them according to his custom.

[3] But the chief priests stirred up *the crowd* to have him release Barabbas for them instead.

[4] So Pilate, wishing to satisfy *the crowd*, released Barabbas for them; and after flogging Jesus, he handed him over to be crucified. (Mark 15:6–8, 11, 15)

That mini-story is parable rather than history. Mark's purpose was to say—in retrospect after the terrible Jewish war with Rome of 66–74 CE—that Jerusalem had chosen the wrong option. It had chosen the violent revolutionary Barabbas—"son of the father"— over the nonviolent revolutionary Jesus—"Son of the Father." But my present concern is how Matthew adopted and adapted his Markan source:

[1] Now at the festival the governor was accustomed to re- lease a prisoner for *the crowd*, anyone whom they wanted. At that time they had a notorious prisoner, called Jesus Barabbas.

[2] Now the chief priests and the elders persuaded *the crowds* to ask for Barabbas and to have Jesus killed.

[3] So when Pilate saw that he could do nothing, but rather that a riot was beginning, he took some water and washed his hands before *the crowd*, saying, "I am innocent of this man's blood; see to it yourselves."

[4] Then *the people as a whole* answered, "His blood be on us and on our children!" So he released Barabbas for them; and after flogging Jesus, he handed him over to be crucified. (Matt. 27:15–16, 20, 24–26)

Matthew changes Mark in two very significant and equally obvi- ous ways. First, Mark consistently uses a singular noun, "the crowd

. . . the crowd . . . the crowd," throughout his account (15:8, 11, 15). But Matthew develops that into: "the crowd . . . the crowds . . . the crowd . . . the people as a whole" (27:15, 20, 24, 25). Not only does "the crowd" become "the crowds," but they both eventually become "the people as a whole." That final escalation is by far the most important one, because "people" is the Greek word *laos*, which designates not just the "people" present, but "the people as a whole" (*pas ho laos*).

Second, Matthew, and only Matthew in the entire New Testament, contrasts the blood innocence of Pilate (27:24) with the blood responsibility of "the people as a whole" (27:25). You can see immediately where Matthew has internally changed and externally expanded Mark. There is no evidence that he has a separate tradition on that subject. He has only Mark and his own escalation but, in this my final example, it is rhetorical violence *against* rather than *from* Jesus that Matthew emphasized.

In conclusion, therefore, Matthew not only intensifies rhetorical violence *by* Jesus against his opponents, but, as in that final case study, the general atmosphere of ideologically based rhetorical violence is turned on themselves by those very opponents. It has taken almost two thousand years to negate the baleful implications of that single Matthean sentence and to insist that it did not and could not apply to all other Jews, earlier, later, or ever.

MY FOURTH POINT ASKS whether that intensification of rhetorical invective opens up our understanding of the time and place, problems and concerns of Matthew's whole parable gospel. And the fifth point asks whether Matthew's Jesus is presented through a challenge or attack parable. I answer both those questions together, as they are closely interconnected.

In the years after the Roman destruction of Jerusalem in 70 CE, the centrality of priests and sacrifice in the Temple was replaced— forever—by that of rabbis and study of the Torah. Matthew wrote his gospel within that paradigm shift. It represents an *intra*-familial clash *in Judaism* between Christian-Jewish scribes and Pharisaic-Jewish scribes because, as Matthew says later, "Every scribe who has been trained for the kingdom of heaven is like the master of a household who brings out of his treasure what is new and what is old" (13:52).

Strife within the family can, of course, be extremely bitter, since opposition can never create total separation. Still, even in that tense situation, Matthew is careful to attack Pharisaic practice rather than theory: "The scribes and the Pharisees sit on Moses' seat; therefore, do whatever they teach you and follow it; but do not do as they do, for they do not practice what they teach" (23:2–3). Still, within the tactics of ancient invective, we should presume that Pharisaic opponents were just as nasty about Matthew as he was about them. And both sides were wildly caricaturing opposition rather than accurately describing character.

On the one hand, therefore, rhetorical invective was probably quite mutually nasty and equally bitter on both sides of the debate between Christian Judaism and Pharisaic Judaism in the first century. On the other hand, there is a very special problem with the rhetorical violence placed by Matthew on the lips of Jesus (or against him, as in that final case).

The problem is not just that Matthew has so enthusiastically escalated the violent rhetoric of the Q Gospel's Jesus over the far milder language of Mark's Jesus—even or especially when Mark is severely criticizing the Twelve. The major difficulty—and my own criticism—is the glaring discrepancy between, say, Matthew 5 and Matthew 23. How can Matthew have Jesus begin with forbidding anger, insult, and name-calling, begin with demanding greetings, prayers, and love for enemies, and then do exactly the opposite throughout the rest of the gospel?

I do not think that Matthew sees himself as outside the Jewish community. Indeed, the very nastiness of his language indicates a stern family feud in the 80s between Christian Jewish scholars and

Pharisaic Jewish scholars. But, with the fourth question answered like that, the fifth is answered as well.

Matthew's presentation of Jesus is not a *challenge parable*, but an *attack parable*. The unfortunate result of his gospel as attack—especially in the light of Matthew 23 *versus* Matthew 5—is that he has created a Jesus ultimately open to Matthew's own favorite accusation—hypocrisy. That gives a very clear answer to this chapter's basic question. *The Jesus of Matthew is regularly and rhetorically violent, but that is not Jesus himself; it is Matthew who is speaking.* Still, we should be grateful that Matthew accurately revealed the Jesus of the *challenge parable* in Matthew 5 before steadily changing him into the Jesus of the *attack parable* in Matthew 23.

What, then, comes next? Mark depicts Jesus through a pedagogical challenge parable, but Matthew has changed that image by writing a polemical attack parable. What about Luke-Acts? Why, to begin with, do I combine what we call the Gospel according to Luke with the Acts of the Apostles to speak of the Gospel according to Luke-Acts? Is that combination challenge or attack or both? And, whichever it is, to whom is it directed?

CHAPTER 9

Rome as the New Jerusalem

THE PARABLE GOSPEL
ACCORDING TO LUKE-ACTS

"APHRODISIAS," SAID OCTAVIAN, WHEN not yet Caesar Augustus,
"is the one city from all of Asia I have selected to be my own," and
its citizens carved that accolade on the archive wall of their theater.
Since the Greek goddess Aphrodite was the Roman goddess Venus,
from whom Augustus's family was allegedly descended, that city was
most fortunately named at that precise historical moment. Two thousand years later, Kenan Erim, who excavated the site and is buried
inside the gate of Aphrodite's temple, claimed, "Of all the Graeco-
Roman sites of Anatolia, Aphrodisias is the most hauntingly beautiful." And the poet L. G. Harvey proclaimed it "beautiful enough to
last forever."

Located in ancient Caria, Aphrodisias is about 150 miles inland
from the mid-Aegean coast of Turkey. In the first century, it contained a unique monumental passageway with three levels on either
side. On both sides, the two top levels were adorned with bas-relief
carvings that smoothly integrated Greek tradition with Roman
domination. It was dedicated to the "Olympian Imperial Gods" of
the Julio-Claudian dynasty (*Theoi Sebastoi Olympioi*). That was the

only time I ever saw the imperial divinities described as "Olympian."

In the twenty-first century, Aphrodisias contains—from that ruined Augusteum or Sebasteion structure—the greatest museum of Roman bas-reliefs in the world. But my present focus is not on any of that, but rather on an inscription from the city's Jewish synagogue discovered in 1966. It is, by the way, the longest Jewish inscription from antiquity.

In the early 200s the right-hand doorpost was carved with the names of those who had donated money to that building. The full list—complete with each individual's family relations or job description—contains 126 names identified in three classes according to their relationship to Judaism. But watch very carefully the comparative statistics of those relationships. Of those 126 persons, 69 individuals (55 percent) are Jews, 3 individuals (2 percent) are "proselytes" or converts, and 54 individuals (43 percent) are "God-worshipers." There is only one women named, but that "Jael"—recall Judges 4–5—comes first as "sponsor" of the whole operation. Furthermore, the first 9 persons in the "God-worshipers" list are all identified as city councilors.

The first category is quite clear; it is those who were born Jews. So is the second; it is those who had converted from paganism to Judaism and had, since they are males, been circumcised. But who were those "God-worshipers," of whom nine belonged to the city council? *They were Gentiles who, while remaining as such—that is, if males, uncircumcised—had accepted Jewish monotheism and Jewish morality and regularly attended the synagogue.*

"On the seventh day," wrote the Jewish philosopher Philo in *The Special Laws*, "there are spread before the people in every city . . . the regulating of one's conduct toward God by the rules of piety and holiness, and of one's conduct toward men by the rules of humanity" (2.15.62–63). And the Jewish historian Josephus notes in his *Jewish Antiquities* that the wealth of Jerusalem's Temple comes from "all the Jews throughout the habitable world, and worshipers of God (*sebomenōn tōn theōn*), even those from Asia and Europe" (14.110).

Still, those Aphrodisias statistics are rather stunning. Almost half of those ready, able, and willing to support its synagogue financially were Gentile "God-worshipers." On any Sabbath day at the Aphrodisias synagogue was the congregation half Jewish and half Gentile? If so, was that an exceptional case or fairly representative of any city in at least the eastern Roman Empire? We have no evidence that Aphrodisias was radically exceptional, so my working hypothesis—pending evidence to the contrary—is that a fairly heavy representation of "God-worshiping" Gentiles was part of normal synagogue life.

There was, in other words, a very significant middle way or third option between, on the one hand, those born Jewish or converted and, on the other, pure Gentiles in the ancient world. Furthermore, if Aphrodisias may be taken as representative, synagogue participation by those middle-way or third-option Gentile "God-worshipers" was public, powerful, prominent, and permanent.

THIS CHAPTER WILL HAVE, like the two preceding ones, five main points, five major questions. The first point is a preliminary one. Why do I speak of Luke-Acts? Are they two separate, even if consecutive, books by the same author we call "Luke"? Or are they a single work conceived, planned, integrated, and published in two volumes? If so, how and why were they ever separated as in our present New Testament?

The second point picks up that emphasis on "God-worshiping Gentiles" in the overture and asks this basic and constitutive question: *Was that unknown author, whom we call "Luke," himself a Gentile God-worshiper before he became a Christian?* I answer that question affirmatively and give you my basic evidence for it.

The third point has, once again, two steps, one negative and one positive. The first step concerns the negative attitude of Luke-Acts toward Jews and the Jewish religion. Whether dealing with Jesus in the first volume or Paul in the second one, Jews are presented as riotous and even murderous. The second step concerns the positive attitude of Luke-Acts toward the Roman Empire; these volumes regularly, explicitly, and officially declare Christianity innocent of any religio-political wrongdoing or troublemaking.

The fourth and fifth points ask the same final questions that concluded the preceding chapters on Mark and Matthew. The fourth asks: How do those preceding two steps help us understand the general purpose and overall intention of Luke-Acts as a two-volume parable gospel? The fifth asks: Is Luke-Acts best seen as challenge, attack, or some combination of the two—and, if so, to whom is each directed?

MY FIRST POINT CONCERNS the validity of the title, "The Parable Gospel according to Luke-Acts," and my insistence that it be taken, not as two distinct works, but as a single two-volume parable gospel. How do I know that? There are two major pieces of evidence.

First of all, the opening words of the second volume (our Acts) connect back explicitly to those of the first volume (our Luke). Both are dedicated to the same person or personification. The first volume says: "I too decided, after investigating everything carefully from the very first, to write an orderly account for you, most excellent Theophilus" (Luke 1:3). The second volume says: "In the first book, Theophilus, I wrote about all that Jesus did and taught from the beginning" (Acts 1:1). That proves that the latter volume was intended as a complement to the former, but does not yet prove they were initially planned as a single two-volume gospel. Maybe, the second one was an afterthought, an add-on because the first one was so successful?

Second, then, as in all such cases, it is not how the second volume begins, but how *the first one ends* that indicates an initial two-volume plan rather than simply one book after another. These are the key questions: Is the former volume incomplete without the second one? Does the former leave questions dangling and readers hanging?

Luke's first volume ends with Jesus's ascension into heaven after this parting command: "I am sending upon you what my Father promised; so stay here in the city until you have been clothed with power from on high" (Luke 24:49). At this point, as it were, we are not told and do not know what "my Father promised" and the "power from on high" are. We are, as it were, left hanging, wondering, waiting.

Luke's second volume opens with another account of Jesus's ascension, but now both those enigmatic terms—"promise" and "power"—are explained. First, the *promise* is explained: "While staying with them, he ordered them not to leave Jerusalem, but to wait there for the promise of the Father. 'This,' he said, 'is what you have heard from me; for John baptized with water, but you will be baptized with the Holy Spirit not many days from now'" (Acts 1:4–5). Next, the *power* is explained: "You will receive power when the Holy Spirit has come upon you." In other words, what they were left awaiting in Luke 24:49 is explained here in Acts 1:4–5 as the coming of the Holy Spirit at Pentecost in Acts 2.

I conclude as a working hypothesis that Luke-Acts was conceived by its author as a single two-volume parable gospel. But, then, why have it in two volumes to begin with? Why not a single very large volume that could not be so easily broken apart by those who created our New Testament? The reason is rather prosaic.

An ancient papyrus scroll could only be so long—about 30 feet—before the glued pages tore apart under the strain of size and usage on its back or unwritten side. Ancient books were therefore divided into multiple volumes—from Latin *volumen*, meaning "scroll." The Jewish historian Josephus, for example, needed seven scrolls, or volumes, for his *Jewish War* and twenty for his *Jewish Antiquities*.

Matthew, Mark, and John needed only one scroll, or volume, for their gospels. But Luke's gospel was so much longer that he required two scrolls, or volumes. His gospel included what later tradition called "The Gospel according to Luke" and the "Acts of the Apostles." Luke would have been greatly surprised, of course, to find

"The Gospel according to John" placed in between the two volumes of his own gospel!

Never, ever, therefore, and despite its present title, think that Luke's gospel is just Luke 1:1–24:53, or you will completely misjudge its purpose. But, emphatically for now, Luke's gospel is all of both volumes as an integrated and intended whole, from *our* Luke 1:1 all the way to *our* Acts 28:31. That is why I insist on calling it the Gospel according to Luke-Acts, and I always interpret any part of either volume in the light of that whole.

My SECOND POINT CONCERNS the identity of that unknown author called "Luke" since the second century. Why do I propose that he was not a Jew who converted to Christianity, but rather a Gentile God-worshiper who did so? Here are two pieces of evidence, one from each of his two volumes.

I begin with a story that is not in Mark, but is found in Matthew 8:5–13, in Luke 7:1–10, and somewhat differently in John 4:46–53. An important official at Capernaum asks Jesus to save someone back at home, and Jesus does so instantly—even from a distance. My present point concerns *who* asks the miracle from Jesus. Here are the three versions:

> *Matthew:* When he entered Capernaum, a centurion came to him, appealing to him and saying, "Lord, my servant is lying at home paralyzed, in terrible distress." (8:5–6)

> *Luke:* He entered Capernaum. A centurion there had a slave whom he valued highly, and who was ill and close to death. When he heard about Jesus, he sent some Jewish elders to him, asking him to come and heal his slave. When they came to Jesus, they appealed to him earnestly, saying, "He is worthy of having you do this for him, for he loves our people, and it is he who built our synagogue for us." (7:1–5).

John: There was a royal official whose son lay ill in Capernaum. When he heard that Jesus had come from Judea to Galilee, he went and begged him to come down and heal his son, for he was at the point of death. (4:46–47)

Both Matthew and John have the official make the request *directly* to Jesus, but Luke does it *indirectly*. Luke has him do it through "Jewish elders" and "friends," because that Gentile had "built [their] synagogue for [them]." Luke certainly adds that insert to describe and applaud the ideal God-worshiper, but I think it also indicates his own pre-Christian status as God-worshiper and synagogue supporter.

Next, throughout what we call Acts, Luke speaks not only of "Jews" and "Gentiles," but also of a third group, an in-between group who are "both/and" rather than "either/or." He calls those ambiguous individuals or groups "those fearing God" or "God-fearers" four times (10:2, 22, 35; 13:16). He also calls them "those worshiping" or "worshipers" four times (13:43, 50; 17:4, 17), and, more fully, "those worshiping God" or "God-worshipers" twice (16:14; 18:7). Recall also the name of the person to whom Luke-Acts was dedicated: Theophilus, which in Greek means "God-lover." That could be—either personally or communally—a third name for such synagogue-attending Gentiles.

In any case, those Gentiles are clearly distinguished from Jews in these phrases: "Israelites, and others who fear God" (13:16), "Jews and *devout* converts" (13:43), "Jews incited the *devout* women" (13:50), "Jews . . . *devout* Greeks (17:1, 4), and "Jews and the *devout* persons" (17:17). In all those cases, by the way, that word *devout* is "(God-) worshipers" in Greek.

Furthermore, those in-between "Gentile Jews" are sometimes indicated by Luke without being directly named as either "God-fearers" or "God-worshipers." For example, the "Ethiopian eunuch, a court official of the Candace, queen of the Ethiopians, in charge of her entire treasury [who] had come to Jerusalem to worship" in Acts 8:27 was most likely a God-worshiper.

Why, in both volumes of his gospel, is Luke—and Luke alone in the entire New Testament—so explicitly interested in those Gentile Jews or Jewish Gentiles? My answer to this first question can only be educated guesswork and scholarly conjecture. But my proposal is that "Luke," the unknown author of that two-volume gospel we now call Luke-Acts, was *originally* a Gentile God-worshiper and synagogue supporter before he converted to Christianity. Keep, then, this question in the back of your mind throughout the discussion that follows. *What might a Gentile God-worshiper who was converted to Christianity think about the Jewish community, on the one hand, and the Roman Empire, on the other?*

I TURN NOW TO my third point, which will have two steps, presented as case studies. First, I explore the very negative attitude of Luke-Acts toward the Jewish religion; then, second, I look at the very positive attitude of Luke-Acts toward the Roman Empire. My focus will be on Jesus in the book of Luke and on Paul in Acts, but I will always be thinking of Luke-Acts as a single two-volume parable gospel.

My primary example of Luke's very *negative* attitude toward Judaism concerns a structural pattern established inaugurally with Jesus in the synagogue at Nazareth, but later extending to Paul in synagogues from Pisidian Antioch in modern Turkey to Macedonian Thessalonica in modern Greece. In both cases, watch carefully why and how that negative response is formulated.

I begin with Jesus in the Jewish homeland. You will recall the difficulties experienced by Jesus in his native Nazareth and his proverbial comment that prophets are honored everywhere but in their own hometown. The story comes from Mark (6:1–6) and is copied closely by Matthew (13:54–58—with a change from "carpenter" to "carpenter's son"). But Luke both cites that proverbial comment (4:23–24) and changes the whole story (4:16–30), so that it becomes a programmatic emphasis for all of Luke-Acts.

To begin with, Luke has Jesus enter the synagogue at Nazareth on the Sabbath and read from Isaiah 61:1 proclaiming a jubilee year of liberation for the poor and the enslaved, the blind and the oppressed (4:16–19). I think, by the way, that this is parable rather than history, because it is extremely unlikely that Nazareth had wealth enough for both a synagogue building and prophetic scrolls. In any case, the audience's immediate response is very good: "All spoke well of him and were amazed at the gracious words that came from his mouth. They said, 'Is not this Joseph's son?'" (4:22).

That final question is more wonder than dismissal. But then Jesus himself initiates the overt attack:

> He said to them, "Doubtless you will quote to me this proverb, 'Doctor, cure yourself!' And you will say, 'Do here also in your hometown the things that we have heard you did at Capernaum.'" And he said, "Truly I tell you, no prophet is accepted in the prophet's hometown." (4:23–24)

Why did Luke place that dismissal on the lips of Jesus rather than on those of his audience, as in Mark 6:2–3 and Matthew 13:54–57? Because Luke uses it to continue this even greater provocation—still on the lips of Jesus:

> But the truth is, there were many widows in Israel in the time of Elijah, when the heaven was shut up three years and six months, and there was a severe famine over all the land; yet Elijah was sent to none of them except to a widow at Zarephath in Sidon. There were also many lepers in Israel in the time of the prophet Elisha, and none of them was cleansed except Naaman the Syrian. (4:25–27)

That is, to put it bluntly, an unprovoked provocation from Jesus. It escalates the situation far beyond anything in Luke's Markan source. Jesus cites instances in which two famous Old Testament prophets, first Elijah in 1 Kings 17 and then Elisha in 2 Kings 5, were sent to the aid not of Jews, but of Gentiles. The hint is that God—then and now?—prefers Gentiles to Jews. This is the result of that insult: "When they heard this, all in the synagogue were filled with rage. They got up, drove him out of the town, and led him to the brow of the hill on which their town was built, so that they might hurl him off the cliff" (4:28–29).

Luke created that fictional scene in the synagogue at Nazareth to make—inaugurally and paradigmatically—this theological point: Jesus was accepted initially by his fellow Jews until he claimed that God showed interest in, and even preference for, Gentiles. The result was a murderous riot.

I turn next to Paul in the Jewish diaspora (outside the homeland). With Jesus—and right at the start of Luke-Acts—we are given, as we just saw, *a situation in a Jewish synagogue where divine preference for Gentiles causes a lethal Jewish riot.* That will certainly not keep recurring with Jesus in Luke's first volume, but it will be a dominant motif for Paul in the second volume. Luke has even structured his account of Jesus at Nazareth as a paradigm for that of Paul at both Pisidian Antioch in the east and at Thessalonica in the west:

Sequence	Jesus in Luke	Paul in Acts	Paul in Acts
Synagogue situation	4:16–17	13:14–16a	17:1–2a
Scriptural fulfillment	4:18–21	13:16b–41	17:2b–3
Initial acceptance	4:22	13:42–43	17:4
Eventual rejection	4:23–28	13:44–49	17:5a
Lethal attack	4:29–30	13:50–52	17:5b–9

That parallelism is crucially important for understanding—and assessing—the megaparable of Luke-Acts. Notice the precise turning points from acceptance to rejection in Acts:

The next sabbath almost the whole city gathered to hear the word of the Lord. But when the Jews saw the crowds [i.e., the

Gentile God-worshipers from 13:43], they were filled with *jealousy;* and blaspheming, they contradicted what was spoken by Paul. (13:44–45; my italics)

Some of them were persuaded and joined Paul and Silas, as did a great many of the devout Greeks and not a few of the leading women [i.e., Gentile God-worshipers]. But the Jews became *jealous,* and with the help of some ruffians in the marketplaces they formed a mob and set the city in an uproar. (17:4–5a; my italics)

Luke had, in fact, already used that "jealousy" to explain Jewish opposition to apostolic preaching in the Temple at Jerusalem: "The high priest took action; he and all who were with him (that is, the sect of the Sadducees), being filled with *jealousy,* arrested the apostles and put them in the public prison" (5:17–18).

In summary, Luke used Jesus's experience in the hometown synagogue at Nazareth as a preparation for what would happen to Paul in later diaspora synagogues. Judaism rejected Christianity, he claims, out of "jealousy," because of its success with Gentiles and especially with those in-between Gentile-Jewish God-worshipers. The whole sequence from Jesus in Luke 4 through Paul in Acts 13 to Paul in Acts 17 is a first warning to be very careful and critical about the negative and accusatory attitude toward Jews and Judaism in Luke-Acts.

Paul himself, by the way, explained the rejection of Christianity "by a part of Israel" not as human jealousy, but as divine mystery in Romans 11:25—which, to put it mildly, is a rather different assessment from what we have just seen in Luke. In other words, Luke-Acts tells us far, far more about "Luke" at the start of the second century than it does about either Jesus at the start or Paul at the middle of the first century.

That first step showed Luke-Acts' *negative* attitude toward Jews and the Jewish religion—first for Jesus and then for Paul. I turn next in the second step to show Luke-Acts' *positive* attitude toward Romans and the Roman Empire—focusing first on Jesus and then on Paul.

Luke-Acts insists repeatedly that Rome finds no fault with Christianity and Roman representatives proclaim its innocence legally, officially, and publicly. Both Jesus in Luke and Paul in Acts are declared innocent of all guilt by the highest Roman officials they encounter.

Once again I begin with Jesus in Luke's first volume. Jesus's only confrontation with direct Roman authority is in his trial before Pilate. All the gospel writers have Pilate declare Jesus innocent, but Luke, *and only Luke*, has Pilate insist *three times* that Jesus is free of any crime. Luke even counts out Pilate's declarations of Jesus's innocence, in case you might miss that emphasis:

> [1] Pilate said to the chief priests and the crowds, "I find no basis for an accusation against this man." (23:4)
>
> [2] Pilate . . . said to them, "You brought me this man as one who was perverting the people; and here I have examined him in your presence and have not found this man guilty of any of your charges against him. Neither has Herod, for he sent him back to us. Indeed, he has done nothing to deserve death." (23:13–15)
>
> [3] A third time Pilate said to them, "Why, what evil has he done? I have found in him no ground for the sentence of death." (23:22)

Note that explicit count of "a third time." Furthermore, Luke, and only Luke, has Jesus appear before both Pilate and Antipas.

Both Pilate and Antipas, both the Rome-appointed subgovernor and the Rome-appointed tetrarch, agree that Jesus is not guilty of any crime worthy of execution. That sets the pattern for what will be repeated like a refrain throughout Acts.

I move next to Paul in Luke's second volume. The drumbeat begins obliquely at Paphos, capital of the Roman province of

Cyprus. Its governor, "the proconsul, Sergius Paulus, an intelligent man, summoned Barnabas and Saul and wanted to hear the word of God" (Acts 13:7). They temporarily blinded their opponent, "a certain magician, a Jewish false prophet, named Bar-Jesus," and, "when the proconsul saw what had happened, he believed, for he was astonished at the teaching about the Lord" (13:12). That is parable, not history. (That is also the moment of transition when— after Acts 13:9—"Saul" becomes "Paul," when his Jewish name is replaced by a Roman name. I judge that a microsymbol in Luke-Acts of Judaism becoming Christianity and Jerusalem becoming Rome.)

The next proconsul Paul meets is Gallio at Corinth, capital of the Roman province of Achaia. He was the elder brother of the philosopher Seneca, and both died under Nero. What happened there depicts the ideal Roman attitude toward Jews and Christians according to Luke-Acts:

> When Gallio was proconsul of Achaia, the Jews made a united attack on Paul and brought him before the tribunal. They said, "This man is persuading people to worship God in ways that are contrary to the law." Just as Paul was about to speak, Gallio said to the Jews, "If it were a matter of crime or serious villainy, I would be justified in accepting the complaint of you Jews; but since it is a matter of questions about words and names and your own law, see to it yourselves; I do not wish to be a judge of these matters." And he dismissed them from the tribunal. Then all of them seized Sosthenes, the official of the synagogue, and beat him in front of the tribunal. But Gallio paid no attention to any of these things. (18:12–17)

Once again, according to the standard accusation of Luke-Acts, it is "the Jews" who cause trouble, not "the Christians," but since the dispute concerns Jewish and not Roman "law," wise governors should act like Gallio. Once again, that is parable not history.

After those deliberately model reactions by Roman governors at Paphos and Corinth, the next officials to join Luke's consensus are at Ephesus, capital of the Roman province of Asia Minor. There is danger of a riot against Paul, because Christianity is bad for image-making commerce surrounding that city's famous temple to Artemis/Diana.

First, "Even some officials of the province of Asia (*asiarchoi*), who were friendly to Paul, sent him a message urging him not to venture into the theater" (19:31). That is, of course, rather important imperial sponsorship. Second, when Paul's opponents gather in the theater, "the town clerk of Ephesus" warns them sternly, "You have brought these men here who are neither temple robbers nor blasphemers of our goddess" (19:37).

This entire consensus of imperial approval reaches its climax when Paul is finally taken into Roman custody in Jerusalem. To begin with, says Luke-Acts, it was not punitive, but protective custody. Claudius Lysias, the military tribune at Jerusalem, heard that "the Jews" planned to kill Paul (23:12–22), so "he summoned two of the centurions and said, 'Get ready to leave by nine o'clock tonight for Caesarea with two hundred soldiers, seventy horsemen, and two hundred spearmen. Also provide mounts for Paul to ride, and take him safely to Felix the governor" (23:23–24). Once again, of course, the lethal problem arose from "the Jews." (It is in this context, by the way, that Acts 22:25–29 proclaims Paul to be a Roman citizen. But Paul himself admits in 2 Corinthians 11:25 that he was "three times . . . beaten with rods," a Roman punishment forbidden to be used on Roman citizens.)

Furthermore, the tribune even wrote a letter to the governor explaining his action—and Luke-Acts gives it all in direct quotation! The letter "found that Paul was accused concerning questions of their law, but was charged with nothing deserving death or imprisonment" (23:29). Furthermore, that letter certifies that Paul was "a Roman citizen" (23:27).

Next, the governor Felix kept Paul for two years, since "he hoped that money would be given him by Paul, and for that reason he used to send for him very often and converse with him" (24:26). The problem this time is with Felix—called a tyrant by the Roman historian Tacitus—and not, of course, with Paul. He is innocent and held in custody illegally.

Then, the new governor, Porcius Festus, arrived around 60 CE. "The Jews . . . from Jerusalem . . . [brought] many serious charges against Paul, which they could not prove" (25:7). Festus offered him a trial in Jerusalem, but Paul, fearing assassination there, appealed to the emperor Nero in Rome. When the Herodians Agrippa II and his sister Bernice came on official welcome to the new governor, Festus told them, "When the accusers stood up [against Paul], they did not charge him with any of the crimes that I was expecting. Instead they had certain points of disagreement with him about their own religion and about a certain Jesus, who had died, but whom Paul asserted to be alive" (25:18–19).

Next, after Paul had defended himself publicly before all three of them, they agreed that "this man is doing nothing to deserve death or imprisonment" (26:31). Agrippa said to Festus, "This man could have been set free if he had not appealed to the emperor" (26:32). As with Jesus in his first volume, so also with Paul in this second one: Luke has a Herodian ruler agree with a Roman governor on the innocence of the accused.

Finally, that story about Paul and all that Roman certification of Christian innocence comes to a climax when Paul eventually reaches Rome:

> Paul lived there two whole years at his own expense and welcomed all who came to him, proclaiming the kingdom of God and teaching about the Lord Jesus Christ with all boldness and without hindrance. (28:30–31)

Even though, from Acts 21 through Acts 28, we have watched a captive Paul move inexorably from Jerusalem to Rome, Luke never tells us how it all ended. Or, better, he does so by the way he concludes Luke-Acts. Luke's climactic manifesto is that God and Christ are proclaimed openly in Rome itself and without any imperial Roman hindrance.

We can now see how these two steps come together. The *negative* image for Luke-Acts is that a riotous and murderous Jewish religion opposes Christianity (first step). Accordingly, it is the *positive* Roman law, order, and administrative justice that protect and defend that embattled Christianity (second step)—from Judaism.

MY FOURTH POINT ASKS how those preceding steps help to establish the overall purpose and intention of Luke-Acts. How is its *defense of Christianity* worked out throughout the two-volume parable gospel?

Luke-Acts had two immediate problems in creating its vindication of Christian innocence. One was external, political, and religious; the other was internal, structural, and compositional. I take them in that order.

First the external problem. When and if Christianity emerged from under the protective umbrella of Judaism, Rome might ask it these questions: "Are you people Jews or Christians? As far as we are concerned, you are both atheists, that is, people who neither honor nor worship our imperial gods. You Jews are at least ancient atheists, and we have learned to live with you. But you Christians, are you not some new breed of atheists—whose founder, by the way, we had finally to execute?" "Jews we know from of old and have given them special privileges," Rome might say, "but who are you Christians? You are newcomers, and all we ever hear about you spells trouble— from your Jewish leader under Tiberius to your Christian arsonists under Nero. Who are you, and what are you?" So how does Luke-Acts answer all those dangerous questions so threatening to the continued existence of Christianity within the Roman Empire?

The fundamental response is that Christians are now the only true Jews, because Jews rejected their own Messiah and therefore their own destiny. Accordingly, Christians should now be full heirs to all those ancient privileges and religious exemptions once given by Rome to Judaism. Christianity is, says Luke-Acts, the true Judaism, the only valid continuity of that ancient and revered religion and not the arrival of some upstart new religion.

That is the dominant theme of Luke-Acts, but there is also the subordinate theme we have just seen. Riots and threats of rioting come not from Christians—who are always peaceful—but from Jews—who are always jealous—according to Luke-Acts. Would that not remind the empire of the homeland Jewish war against Rome of 66–74 CE and/or—depending on the date of Luke-Acts—of the Jewish diaspora war against Rome of 115–17 CE? That could play dangerously into actual and potential Roman anti-Judaism. In any case, says Luke-Acts, if peaceful Christianity is the true continuation of Judaism, because what purports to be Judaism has now become riot-prone, how can Rome not reject the "old" Judaism, accept Christianity as the "new" Judaism, and transfer any privileged toleration from the former to the latter religion?

Next the internal problem in comparing Luke-Acts. Granted that defensive manifesto was necessary as Christianity emerged from Judaism on the religio-political level, there were still major literary difficulties for Luke-Acts on the structural and compositional level. In other words, I turn now from this fourth point's first to its second step.

Think, for a moment, about Luke's preliminary literary problems in composing his two-volume gospel. Jesus will be gone by the end of the first volume, so who will be the major protagonist of the second? Will it be the Twelve, Peter and Paul in tandem, or Paul alone? And would that second protagonist not create a dangerous parallelism with Jesus, making the two to be equivalent "heroes"? Watch, in what follows, how Luke-Acts solves that compositional challenge with two interwoven motifs—that of the *journey* and that of the *Spirit*—and watch especially how he combines them as the *journey of the Spirit*.

The first volume of Luke-Acts records a long, slow journey from Galilee to Jerusalem and ends there with "the eleven and their companions . . . continually in the temple blessing God" (Luke 24:33, 53); the second volume records a long, slow journey from Jerusalem to Rome and ends there with Paul "proclaiming the kingdom of God and teaching about the Lord Jesus Christ with all boldness and without hindrance" (Acts 28:31). In outline:

First Volume (Luke)

In Galilee
(3:1–9:50)

From Galilee to Jerusalem
(9:51, 53; 13:22–23, 33–34; 17:11; 18:31; 19:11, 28)

In Jerusalem
(19:29–24:53)

Second Volume (Acts)

In Jerusalem
(1:1–7:60)

From Jerusalem to Rome
(8:1–28:14a)

In Rome
(28:14b–31)

In that first volume, we are—as indicated above—repeatedly reminded that Jesus is on a long, slow, solemn procession toward Jerusalem. In the second one, there is a similar process—from Judea through Samaria to Syrian Antioch (8:5; 9:31; 11:19); from Antioch through Cyprus to Galatia (13:1–14:6); from Galatia through Greece to Asia (15:40–19:41). But then Paul returns to Jerusalem and starts his last journey—in chains—from Jerusalem to Rome (21:17–28:14a).

You will notice in that outline that Jerusalem is the center of Luke's two-volume gospel parable. If you *mistakenly* read only that first volume as constituting Luke's gospel, you would totally *misinterpret* its conclusion. In its final verses the companions of Jesus are in Jerusalem and in the Temple "continually blessing God" (Luke 24:52–53).

If those verses are taken as terminal to Luke's gospel, Christian Judaism is firmly located within Judaism, Jerusalem, and its Temple.

But Luke 24:52–53 are hinge verses rather than final ones. They are not conclusion, but transition. For Luke-Acts, the "good news" is that Judaism has ceded place to Christianity, and all of the privileges Rome bestowed on Judaism should now be afforded to Christianity. Rome was now God's new holy city. Rome was the new Jerusalem. (That would, of course, have been "news," but not "good news" for Paul or Mark or Matthew.)

I turn next from the *journey* motif to the *spirit* motif in Luke-Acts. As mentioned above, Luke did not want to risk any balanced parallelism between a journeying Jesus in his first volume and a journeying Paul (or anyone else) in his second volume—as if Paul were somehow as important as Jesus. What was his solution? *To emphasize that the one journeying was the Holy Spirit.* Each volume, therefore, had to begin with a balanced arrival of the Holy Spirit down here to earth.

At the start of the first volume, John baptized Jesus, and "the Holy Spirit descended upon him in bodily form like a dove" (Luke 3:22). After that, "Jesus, full of the Holy Spirit, returned from the Jordan and was led by the Spirit in the wilderness" (4:1). At the start of the second volume, the Twelve are "filled with the Holy Spirit," descending in visible form as tongues of fire at Pentecost (2:1–4). Thereafter, far more explicitly than with Jesus, the Holy Spirit is clearly in charge of both theology, for example, "It has seemed good to the Holy Spirit and to us" (15:28), and geography, for example:

> While they were worshiping the Lord and fasting, the Holy Spirit said, "Set apart for me Barnabas and Saul for the work to which I have called them." So, being sent out by the Holy Spirit, they went down to Seleucia; and from there they sailed to Cyprus. (13:2, 4)

> They went through the region of Phrygia and Galatia, having been forbidden by the Holy Spirit to speak the word in Asia. When they had come opposite Mysia, they attempted to go into Bithynia, but the Spirit of Jesus did not allow them. (16:6–7)

Those are only a few examples of an almost drumbeat mention of the Holy Spirit from Acts 1:2 through 28:25.

Putting those two motifs of *journey* and *spirit* together, Luke-Acts records the great journey of God's Holy Spirit from Galilee to Jerusalem in the first volume and then from Jerusalem to Rome in the second. The "good news," *for the author of Luke-Acts*, is that the Holy Spirit has changed headquarters from Jerusalem to Rome. Rome—not Jerusalem—is now the holy city of Christianity. Rome is new Jerusalem.

Imagine it—*but not literally*—this way. Luke-Acts is, as it were, *a defense brief* for Christianity carried by Paul into the imperial court at Rome. Put another way, Luke-Acts promotes a Christianity that is *within* rather than *against* the Roman Empire. Put a third way, Luke-Acts is *a*—and maybe even *the*—first move toward a future of *Roman Christianity* and Constantine. Luke-Acts is not blind—is emphatically not blind—to Christian problems with Rome, but those are to be solved by *negotiation with* and not *negation of* the *Pax Romana*.

I TURN, FINALLY, TO this chapter's fifth point. Granted all of that preceding analysis, and especially its fateful claims about Judaism and Christianity, what type of parable is the Gospel according to Luke-Acts? Is it an internal *challenge* parable like that offered by Mark to the Twelve companions and family relatives of Jesus? Or is it an internal *attack* parable like that proclaimed by the Christian Judaism of Matthew against the Pharisaic Judaism of his opponents? It is actually both *attack and challenge*, but both aspects are more *externally* than internally directed and both are tightly integrated.

First, Luke-Acts as attack. The presentation of Jesus in Luke-Acts is, first of all, an *attack* parable—against the Jewish religion. It is, however, quite different from that seen already in Matthew's portrayal of Jesus. Luke-Acts comes from outside rather than inside Judaism, because "Luke," unlike "Matthew," is now fully outside the Jewish religion. As a converted Gentile God-worshiper, he finds present validity in Judaism only as absorbed into and thereby replaced by Christianity.

On the one hand, Luke-Acts' attack does not have the bitterness and invective so visible in Matthew. Think, for instance, of that single accusatory word "hypocrites": Matthew has it sixteen times (6:2–16; 15:7; 22:18; 23:13–29; 24:51), but Luke has it only twice (12:56; 13:15).

On the other hand, although Matthew's internal attack opposes Christian Judaism to Pharisaic Judaism, Luke-Acts' external attack opposes Christianity to Judaism. As a God-worshiper, "Luke" knows Judaism and its Greek-translation scriptures very, very well, but as a Gentile (and Roman citizen?) his vision is not of a *Christian Judaism* or even of a *Jewish Christianity*, but of a *Roman Christianity* or even a *Christian Rome*.

Luke-Acts is also a challenge parable—but externally to the Roman authorities. The first and major element of challenge is, of course, for Rome to accept Christianity as replacing Judaism, to grant Christianity those imperial tolerances and exemptions once accorded Judaism. That challenge is summed up in the final words of Luke-Acts, in which Paul is *in Rome* "proclaiming the kingdom of God and teaching about the Lord Jesus Christ with all boldness and *without hindrance*" (28:31).

There are also, of course, several elements of ethical challenge to Rome's standard social norms. Notice, for example, what is emphasized in the following conversion story. "In Caesarea there was a man named Cornelius, a centurion of the Italian Cohort, as it was called. He was a *devout* man (from the Greek verb "to worship") who feared God with all his household" (Acts 10:1–2a). In other words, Cornelius was a Gentile God-worshiper or God-fearer. But notice what is emphasized three times about his character:

He was a devout man who feared God with all his household; he gave *alms* generously to the people and prayed constantly to

God. . . . An angel of God . . . [said], "Your prayers and your *alms* have ascended as a memorial before God.". . . A man in dazzling clothes . . . said, "Cornelius, your prayer has been heard and your *alms* have been remembered before God." (10:2–4, 31)

Luke-Acts challenges Rome to compassionate almsgiving, that is, to charitable generosity—but not to distributive justice. Rome, of course, did not crucify those who demanded charity, but rather those who demanded justice.

In summary and conclusion, Luke-Acts is an *attack* on Judaism, but also a *challenge* to Rome. It operates, in other words, on two fronts at the same time by rejecting and denigrating Judaism except as it is now absorbed into Christianity, while, at the same time, proclaiming and rejoicing in Christianity's Roman future. With the Jesus of Mark presented through a *challenge* parable, the Jesus of Matthew conveyed through an *attack* parable, and the Jesus of Luke-Acts presented through an *attack and challenge* parable, we come finally to John. The next and final chapter asks: What type of parable is the Gospel according to John?

CHAPTER 10

The Visionary Dream of God

THE PARABLE GOSPEL ACCORDING TO JOHN

WHEN YOU THINK OF WORLD Heritage Sites, you usually imagine ancient places and ruined cities. But one site is emphatically neither. It is a city planned in the open savannah to become its country's new capital. It is a city only fifty years old that was almost immediately declared a World Heritage location. It is a city whose only antiquity is its Latinized name, Brasilia, capital of Brazil.

Look east from the observation deck of the city's centrally located television tower and imagine that you are on the tail of the plane whose shape inspired the city's design. In front of you, on both sides, are the evenly balanced and deliberately named North Wing and South Wing, city sections that sweep elegantly backward from the plane's central cockpit. On both sides of the cockpit's broad central axis the separate government departments look like so many glass-faced dominoes standing upright on their longer sides. They march in serried ranks toward the cockpit's core in the plane's nose. There, in Three Powers Square, are the judicial, legislative, and executive functions that guide the plane-city of Brasilia and the Federal Republic of Brazil.

My present focus is on a very beautiful building located—along with the National Museum and the National Library—just before the South Wing's line of government departments start their march toward the Three Powers Square. It is Brazil's National Cathedral, the Catedral Metropolitana Nossa Senhora Aparecida, whose circular design, concrete ribs, and stained-glass totality arch upward like hands opened in prayer. You enter the building by going underground outside and then up inside, because doorways would have broken the glass circularity.

You approach those descending stairs by walking between statues of the four evangelists, austere and double-life-size bronzes sculpted by Alfredo Ceschiatti. They are not divided two on each side, as you might expect for an entrance avenue. Neither are all four on one side facing those government complexes to make a religio-political statement. Instead, three on one side face one on the other side of the entranceway.

The east-side triad are what scholars call the *synoptic* evangelists— so-called because you can *view their texts together* in parallel columns. First comes Matthew holding with both hands a scroll opened from right shoulder to left hip across his body. Then Mark, bare-chested, with a closed scroll in his lowered right hand, his lowered left in an open-handed gesture of supplication. Finally, there is Luke, also with a closed scroll in his lowered right hand, but with his left over his heart and his head veiled for worship. On the west side of the entranceway, facing those three synoptic authors, is John. But, unlike them, he holds his scroll in his left hand, so that his right can be raised with palm toward them in the authoritative gesture of speaker, teacher, and witness. (We still make that gesture while swearing to the truth in court.)

In that sculptural complex, all four evangelists are depicted as authors, but it is John alone who teaches the others. It is John who witnesses to the synoptic triad of Matthew, Mark, and Luke. That claim gives me my generative questions for this chapter. If each of the synoptic gospels has created a megaparable—whether it is challenge and/or attack—about Jesus of Nazareth, how does John's parable "instruct" those others? Does it do so by challenge or attack?

Even more important, does it "instruct" them correctly or incorrectly? Throughout this chapter, therefore, those provocatively positioned evangelists from Brasilia's National Roman Catholic Cathedral will remain as a permanent visual matrix.

THE PRESENT CHAPTER WILL proceed—like the three before it—with five linked points. My first point asks whether John is an attack parable. If so, what is attacked and against whom is that directed? And how does its focus of attack compare with those already seen for Matthew and Luke?

My second point is a short probe of the opening words in John's parable gospel. How do those words—and all of John's overture in 1:1–18—compare with and challenge the synoptic overtures in Mark 1:1–8, Matthew 1–2, and Luke 1–2? That probe gives me a working hypothesis to explore the following third point—which has four steps. It asks how John sees the life, death, resurrection, and "return" of Jesus in comparison to what we find in the synoptic tradition of Mark, Matthew, and Luke.

The fourth and fifth points follow the pattern established in the three preceding chapters. The fourth point asks: What do the preceding conclusions reveal about the overall purpose and general intention of John's parable gospel? The fifth point asks: How do attack and challenge coalesce for John? If attack, against whom is it directed? If challenge, to whom is it directed?

THAT FIRST POINT'S QUESTION seems a very easy one to answer. The immediate impression from reading John's gospel is that it is an *attack* parable with obvious parallels to both Matthew and Luke. We saw in Chapter 8 that Matthew's attack was from Christian Judaism against Pharisaic Judaism. Matthew was, in other words, still *inside* Judaism. We saw in Chapter 9 that Luke's attack was from Gentile, and especially God-worshiping Gentile, Christianity against traditional Judaism itself. Luke-Acts was, in other words, already *outside* Judaism. Watch, now, how John combines Matthew and Luke, *as it were*, by escalating his attack from part to whole, from, say, "Pharisees" or "chief priests" to—simply—"the Jews" (as if Jesus and all his companions were not also "Jews"!)

First, with regard to the Pharisees, John is as accusatory as Matthew—and, indeed, even more so. The conflict between Jesus and the Pharisees in John 7–9, for example, concludes like this: "Some of the Pharisees . . . said to him, 'Surely we are not blind, are we?' Jesus said to them, 'If you were blind, you would not have sin. But now that you say, "We see," your sin remains'" (9:40–41). But even the accusation of blindness—as already seen repeatedly in Matthew 23—is not John's most serious attack on the Pharisees.

More seriously, John—and only John—directly involves the Pharisees—and not just the chief priests—in the death of Jesus. And that association starts early in John's narrative: "The chief priests and Pharisees sent temple police to arrest him," and later "the temple police went back to the chief priests and Pharisees, who asked them, 'Why did you not arrest him?'" (7:32, 45). Furthermore, that collaboration continues to its lethal climax: "The chief priests and the Pharisees called a meeting of the council, and said, 'What are we to do? This man is performing many signs'" (11:47). So "the chief priests and the Pharisees had given orders that anyone who knew where Jesus was should let them know, so that they might arrest him" (11:57). Finally, "Judas brought a detachment of soldiers together with police from the chief priests and the Pharisees, and they came there with lanterns and torches and weapons" to arrest Jesus (18:3).

Second, John regularly escalates accusations from part to whole, from Jewish authorities to Jewish people. For example, compare these comments by Mark and John about the early and lethal opposition to Jesus because of his Sabbath-day healings. The former says that the "Pharisees went out and immediately conspired with the Herodians against him, how to destroy him" (Mark 3:6). The latter says that "the Jews were seeking all the more to kill him, because he was . . . breaking the sabbath" (John 5:18). The escalation from part to whole is obvious.

Or again, with regard to name-calling and character assassination, compare Mark and John on the specific accusation of demonic possession. The former records that "the scribes who came down from Jerusalem said, 'He has Beelzebul, and by the ruler of the demons he casts out demons'" (Mark 3:22). But, in the latter gospel, once again, that same accusation escalates to all: "The Jews answered him, 'Are we not right in saying that you are a Samaritan and have a demon?'" (John 8:48). That is attack, not challenge.

Furthermore, with regard to name-calling, Jesus himself does even more of it in John than in Matthew. He had just said this to those same Jews: "You are from your father the devil, and you choose to do your father's desires. He was a murderer from the beginning and does not stand in the truth, because there is no truth in him. When he lies, he speaks according to his own nature, for he is a liar and the father of lies" (8:44).

Finally, watch these different versions of the Roman trial of Jesus and the release of Barabbas in Mark and John. Mark speaks consistently of "the crowd" (15:8, 11, 15), encouraged by "the chief priests" (15:11–12), who prefer Barabbas to Jesus. But John makes this change:

> When *the chief priests and the police* saw him [Jesus], they shouted, "Crucify him! Crucify him!" Pilate said to *them*, "Take him yourselves and crucify him; I find no case against him." *The Jews* answered him, "We have a law, and according to that law he ought to die because he has claimed to be the Son of God." (19:6–7)

In John, the specific phrase "the chief priests and the police" is escalated to "the Jews."

In other words, and on this first point, John's external attack is not just against Pharisaic Judaism, as in Matthew—but against Judaism itself, as in Luke-Acts. The term "the Jews" appears only a few times in the synoptic tradition—mostly as a neutral expression used by non-Jews. But in John—as in Acts—the term is sometimes used neutrally as an ethnic designation, but it more often occurs with an adversarial edge to it.

My SECOND POINT IS a short but crucial probe, like an archaeologist's preliminary sounding on an unexcavated ancient site, into the opening words of John's parable gospel. First of all, every gospel begins with an overture—an initial action that focuses and summarizes the entire following story. Think of them as similar to the overtures of classical operas or musical comedies, which combine themes or melodies to be heard later throughout the following drama. Think also of how those gospel overtures must have helped ancient hearers or readers confronted with wall-to-wall writing, all in uppercase Greek, without paragraphs or headings, and certainly lacking our chapter and verse numbers.

Mark's overture goes back to Isaiah's "prophecy" about John the Baptist (1:1–3), and Matthew's and Luke's overtures are very different versions of the nativity of Jesus in which Matthew goes as far back as Abraham (1:1), and Luke goes all the way back to Adam (3:38). But John's overture begins far back beyond any of those times mentioned by the synoptic authors. It begins not with John, or Isaiah, or Abraham, or Adam. It begins with a visionary dream in the mind of God, a visionary dream that is *with* God and *is* God:

In the beginning was the Word (*ho logos*),
and the Word (*ho logos*) was with God,
and the Word (*ho logos*) was God.
This one (*houtos*) was in the beginning with God. (1:1–2)

We translate the Greek *ho logos* as "the Word," and that is both correct and vacuous. What does *ho logos* or "the Word" mean in the opening words of John's magnificently poetic overture?

It means that God did not come up with a bright new idea called Jesus around 4 BCE. The eternal and generative dream of God was for a world of justice and peace, for an earth unsullied by oppression and injustice, by violence, bloodshed, and war. That hope, vision, dream for the earth was always *with* God and *was* God. But, John claims, it became embodied, incarnated, revealed humanly in Jesus: "*The* Word (*ho logos*) became flesh and lived among us" (1:14). John's overture claims that Jesus of Nazareth is the visionary dream of God as embodied humanly in time, place, and sandals.

Think of it this way. A mighty river pushes steadily against a logjam, but cannot break through except in trickles and rivulets. Then, one day, it breaks through fully and floods forward on its way. It broke through at a specific moment in time, but it was not created at that moment. It was always there, pressing, pressing, pressing. Furthermore, if you could control *all* the variables, you might be able to explain that moment of breakthrough. But it would be a serious mistake downriver to think that the river had just been invented. And that too is a challenge parable.

MY THIRD POINT FOLLOWS directly from that initial probe. It asks whether John's megaparable of Jesus is, despite what we saw in my first point above, not merely an attack parable against Judaism, but even more profoundly a challenge parable to the three synoptic gospels. This present point proposes that John's gospel is a challenge to the life, death, resurrection, and "return" of Jesus as they are presented in the synoptic vision of the other gospels. The next steps of this point will compare those four elements of Jesus's story as they appear in John with those as they appear especially in Mark, as Mark is the major source for Matthew and Luke.

I begin with the *life* of Jesus. My focus here is how differently John interprets the miracles that fill so much of that life in the synoptic gospels. The healing miracles, for example, were cited by Luke to establish and vindicate Jesus's very identity when questioned by the imprisoned Baptist: "Go and tell John what you have seen and heard: the blind receive their sight, the lame walk, the lepers are cleansed, the deaf hear, the dead are raised, the poor have good news brought to them" (7:22). I give just one example to show how differently John interprets those traditional miracles.

The miraculous multiplication of loaves and fishes is told five times in the synoptic gospels (Mark 6:32–44; Matt. 14:13–21; Luke 9:10b–17; Mark 8:1–10; Matt. 15:32–39). I focus here on that first one, in Mark 6:32–44, to compare it with the parallel version in John (6:1–13) and the long discourse by Jesus following it (6:14–59).

The story of the multiplication in Mark is directly and literally about food for the hungry. Furthermore, it is another attempt by Jesus—like those seen already in Chapter 7—to educate the Twelve in their responsibility as community leaders. The difference between Jesus's vision and theirs is emphasized in this opening dialogue after a day of teaching "a great crowd":

> When it grew late, his disciples came to him and said, "This is a deserted place, and the hour is now very late; send them away so that they may go into the surrounding country and villages and buy something for themselves to eat." But he answered them, "You give them something to eat." (Mark 6:35–37a)

The opposing solutions are quite clear:

> From the Twelve: "*Send them away* to buy something for themselves to eat."

> From Jesus: "*You give them* something to eat."

And their response almost mocks him: "They said to him, 'Are we to go and buy two hundred denarii worth of bread, and give it to them to eat?'" (6:37b). Thereafter, Jesus pulls them into the middle between himself and the crowd at every stage of the miracle:

[1] *Seeking:* And he said to them, "How many loaves have you? Go and see." When they had found out, they said, "Five, and two fish." (6:38)

[2] *Seating:* Then he ordered them to get all the people to sit down in groups on the green grass. So they sat down in groups of hundreds and of fifties. (6:39–40)

[3] *Distributing:* Taking the five loaves and the two fish, he looked up to heaven, and blessed and broke the loaves, and gave them to his disciples to set before the people; and he divided the two fish among them all. And all ate and were filled. (6:41–42)

[4] *Gathering:* And they took up twelve baskets full of broken pieces and of the fish. Those who had eaten the loaves numbered five thousand men. (6:43–44)

In other words, and quite deliberately for Mark, the Twelve are forced to abandon their solution (send them away) and participate in every stage of Jesus's solution (give them something to eat).

The point of this miracle parable is, *for Jesus*, that the food already present—already present and not divinely delivered like, say, the manna from heaven as in Exodus 14—is more than enough for everyone when it passes through his own hands exercising God's distributive justice for God's people on God's earth. The point is also, *for Mark*, that the Twelve as community leaders have denied their own responsibility for that process. But the story is always and ever about real food as the material basis of life in this world. It is never *just about food*. It is always *about just food*.

The story about the miraculous distribution in John 6:1–13 is similar to that in Mark—the same already present five loaves and two fishes (6:9), the same "large crowd" of five thousand people (6:10), and the same twelve baskets left over (6:13). But there is one rather minor and one very major difference between Mark's and John's versions.

First, the minor difference. Mark was quite willing to have Jesus ask a question: "How many loaves have you? Go and see" (6:38). But

John is not happy with that implicit ignorance on the part of Jesus. So he starts his parable this way:

> Jesus said to Philip, "Where are we to buy bread for these people to eat?" He said this to test him, for he himself knew what he was going to do. Philip answered him, "Six months' wages would not buy enough bread for each of them to get a little." (6:5–7)

That is only a minor change, although it is also a significant one, because, for John, Jesus knows everything beforehand and asks not to learn, but to test.

Next, here is the major difference between Mark and John in this miracle parable. The remainder of John 6 reduces—that verb is carefully chosen—that story to a *visual aid* for the long discourse that follows it (6:14–59). And that discourse by Jesus refers exclusively to the loaves and not to the fishes. You can already see those fishes disappearing in John by comparing the end of the action in Mark with this transition from action to discourse in John:

> They took up twelve baskets full of broken pieces and of the fish. Those who had eaten the loaves numbered five thousand men. (Mark 6:43–44)

> They gathered them up, and from the fragments of the five barley loaves, left by those who had eaten, they filled twelve baskets. (John 6:13)

For John, the fishes can go because, in the following discourse, Jesus is the *bread*—but not the *fish*—of life. Here is what happens in the bread-of-life discourse.

First, negatively. Jesus admonishes the people for any interest in the reality of the loaves as bread, as actual food: "You are looking for me, not because you saw signs, but because you ate your fill of the loaves" (6:26). Or, again: "Do not work for the food that perishes, but for the food that endures for eternal life" (6:27).

Second, positively. When you read the discourse for yourselves, notice how it is structured around Jesus's repeated claim to be *the bread of life that came down from heaven*:

> Jesus said to them, "I am the bread of life. Whoever comes to me will never be hungry, and whoever believes in me will never be thirsty." (6:35)

> The Jews began to complain about him because he said, "I am the bread that came down from heaven." (6:41)

> "I am the bread of life. Your ancestors ate the manna in the wilderness, and they died. This is the bread that comes down from heaven, so that one may eat of it and not die." (6:48–50)

> "I am the living bread that came down from heaven. Whoever eats of this bread will live forever; and the bread that I will give for the life of the world is my flesh." (6:51)

By the time you reach the end that discourse in John 6, you will have forgotten the actual loaves—and fishes—that served, for John, as a simple visual aid and symbolic referent to Jesus himself as divine food from heaven.

One final emphasis. The difference between Mark and John is not simply between *Jesus giving actual or physical bread* and *Jesus being symbolic or spiritual bread*. Both stories are symbolic. Mark's story symbolizes—and effects—God's gift of food. John's story symbolizes—but does not effect?—God's gift of Jesus. We now read Mark and John and get both. But John intended to challenge Mark and have the story read in his own divergent version.

John interprets all the physical or restorative miracles of Jesus as symbolic of what God *is* in Jesus rather than of what God *does* in Jesus. Look back, for example, at John 4 and note how physical drinking in 4:7–15 and physical eating in 4:31–38 become spiritual symbols of Jesus. Or, again, do you really think that Cana was just about wine?

My second step concerns the *death* of Jesus. Three examples will suffice to show the immense differences between Mark and John concerning the death of Jesus: first in the garden; then on the cross; and finally at the tomb.

For Mark, Jesus is almost out of control in the Garden of Gethsemane. Notice the three themes of *ground, cup,* and *disciples:*

Ground: He began to be distressed and agitated. . . . And said to them, "I am deeply grieved, even to death." . . . And going a little farther, he threw himself on the *ground* and prayed that, if it were possible, the hour might pass from him. (14:33–35)

Cup: He said, "Abba, Father, for you all things are possible; remove this *cup* from me; yet, not what I want, but what you want." (14:36)

Disciples: All of them deserted him and fled. (14:50)

Watch those three italicized themes and compare how John retells that story and changes each of them quite completely:

Ground: Judas brought a detachment (*speira*) of soldiers together with police from the chief priests and the Pharisees, and they came there with lanterns and torches and weapons. Then Jesus, knowing all that was to happen to him, came forward and asked them, "Whom are you looking for?" They answered, "Jesus of Nazareth." Jesus replied, "I am he." Judas, who betrayed him, was standing with them. When Jesus said to them, "I am he," they stepped back and fell to the *ground.* (18:3–6)

Cup: Simon Peter, who had a sword, drew it, struck the high priest's slave, and cut off his right ear. The slave's name was

Malchus. Jesus said to Peter, "Put your sword back into its sheath. Am I not to drink the *cup* that the Father has given me?" (18:10–11)

Disciples: Again he asked them, "Whom are you looking for?" And they said, "Jesus of Nazareth." Jesus answered, "I told you that I am he. So if you are looking for me, *let these men go.*" (18:7–8)

That is—from Mark to John—an absolutely extraordinary reversal. Jesus is not out of control, but totally in control. He is, in fact, managing his own arrest. His humanity has ceded overt and total place to his divinity. Notice the elements in John's version.

First of all, that vague word "detachment" is quite specific in Greek—it is *speira*, a cohort, that is, six hundred troops. John's very deliberate emphasis is certified by that word's repetition at the end of the passage: "The soldiers (*speira*), their officer (*chiliarchos*), and the Jewish police arrested Jesus and bound him" (18:12). That officer is a tribune or, literally, commander of a thousand soldiers. It takes all of that to arrest Jesus—when he lets them up off the ground.

Next, there is no mention by Jesus—even with total submission and obedience—of having the cup of suffering pass him by—as in Mark. Instead, there is that rhetorical question in John: "Am I not to drink the cup?"

Finally, the disciples do not desert Jesus and flee, as in Mark. Instead, in John, Jesus commands those arresting him to "let these men go." It is not that they abandon Jesus, but that Jesus protects and saves them. And that was "to fulfill the word that he had spoken, 'I did not lose a single one of those whom you gave me'" (18:9), recalling his earlier word that "not one of them was lost except the one destined to be lost," that is, Judas (17:12).

What about the crucifixion of Jesus? Think of John's account of Jesus's death as Mark's desolate human darkness rewritten in translucent divine light. What we have just seen in the garden is continued on the cross. Here is Mark's version—and watch the purpose of the sour wine:

> At three o'clock Jesus cried out with a loud voice, "Eloi, Eloi, lema sabachthani?" which means, "My God, my God, why have you forsaken me?" When some of the bystanders heard it, they said, "Listen, he is calling for Elijah." And someone ran, filled a sponge with *sour wine*, put it on a stick, and gave it to him to drink, saying, "Wait, let us see whether Elijah will come to take him down." Then Jesus gave a loud cry and breathed his last. (15:33–37)

That drink of sour wine is to revive Jesus and keep him alive long enough to see if Elijah comes to his aid. For Mark, Jesus dies amid external mockery and internal—how strong should the word be—despair? But that must, of course, be balanced for Mark by what also happens externally: "The curtain of the temple was torn in two, from top to bottom. Now when the centurion, who stood facing him, saw that in this way he breathed his last, he said, 'Truly this man was God's Son!'" (15:38–39).

In any case, the parallel scene in John is—as you expect by now—the precise opposite of Mark's. For John, Jesus is once again in total and final control even of his own death. Watch that incident of the sour wine:

> When Jesus knew that all was now finished, he said (in order to fulfill the scripture), "I am thirsty." A jar full of *sour wine* was standing there. So they put a sponge full of the wine on a branch of hyssop and held it to his mouth. When Jesus had received the wine, he said, "It is finished." Then he bowed his head and gave up his spirit. (19:28–30)

The proffered wine is now given not to mock Jesus, but to obey him. Jesus is portrayed as in control of his arrest by his commanding the arresters and of his execution by commanding the executioners, so that the scriptures are all fulfilled. And, needless to say, there is no loud death cry in John. Jesus dies when all is finished, and he is ready to give up his spirit. The Jesus of Mark dies in human agony. The Jesus of John dies in divine radiance.

With regard to entombment, in Mark, Jesus is buried swiftly and somewhat inadequately, "since it was the day of Preparation, that is, the day before the sabbath" (15:42). It is not a dishonorable burial, because Joseph of Arimathea "bought a linen cloth, and taking down the body, wrapped it in the linen cloth, and laid it in a tomb that had been hewn out of the rock. He then rolled a stone against the door of the tomb" (15:46). But there was no time for proper anointing or full mourning, so "when the sabbath was over, Mary Magdalene, and Mary the mother of James, and Salome bought spices, so that they might go and anoint him" (16:1).

That was at least a *decent* burial, but in John it escalates into a *royal* or even a *divine* burial. Note the differences. John begins, first, with Joseph of Arimathea's request for Jesus's body from Pilate (19:38), just as Mark did (15:42–45). Then John reintroduces Nicodemus, whom we have not seen since 3:1–9 and 7:50–52. That allows John to add two major new aspects to that burial:

> Nicodemus, who had at first come to Jesus by night, also came, bringing a mixture of myrrh and aloes, weighing about a hundred pounds. They took the body of Jesus and wrapped it with the spices in linen cloths, according to the burial custom of the Jews. Now there was a garden in the place where he was crucified, and in the garden there was a new tomb in which no one had ever been laid. (19:39–41)

That the tomb was *new and unused* is present in both Matthew (27:60) and Luke (23:53), but not in Mark (15:42–44). That the tomb was in a *garden*, that is, in the ideal and idealized location for a burial site, is unique to John. (We are back, by the way, where the death story of Jesus began—in a *garden*.) But, of course, John's major addition is that anointing with "a mixture of myrrh and aloes, weighing about a hundred pounds."

If we did not have John's gospel, we could imagine composing it like this. Take Mark, turn any negative into positive, any darkness into light, and any humanity into divinity. Then, put Jesus in full and total control of his own execution—all happens as Jesus wills it and when he is completely ready. Finally, bury Jesus not inadequately, but superadequately. Do not give him a hasty and unanointed burial, but a slow, fully anointed, and regally if not divinely magnificent one.

My third step focuses on the *resurrection* of Jesus. It was relatively easy to see how John challenged the synoptic tradition of the life and death of Jesus. It is much harder to understand how he does the same with its general tradition of Jesus's resurrection and return. Whatever he does there is much more oblique and very, very ambiguous.

To begin with, think about the story of Lazarus. On the one hand, it is a spectacularly clear miracle of resurrection as resuscitation. Jesus deliberately waits until Lazarus is securely dead: "After having heard that Lazarus was ill, he stayed two days longer in the place where he was" (11:6), so that "when Jesus arrived, he found that Lazarus had already been in the tomb four days" (11:17). Next, Martha protests that "already there is a stench because he has been dead four days" (11:39). Finally, Jesus commands Lazarus to "come out," and "the dead man came out, his hands and feet bound with strips of cloth, and his face wrapped in a cloth. Jesus said to them, 'Unbind him, and let him go'" (11:44).

It is hard to avoid that insistence on the reality of bodily death and decay. "Life" and "death" in John 11 are very literal words referring to very literal facts. Yet in the middle of that reality we find this interchange between Jesus and Martha:

Jesus said to her, "Your brother will rise again." Martha said to him, "I know that he will rise again in the resurrection on the last day." Jesus said to her, "I am the resurrection and the life. Those who believe in me, even though they die, will live, and *everyone who lives and believes in me will never die.* Do you believe this?" She said to him, "Yes, Lord, I believe that you are the Messiah, the Son of God, the one coming into the world." (11:23–27)

Those italicized words indicate a shift from the literal to some metaphorical meaning of "life" and "death." Furthermore, Martha does not exactly answer Jesus's question. She believes he is the Messiah, the Son of God, but does she believe that *everyone who lives and believes in Jesus will never die*? What does it mean *to never die*?

Is Lazarus, *for John*, a positive or negative parable? Is his raising a positive model for that of Jesus or a negative model almost lampooning resuscitation mistaken for resurrection? Is John 11 similar to John 6: Is the physical miracle not important in itself, but only present as a visual aid to the spiritual challenge of Jesus as "the bread of life" (6:35, 42, 48, 51) or "the resurrection and the life" (11:25)? I think that John is using Lazarus in John 11 as a negative foil for Jesus in John 20. Watch, next, what happens there—as a challenge to the synoptic accounts.

Two—possibly *the* two?—most important early Christian leaders known from the synoptic tradition, Mary and Peter, are flatly challenged concerning the resurrection of Jesus in this chapter. They are almost woven together: Mary in 20:1–2 and 20:11–18 frames Peter in 20:3–10.

First, Peter. Luke told the story like this: "Peter got up and ran to the tomb; stooping and looking in, he saw the linen cloths by themselves; then he went home, amazed at what had happened" (24:12). But John rephrases it like this:

Peter and the other disciple ["the one whom Jesus loved" from 20:2] set out and went toward the tomb. The two were running together, but the other disciple outran Peter and reached the tomb first. He bent down to look in and saw the linen wrappings lying there, but he did not go in. Then Simon Peter came, following him, and went into the tomb. He saw the linen wrappings lying there, and the cloth that had been on Jesus's head, not lying with the linen wrappings but rolled up in a place by itself. Then the other disciple, who reached the tomb first, also went in, and *he saw and believed;* for as yet *they* did not understand the scripture, that he must rise from the dead. (20:3–9)

The Beloved Disciple gets there first, looks in first, and believes first—or even alone (note my italics). All Peter gets to do is—in ultimate deference to Luke 24:12—*enter* first. But, says John in a challenge to the synoptic tradition, an empty tomb and abandoned death wrappings *may or may not* inspire belief in the resurrection of Jesus.

Next, Mary. Neither is the empty tomb enough for Mary to believe in resurrection. Three times John has her interpret it incorrectly—as a case of grave robbery:

[1] She ran and went to Simon Peter and the other disciple, the one whom Jesus loved, and said to them, "They have *taken* the Lord out of the tomb, and we do not know where they have laid him." (20:2)

[2] They [the angels in the tomb] said to her, "Woman, why are you weeping?" She said to them, "They have *taken away* my Lord, and I do not know where they have laid him." (20:13)

[3] She turned around and saw Jesus standing there, but she did not know that it was Jesus. Jesus said to her, "Woman, why are you weeping? Whom are you looking for?" Supposing him to be the gardener, she said to him, "Sir, if you have *carried him away*, tell me where you have laid him, and I will take him away." (20:14–15)

That last scene is quite extraordinary. Even a risen vision is not enough until Jesus calls her by her name: "Jesus said to her, 'Mary!' She turned and said to him in Hebrew, 'Rabbouni!' (which means

Teacher)" (20:16). An empty tomb is ambiguous, says John, and so—just in itself—is a risen vision. *Both* empty tomb *and* risen vision require interpretation—by faith.

One final point on Mary. She is not told by Jesus *noli me tangere*, "Do not touch me," as in the traditional Latin translation. The Greek is importantly different: "Jesus said to her, 'Do not hold on to me, because I have not yet ascended to the Father. But go to my brothers and say to them, "I am ascending to my Father and your Father, to my God and your God"'" (20:17). In other words, the risen apparitions that count are *not before, but after* the ascension of Jesus into heaven. When Jesus appears in 20:19 and again in 20:24, he has ascended and is *appearing from* heaven above and not from an empty tomb below. That is John's ultimate challenge to the synoptic apparition tradition, and it leads directly into my next section.

My fourth and final step involves the so-called *return* of Jesus. In the synoptic tradition, the consummation of the kingdom's presence was understood as the return of Jesus in the imminent future. Jesus says in Mark, "There are some standing here who will not taste death until they see that the kingdom of God has come with power" (9:1). And Jesus says in Matthew, "You will not have gone through all the towns of Israel before the Son of Man comes" (10:23). But the counterchallenge of John to the synoptics is that the return of Jesus has already happened. Jesus is already back—in the Holy Spirit.

When Jesus appeared to all the disciples *from heaven* in John 20:19–23, he "breathed on them and said to them, 'Receive the Holy Spirit'" (20:22). That mention of their receiving the Hoy Spirit directs our minds back to the great final discourse of Jesus in John 13–17. In that long section, the Holy Spirit—well-known from the synoptic tradition—is uniquely renamed as the Advocate, the Defender, the Comforter (Greek *paraklētos*):

> I will ask the Father, and he will give you another *Advocate*, to be with you forever. This is the *Spirit of truth*, whom the world cannot receive, because it neither sees him nor knows

him. You know him, because he abides with you, and he will be in you. (14:16–17)

The *Advocate, the Holy Spirit*, whom the Father will send in my name, will teach you everything, and remind you of all that I have said to you. (14:26)

When the *Advocate* comes, whom I will send to you from the Father, the *Spirit of truth* who comes from the Father, he will testify on my behalf. (15:26)

First, the Holy Spirit or Spirit of Truth is renamed as the divine Advocate in the legal and forensic sense of an attorney who defends Christians against "the ruler of this world" (16:11). Furthermore, it is "*another* Advocate," so that Jesus himself was also an earlier Advocate. Finally, *sent by the Father in the name of Jesus* (14:26) is the same as *sent by Jesus from the Father* (15:26).

Immediately after that first citation above, Jesus continues with this promise: "I will not leave you orphaned; I am coming to you. In *a little while* the world will no longer see me, but you will see me; because I live, you also will live" (14:18–19). That phrase "a little while" is later repeated like a dramatic refrain. Indeed, it is not just repeated, but pounded on:

"*A little while*, and you will no longer see me, and again *a little while*, and you will see me." Then some of his disciples said to one another, "What does he mean by saying to us, '*A little while*, and you will no longer see me, and again *a little while*, and you will see me'; and 'Because I am going to the Father'?" They said, "What does he mean by this '*a little while*'? We do not know what he is talking about." Jesus knew that they wanted to ask him, so he said to them, "Are you discussing among yourselves what I meant when I said, '*A little while*, and you will no longer see me, and again *a little while*, and you will see me'?" (16:16–19)

That phrase "a little while" is cited seven times in those four verses. Why is it so important for John?

My proposal is that John is challenging and correcting the "little while" until the return of Jesus as imagined by the synoptic tradition. The first "little while" is, for John, the time until Jesus is crucified and he is gone from his companions—Holy Thursday to Good Friday for Christians today. The second "little while" is, for John, the time until Jesus is resurrected and returns not for a day or even forty days but permanently in the Spirit Advocate—Good Friday to Easter Sunday for us. A "little while" means days—at the most.

In other words, John's challenge to the synoptic tradition is that *the return of Jesus has already happened in the heavenly gift of the Holy Spirit.* "I tell you the truth: it is to your advantage that I go away, for if I do not go away, the Advocate will not come to you; but if I go, I will send him to you" (16:7). Nobody has seen God, but Christians see God in Jesus. Jesus is gone, but Christians have him—or, better, he has them—in the divine Advocate as the Holy Spirit of Truth. That mystery of the Trinity is at the same time terribly obvious and wholly mysterious.

MY FOURTH POINT ASKS, as usual, about situation and location with regard to those preceding points. Granted what we have just seen of John as *attack* against Judaism and, even more so, as *challenge* to synoptic Christianity, where was John standing to launch such a two-front operation? It seems clear that John, unlike Matthew but like Luke, speaks from *outside* Judaism. But from where exactly? Is he just now outside or *was he—like Luke—never fully and completely inside?*

Here is my very best—but not at all original—conjectural answer. John's gospel speaks so readily of—and against—"the Jews," because it comes *not from a Jew converted to Christianity, but from a Samaritan converted to Christianity.* My proposal is that a *Christian Samaritan* can both *attack* Judaism and *challenge* Jewish—or Gentile—Christianity with equal knowledge on both fronts.

Was "John" a Samaritan converted to Christianity? Notice, for example, how John differs from the other gospels with regard to Samaria and Samaritans. (You will recall, by the way, the tensive relationship between Jews and Samaritans from Chapter 3.)

Mark never mentions either Samaria or the Samaritans. Matthew has Jesus warn his companions: "Go nowhere among the Gentiles, and enter no town of the Samaritans" (10:5). The first volume of Luke-Acts speaks of Samaritans both positively (Luke 17:11–19) and negatively (9:51–56). But in the second volume everything about Samaria is extremely positive. The risen Jesus promises his companions: "You will receive power when the Holy Spirit has come upon you; and you will be my witnesses in Jerusalem, in all Judea and Samaria, and to the ends of the earth" (Acts 1:8). That geographical mandate then moves from Judea (Acts 1–7), through Samaria (Acts 8), and on, slowly but surely, to Rome (Acts 9–28). For Luke-Acts' vision of Christian destiny, Samaria is a crucial step in the transition from Judea to Italy, from Jerusalem to Rome, and from Jew to Gentile (Acts 8:5–25; 9:31; 15:3).

John, however—and John alone—tells that special story about Jesus and the Samaritan woman at Jacob's well. Jesus "had to go through Samaria. So he came to a Samaritan city called Sychar, near the plot of ground that Jacob had given to his son Joseph. Jacob's well was there, and Jesus, tired out by his journey, was sitting by the well. It was about noon" (4:3–6).

The Samaritan woman recognizes Jesus as "a prophet" (4:19), and Jesus then reveals to her that he is "the Messiah/Christ" (4:25–26). Next, "the woman left her water jar and went back to the city. She said to the people, 'Come and see a man who told me everything I have ever done! He cannot be the Messiah, can he?' They left the city and were on their way to him." (4:29–30). Finally, there is this climactic conclusion:

Many Samaritans from that city believed in him because of the woman's testimony, "He told me everything I have ever done." So when the Samaritans came to him, they asked him to stay with them; and he stayed there two days. And many more believed because of his word. They said to the woman, "It is no longer because of what you said that we believe, for we have heard for ourselves, and we know that this is truly the Savior of the world." When the two days were over, he went from that place to Galilee. (4:39–43)

The escalation of Jesus's identity is from "prophet" (4:19) to "Messiah/Christ" (4:25, 29) to "Savior of the world" (4:42). But the point of this story is to tell the conversion of the Samaritans to Christianity in miniature, microcosm, and parable.

We could understand how, if "Luke" was a Gentile God-worshiper converted to Christianity, he could know so much about Judaism and still reject it profoundly. Similarly here. "John" as a Samaritan converted to Christianity is no more than a possibility, but it is one that at least explains how he can know so much about Judaism and be so clearly outside it and against "the Jews."

THE FIFTH POINT FOR this chapter asks, as always, whether the gospel involved here is attack, challenge, or some combination of both. In this case, you already have my answer. It is a bitter attack on Judaism, from outside it, possibly from a Samaritan tradition. It is also a serenely sweeping challenge to all aspects of the synoptic Jesus in Mark, Matthew, and Luke. And, by the way, when Jesus says, "In my Father's house there are many dwelling places" (14:2), John is not proposing toleration for other interpretations of Christianity. The author of the fourth gospel is demanding toleration for his own divergent vision as the synoptic tradition becomes more and more ascendant, more and more normative.

Finally, John's gospel is also a challenge parable to Roman imperial authority. You can see that most clearly in the climactic interchange between Pilate and Jesus. Notice how John formats this miniparable:

My kingdom is not from this world.

> If my kingdom were from this world,
>
> my followers would be fighting
>
> to keep me from being handed over to the Jews.

But as it is, my kingdom is not from here. (18:36)

You can read and then ignore John's usual anti-Judaic phrasing "handed over to the Jews"—as if Pilate were not legally, officially, and operationally in charge of the crucifixion. But my present focus is on those twin frames concerning "my kingdom."

We often quote only that first line, "My kingdom is not from this world," and thereby leave it open to several possible misunderstandings. Does Jesus mean that the kingdom of God is not about the earth, but about heaven? Or that it is not about the present, but about the future? Or that it is not about the exterior, but only about the interior life?

But, actually, Jesus continues and makes his meaning emphatically clear. "The difference, Pilate, between the kingdom of Rome and the kingdom of God—here below upon this one and only earth, in this one and only world—is that yours is based, supported, and defended by violence, and mine is not. No, not even to free me from you, Pilate, would or could my followers ever fight and use violence."

John's megaparable is, in conclusion, both an attack parable directed against and from outside Judaism—like Luke-Acts—but also, and even more so, a challenge parable directed against but from inside Christianity—like Mark. It is also, as are all the gospels in their different ways, a challenge parable to the Roman Empire. We saw this sort of challenge already in Luke-Acts, but John's is a more subversive version than Luke-Acts'. It does not simply request noninterference as Christianity replaces Judaism with Roman approval. It is not about accommodation with Rome's violence, but about replacement or transformation of that imperial normalcy.

History and Parable

THIS EPILOGUE HAS TWO SECTIONS. The first section is a summation of what I have proposed in this book about the *parabling* of Jesus. The second section raises two new and concluding questions about Jesus himself, about the *Jesus* of that parabling. I begin with a review of what we have done.

First, parable is story, that is, a tensive sequence of beginning, middle, and end in a narrative that lures you into its plotted micro-world to *participate as an outsider-insider* in its ongoing adventure. (If you say of a story, "I can't get *into* it," participation has failed.) Some stories, of course, demand participation without thought, since thinking might reveal a story's utter implausibility or even sheer vacuity.

Second, metaphor is "seeing as," and metaphors extend from the most trivial clichés ("the sun rises") to imagining worlds and proposing reality itself ("liberty and justice for all"). Here also, the purpose of metaphor is participation. Metaphors invite us to recognize the human necessity of "seeing as," the dangerous and vertiginous necessity to create the ground we stand on. But, once again, metaphors can become clichés, and then we forget their inevitability.

But, still, try this, for example. Look in a mirror and see if you can see yourself without seeing your eyes seeing yourself. We swim in metaphor like fish in the sea. Do fish know about the sea? The hidden question of metaphor is this: Can we humans ever see without "seeing as"?

Third, a parable is a metaphorical story and, as such, it tends to generate a special mode of participation by hearers or readers. It does not want you to get *into* its story, but to get *out of* it. The Sower parable does not want you to get *into* sowing and ponder agricultural data. It wants you to *get out* of sowing—but into what? Parables are traps for thought and lures for participation. You are seduced or even provoked into thinking like this: If sowing is not sowing, what is it?

Fourth, I proposed a basic threefold typology for the genre of parable. *Riddle* parables (or allegories) are stories in which each element points outside itself to elements in some other hidden story. In Mark's Sower parable, for instance, "the birds" (4:4) mean "Satan" (4:15). With riddles, participation involves discovering hidden knowledge and decoding secret information.

Example parables are ethical models, moral cases, or practical instances inviting participation by comprehension and imitation. In Luke, for example, seeking the lost sheep and rejoicing over its recovery (15:6) is a model for how Jesus acts toward sinners (15:1–2, 7) and, presumably, how we should act as well.

Challenge parables are the ones within my proposed threefold spectrum in which I am primarily interested—from the written book-length ones of Ruth, Jonah, and Job in the Christian Old Testament to the hour-long oral ones of Jesus in our New Testament. In all those case studies I emphasized the oblique and indirect, the delicate and gentle way in which great sweeping absolutes of habit and custom, law and culture, presumption, presupposition, and prejudice were subverted by simple parabolic narrative that recorded a single, but different vision.

No Moabite, says the absolute law of God, may ever enter the people of God. But, says the challenge parable of Ruth, a Moabite woman was the great-grandmother of David, the anointed of God, the once and future king of Israel. What about that? No attack is launched on Deuteronomic theology or on the Torah-based divorces demanded by Ezra and Nehemiah. But Ruth the Moabite is in the genealogy of David—and later of Jesus. So how about that?

Similarly, for Jesus. The "good Samaritan," like the "good Moabite," challenges ethnic absolutes and religio-political discriminations—not just in the Jewish, but in any world. What if your plural ethnic "good guys"—the priest and Levite—fail to act compassionately, and only your singular ethnic "bad guy"—a Samaritan—does so successfully? Is that the exception that proves the rule or the exception that subverts the rule? Think about it.

Further, to conclude the book's first part, I wondered if, granted parables as participatory pedagogy, there was some profoundly intrinsic link between the medium and the message of Jesus, between the *medium* of challenge parables and the *message* of God's kingdom. In response I had two equally important correlations.

All parables are *participatory pedagogy.* The first correlation was based on this proposal: Jesus proclaimed a participatory or collaborative eschatology by announcing that the kingdom of God was not an act of unilateral intervention by divinity, but an act of bilateral cooperation between divinity and humanity (Desmond Tutu: "God, without us, will not; as we, without God cannot.")

But a participatory eschatology demanded a participatory pedagogy, a collaborative message demanded a collaborative medium. In other words, parables were the perfect—even necessary and inevitable—medium for that precise message. That raises, however, one further question. Why did Jesus prefer *challenge* parables rather than *riddle* or *example* parables, since *all* parables demand participation? All those three types are participatory, collaborative, and interactive media. So why did Jesus choose challenge parables in particular?

Challenge parables are *nonviolent pedagogy.* We saw that God's kingdom was, for Jesus, not just a collaborative venture, but also a nonviolent one. (Thank you, Pilate, at least for getting that right.) I consider those two aspects as equally important and equally necessary for his visionary world of justice and peace. A *challenge* parable confronts metaphorically, of course, but also delicately and gently. It is, after all, only a single story, so how can it stand up to a sweeping legal absolute, ancient ethnic stereotype, established religio-political presumption, and especially a divinely sanctioned mandate? It will, it can, and it does. Because that is the *power* of the challenge parable.

Fifth, before turning from parables *by* Jesus in Part I to those *about* Jesus in Part II, I presented an Interlude on Caesar at the Rubicon. In that former part we were looking at fictional characters in fictional stories, parabolic protagonists in parabolic narratives. But that Interlude introduced the possibility—indeed, actuality—of factual characters in fictional stories, historical characters in parabolic stories. Julius Caesar certainly existed, and to get from Ravenna to Rimini in 49 BCE he certainly crossed the river Rubicon. That Interlude was, of course, a deliberate preparation to move from fictional characters in fictional stories—that, is parables *by* Jesus in Part I—to factual characters in fictional stories—that is, parables *about* Jesus in Part II.

Sixth, without attempting in any way to summarize the four chapters of Part II, I emphasize one conclusion from that sweep from Mark, through Matthew and Luke-Acts, to John. Mark presented Jesus through a challenge megaparable, but in Matthew the presentation morphed into an attack megaparable. Next, Luke-Acts and John both, but in divergent ways, combined challenge parable with attack parable.

In other words, even if only on the level of rhetoric, the nonviolence of challenge parable has become—progressively throughout the four gospels—the violence of attack parable. Attack is not just a new and fourth type of parable. It is an antiparable to the challenge-parable mode of Jesus himself. Parable has turned—at least rhetorically—violent.

I pause for a moment to emphasize one final time how I understand the *challenge parable* as used throughout this book—and especially as distinct from the fourth type, the *attack parable*. For me, the trajectory of human violence escalates almost inevitably from the ideological through the rhetorical to the physical. Granted that understanding of human violence, I see the challenge parable as an attempt to question ideological absolutes—whether they are ethnic or legal, social or cultural, religious or political—without reverting to an equally absolute countervision. A challenge parable is a narrative and, as such, can only tell a single story. But that single story dares you—*with nonviolent rhetoric*—to reconsider presumptions, presuppositions, and prejudices taken all too often as unalterable reality. The *power of the challenge parable* is the power of nonviolent rhetoric to oppose violence without joining it.

I TURN NEXT TO the second subject in this Epilogue and, by now, you have probably guessed the content of my two final questions. If parables involve fictional characters in fictional stories (challenge stories *by* Jesus) and factual characters in fictional stories (gospel stories *about* Jesus), are there also fictional characters in factual stories? In other words, and for my present focus, did *Jesus himself exist* as a historical figure, or did he never exist factually, but only fictionally? Furthermore, does that make any difference for the Christian vision of the "good news"? Two questions, therefore: Did Jesus exist? And is the answer important either way?

The first question is did Jesus ever exist as a historical figure in time and place? Is he like Julius Caesar—a factual figure, but enveloped in clouds of parable? Or is he like the Good Samaritan—an entirely fictional character of Christianity's parabolic imagination? My answer is that *Jesus did exist as a historical figure.* That conclusion derives from two historical considerations—two types of proof, one external, the other internal. It does not arise from any dogmatic presuppositions.

The *external reason* is the basic agreement about Jesus between the Jewish historian Josephus at the end of the first century and the Roman historian Tacitus at the start of the second century. Both were writing at Rome and indicate what at least some educated elites knew about "Christians" as followers of a "Christ"—like Platonists followed Plato or Aristotelians followed Aristotle. Who, then, was this "Christ"?

There is a general scholarly consensus that the explanation about Jesus in Josephus's *Jewish Antiquities* was "improved" by later Christian editors and, in citing it, I italicize those assumed additions. It is a deliberately neutral report from Rome in the 90s CE with these four main points:

Movement: About this time there lived Jesus, a wise man, *if indeed one ought to call him a man*. For he was one who wrought surprising feats and was a teacher of such people as accept the truth gladly. He won over many Jews and many of the Greeks. *He was the Christ.*

Execution: When Pilate, upon hearing him accused by men of the highest standing amongst us, had condemned him to be crucified,

Continuation: those who had in the first place come to love him did not give up their affection for him. *On the third day he appeared to them restored to life, for the prophets of God had prophesied these and countless other marvelous things about him.*

Expansion: And the tribe of the Christians, so called after him, has still to this day not disappeared. (18.63–64)

I agree that those italicized sections are Christian "improvements," save for one case. Josephus must have mentioned "Christ" earlier in that text, since he concludes that "Christians" are "called after him," namely, after Christ, but only "Jesus" has been given as a name for the movement's founder. So I think it very likely that the phrase, "He was [called?] the Christ," was originally there as a

Josephan explanation rather than added as a Christian confession.

Furthermore, later in his *Jewish Antiquities* Josephus speaks of "Jesus who was called the Christ" (20.200). So my proposal is that in 18.63–64 he also said, "He was called the Christ." Christian editing involved only the omission of "called" and not the insertion of the entire sentence.

Be that as it may, Tacitus writing his *Annals* of the Julio-Claudian dynasty in the 110s, explained "Christians" as followers of "Christ" under those same four rubrics:

Movement: Christus, the founder of the name,

Execution: had undergone the death penalty in the reign of Tiberius, by sentence of the procurator Pontius Pilatus,

Continuation: and the pernicious superstition was checked for the moment, only to break out once more,

Expansion: not merely in Judaea, the home of the disease, but in the capital itself, where all things horrible or shameful in the world collect and find a vogue. (15.44)

Externally, therefore, two historians at the turn of the first to second century explain "Christ" as the founder of a movement that was not stopped by his execution, but spread in time and place— whether as "an unbroken love" with Josephus or as a "pernicious superstition" with Tacitus. That is the external proof of the factuality of Jesus, but, for me at least, the internal one is even more decisive.

The *internal argument* starts with what we have already seen throughout the sequence of the gospels from Mark, through Matthew and Luke, to John. We saw that Jesus presented through a challenge parable morphed steadily into Jesus presented through an attack parable. Recall, as just one example, how Jesus started off in Matthew 5 forbidding character assassination or even insulting language and commanding forgiveness and love of one's enemies. But by Matthew 23 that same Jesus is repeatedly declaring, "Woe to you, scribes and Pharisees, hypocrites!" We saw, through the successive gospels, how rhetorical invective increases steadily on the lips of Jesus.

Think of another example, from a wider, overall New Testament perspective. Jesus enters Jerusalem on a donkey at the start of his last week (our Palm Sunday). First of all, Matthew has Jesus ride a *nursing* female donkey with her little colt trotting by her side (21:2). Next, that happens, Matthew 21:4 says, "to fulfill what had been spoken through the prophet" about the Messiah's advent in Zechariah 9:9.

Finally, then, why a donkey? Because such a nonviolent entry meant that the Messiah "will cut off the chariot from Ephraim and the war-horse from Jerusalem; and the battle bow shall be cut off, and he shall command peace to the nations; his dominion shall be from sea to sea, and from the River to the ends of the earth" (Zech. 9:10). That non-violent entry was a parabolic lampoon on the violent imperial mode of entering a conquered city through shattered walls or opened gates.

But turn now to the final book of the New Testament, the Apoca-lypse or Revelation. In Revelation 19 the return of Jesus is no longer on a nursing female donkey, but on a white battle horse:

> I saw heaven opened, and there was a white horse! Its rider is called Faithful and True, and in righteousness he judges and makes war. . . . I saw the beast and the kings of the earth with their armies gathered to make war against the rider on the horse and against his army. . . . And the rest were killed by the sword of the rider on the horse, the sword that came from his mouth; and all the birds were gorged with their flesh. (19:11, 19, 21)

The nonviolent incarnate Jesus has become the violent apocalyptic Jesus. The nursing donkey and her colt have been replaced by the warhorse or battle charger.

That is my second, internal, and far more definitive reason for accepting Jesus as a historical figure—no matter how creatively he has been portrayed in parable in small ways and large throughout the four gospel versions. Here is the point: *If you are inventing a nonhistorical figure, why invent one you cannot live with, but must steadily and terminally change into its opposite?* In other words, I find it much more likely that Jesus was an actual historical figure whose radical insistence on nonviolent distributive justice was both accepted and negated by the tradition it engendered. I conclude that Jesus was an actual, factual, historical figure and not a metaphorical, symbolic, or parabolic invention by his first-century Jewish contemporaries.

For those two reasons, one external and one internal, and along with the consensus of modern scholarship, I conclude that Jesus really existed, that we can know the significant sequence of his life—from John the Baptist to Pilate the prefect—but that he comes to us trailing clouds of fiction, parables *by* him and *about* him, particular incidents as miniparables and whole gospels as megaparables.

My second concluding question is: What, if any, difference would it make for the Christian vision if we discovered—with absolute certainty—that Jesus was never a historical figure? Apart from accusations of original lies or inaugural conspiracies, what if "Jesus" had been as deliberately and honestly invented as was, say, the "Good Samaritan" or the "Prodigal Son"? What—if anything—would have been lost to Christianity? Nothing more or less than *an actual life* of nonviolent distributive justice as the revelation of the character of God. But could you not get that just as well from a nonhistorical figure in a magnificent parable? Not really. But why? What is at stake?

Imagine if the "Reverend Martin Luther King Jr." had been simply a nonhistorical character whose life and ideas were portrayed in a *New York Times* bestseller novel, a fictional tale that won all types of prizes and immediately became a motion picture. Its vision would have been absolutely valid for American destiny, but could have been dismissed with the offhand comment that it was all very lovely, but would not work—not now, not here, and maybe not anywhere, ever. It was just fictional entertainment, a dream from which one woke to a reality that negated it even as a human possibility. People, it might have been objected, would always strike back—at least by the second or third day, at least by the second or third murder.

But because Dr. King was an actual person who did it—rather than just a character in a parabolic novel who imagined it—his vision could not be so easily dismissed. If it were done, it could be done again—and by others. That, of course, is the challenge of Jesus as an actual, factual, historical figure. If any one human being can do anything in life and death, other human beings can do likewise.

The *power* of Jesus's parables challenged and enabled his followers to co-create with God a world of justice and love, peace and nonviolence. The *power* of Jesus's historical life challenged his followers by proving at least one human being could cooperate fully with God. And if one, why not others? If some, why not all? "Ashes denote," wrote Emily Dickinson, "that fire was." And if fire ever was, fire can be again.

Scripture Index

Scripture references are in bold.

Old Testament

Exodus
1–2, **178, 179, 181**
7:13–14, 22, **21**
8:15, 32, **21**
8:19, **21**
9:7, 35, **21**
9:12, **21**
9:29, **106**
9:34, **21**
10:1, 20, 27, **21**
11:10, **21**
14, **227**
14:8, **21**
22:25, **104**
22–23, **104**
24:1, **106**

Leviticus
17–26, **104**
25:36–37, **104**

Deuteronomy
1:16, **73**

12–26, **104**
23:3–4a, **72, 73**
23:19, **104**
28, **81, 84, 85, 121**
28:2, **84**
28:4, **84**
28:18, **84**
28:25, **84**

Judges
9, **33**
9:1–3, **33**
9:8–15, **33**
9:15, **33**
9:49, **33**
9:53, **34**
13–16, **16**
14:1, **16**
14:3, **16**
14:6, **17**
14:12–13, **17**
14:14, **17**
14:15, **17**
14:18, **17**
14:19, **17**

15:5, **18**
15:6, **18**
15:8, **18**
16:1, **17**
16:4, **17**

Ruth
1:1, 2, 6, 22, **71**
1:4, **71**
1:5, **69**
1:16–17, **70**
1:22, **70, 71**
2:1, **70**
2:2, 21, **71**
2:6, **71**
4:3, 5, 10, **71**
4:5, 10, **71**
4:14–17, **71**
4:17–22, **71**

2 Samuel
11:1, **34**
11:2–3, **34**
11:8, **34**
11:15, **35**

2 Samuel (continued)
12:1–4, **34**, **35**
12:10, **35**
12:13, **35**

1 Kings 17, **206**

2 Kings 5, **206**

Ezra 10:2, 10, 11, 14,
17, 18, 44, **72–73**

Nehemiah
13:1–2, **73**
13:3, 26, 27, 30, **73**

Job
1:1–2:13, **80**, **81**, **82**
1:1–3, **82**
1:2–3, **85**
1:8, **82**
3:1–37:24, **80**, **81**, **84**
6:24, **85**
38:1, **86**
38:1–40:2, **85**
38:1–42:6, **80**, **81**, **85**
40:3–5, **85**
40:6–41:34, **85**
42:1–6, **85**
42:7, **85**
42:7–17, **80**, **81**, **82**
42:10, **81**, **87**

Psalms
15:5, **105**
137:7, **83**

Isaiah
4:11–13, **20**
6:8, **77**

6:10, **20**, **103**
37:33, 35, **78**
45:1, **87**
61:1, **205**

Jeremiah
4:21, **83**
25:15–16, **82**
25:15–26, **82**
25:18, **82**
25:19–21, **82**

Ezekiel
18:8–9, 13, 17, **105**
22:12, **105**

Daniel
1–6, **36**
3, **36**
6, **36**
7, **116**, **117**
7:2–6, **116**
7:7, 19, 23, **116**
7:8, 11, 20, 21, **116**
7:12, **117**
7:14, **117**
7:18, **117**
7:27, **117**, **126**

Obadiah 1, 2, 4, 8, 12,
13, **83**

Jonah
1:1–2, **75**
1:3, **75**
1:10, **75**
1:16, **75**
2:1–9, **75**
2:10, **75**
3:1–2, **75**

3:4, **75**
3:5–9, **75–76**
3:10, **76**
4:1, **76**
4:10, **76**
4:10–11, **76**

Nahum
1:1, **78**
2:8–10, **78–79**
3:1–3, **79**

Zechariah
9:9, **250**
9:10, **250**
10:11, **78**

New Testament

Matthew
1:1, **180**, **224**
1–2, **178**, **179**, **180**,
221
2:2, **179**
3:7–10, **121**
3:13–15, **124**
3:16–17, **124**
4:17, **126**
5, **186**, **187**, **194**,
195, **250**
5:17–20, **182–183**
5:21–26, **183**
5:22, **184**
5:24, **185**
5:27–30, **183**
5:31–32, **183**
5:33–37, **183**
5:38–42, **183–184**
5:43–48, **184**

5:44–45, **129**
5:44–45, 48, **185**
5:48, **129**
5–7, **182**
6:2, 5, 16, **186**
6:2–16, **217**
6:10, **124, 135**
8, **221**
8:5–6, **202**
8:5–13, **202**
8:11–12, **190**
9:15–16, **126**
10:5, **240**
10:10, **130**
10:14, **188**
10:23, **237**
10:31–32, **100**
10:35–36, **132**
11:11, **124**
11:12–13, **126**
11:18–19, **123**
11:20–24, **188**
12:28, **126**
12:38–42, **190**
13:16–17, **126**
13:24–30, 36–43, **190**
13:42, **190**
13:44, **135**
13:44–46, **108**
13:45, **135**
13:47–50, **190**
13:52, **194**
13:54–57, **205**
13:54–58, **204**
14:13–21, **226**
15:7, **217**
15:32–39, **226**
16:1–4, **190**
18:4, **40**
18:6, **40**

18:10–14, **41**
18:12–14, **40**
19:23–24, **124**
19:30, **93**
20:1, **111**
20:1–2, **95**
20:1–16, **95**
20:3, **96**
20:3–7, **96**
20:7, **96**
20:8–15, **96–97**
21:2, **250**
21:4, **250**
21:28–32, **109**
22:1–14, **190**
22:13, **191**
22:18, **217**
22:23–33, **57**
22:34, **58**
22:34–35, **58**
22:34–40, **57**
22:36–40, **58**
22:40, **52, 58**
22:41–46, **57**
23, **186, 187, 194,
 195, 222, 250**
23:2–3, **194**
23:12, **93**
23:13, **186**
23:13–29, **217**
23:15, **186**
23:16, **186**
23:17, 19, **186**
23:23, **186**
23:24, **186**
23:25, 26, **186**
23:27, **186**
23:29, **186**
23:33, **186**
24:45–51, **191**

24:51, **191, 217**
25:1–13, **109**
25:14–18, **99**
25:14–30, **99, 191**
25:19–23, **99–100**
25:20–23, **108**
25:24, 26, **106**
25:24–28, **100**
25:27, **104**
25:30, **191**
27:11, 29, 37, **179**
27:11–37, **179**
27:15, 20, 24, 25, **193**
27:15–16, 24–26, **192**
27:24, **293**
27:25, **193**
27:37, **179**
27:60, **233**

Mark
1:1, **159, 161**
1:1–3, **224**
1:1–8, **221**
1:4–5, **121**
1:9, **123**
1:10–11, **124**
1:14, **171**
1:14–15, **21, 161**
1:14b–15, **126**
1:16, **166**
1:19, **166**
1:25, **164**
2:1, **21**
2:10, 28, **126**
2:19–20, **126**
2–3, **23**
3, **21**
3:6, **21, 222**
3:12, **164**
3:16–17, **166**

Mark *(continued)*
3:16–19, **166**, **174**
3:21–22, **22**
3:22, **223**
3:23, **22**
3:23–27, **22**, **24**
4, **22**, **23**, **24**, **27**, **40**,
   42, **62**
4:1–2, **19**, **24**
4:1–20, **19**
4:3–8, **19**
4:3–9, **9**, **25**
4:4, **244**
4:8, **25**
4:10, **19**, **20**
4:11–13, **24**, **103**
4:14–20, **22–23**, **25**
4:15, **244**
4:20, **25**
4:21–23, **25**
4:33–34, **25**
4:34, **6**
5:1–13, **162**
6:1–6, **204**
6:2–3, **205**
6:8, **130**
6:9, **227**
6:10, **227**
6:11, **188**
6:11–12, **187**
6:13, **227**
6:32–44, **226**
6:35–37a, **226**
6:35–43, **174**
6:37b, **226**
6:38, **227**
6:39–40, **227**
6:41–42, **227**
6:43–44, **227**
6:44, **228**

7, **23**, **180**, **226**
7:1–5, **23**
7:6, 8, **23**
7:14, **23**
7:17, **23**, **24**
8:1–9, **174**
8:1–10, **226**
8:11–13, **189**
8:14–17a, **174**
8:17, **175**
8:17b–21, **174**
8:22–10:52, **163**
8:22–26, **163**
8:27, **173**
8:31, **126**, **164**
8:31–9:1, **164**, **170**
8:31–10:45, **163**
8:31–32a, **164**, **165**
8:32b, **164**, **166**
8:33, **167**
8:33–9:1, **164**
8:34, **168**
8.17b–21, **176**
9:1, **237**
9:2, **167**
9:9, 12, 31, **126**
9:25, **164**
9:31, **164**
9:31–37, **165**, **170**
9:32–34, **164**, **166**,
   167
9:35–37, **164**
10:15, **188**
10:32–16:8, **170**
10:32a, **169**
10:32a–45, **170**
10:33, **164**
10:33, 45, **126**
10:33–34, **164**, **166**
10:33–45, **166**, **170**

10:35–36, 37–38,
   39–40, **167**
10:35–37, **166**
10:35–40, **167**
10:35–41, **164**
10:37, **163**, **167**
10:41, **167**
10:42–44, **162**
10:42–45, **164**, **167**
10:43–44, **175**
10:46–52, **163**
10:52, **163**
10–16, **172**
11:27, **23–24**
11–12, **23**
12, **23**
12:1, 12, **24**
12:1–8, **134**
12:9–12, **134**
12:18–27, **57**
12:28, **58**
12:28–34, **57**
12:29–31, **58**
12:32, **59**
12:32–33, **58**
12:34a, **58**
12:35–37, **57**
13:5–7, 21–22, **173**
14:3–9, **170**, **172**
14:7–8, **171**
14:9, **170**, **171**
14:10–11, **166**
14:12–16, **143**
14:21, 41, **126**
14:22, **4**
14:33, **167**
14:33–35, **230**
14:36, **230**
14:50, **230**
14:63–64, **166**

15:1, **166**
15:3–4, **162**
15:6–8, 11, 15, **191–192**
15:7, **130**
15:8, 11, 15, **193, 223**
15:11–12, **223**
15:15, **162, 166**
15:19, **166**
15:20, **166**
15:24, **166**
15:33–37, **232**
15:37–39, **171**
15:38–39, **232**
15:39, **170**
15:40–41, **169, 171**
15:42, **233**
15:42–44, **233**
15:42–45, **233**
15:46, **233**
15:47, **169**
16:1, **169, 233**
16:1–2, **172**
16:1–8, **170, 171**
16:6, **166, 172**
16:7, **172**
16:7–8, **169, 174**
16:8, **172**
16:9–20, **172**
20:31, **93**

Luke
1:1, **202**
1:1–24; 53, **202**
1:3, **200**
1–2, **221**
2:1–4, **215**
3:1–9:50, **214**
3:10–14, **122**
3:21a, **124**

3:21b–22, **124**
3:22, **215**
3:38, **224**
3–4, **90–91**
3–6, **87–88**
4, **207**
4:1, **215**
4:16–17, **206**
4:16–19, **205**
4:16–30, **204**
4:18–21, **206**
4:22, **205, 206**
4:23–24, **204, 205**
4:23–28, **206**
4:25–27, **205**
4:28–29, **206**
4:29–30, **206**
5:29–32, **39**
5:30, **92**
5:34–35, **126**
6:27–28, 35, **129**
6:36, **129**
7:1–5, **202**
7:1–10, **202**
7:1–18, **122**
7:19, **122**
7:22, **226**
7:22–23, **122**
7:28, **124**
7:34, **92**
8:8, **26**
8:15, **26**
9, **221**
9:3, **130**
9:5, **188**
9:10b–17, **226**
9:51, 53, **214**
9:51–56, **240**
9:52–56, **61**
10, **62**

10:12–15, **188**
10:23b–24, **126**
10:25, **48**
10:25–29, **49, 57, 59**
10:26, **48**
10:27, **49, 52, 58**
10:28, **49, 59**
10:29, **49, 52, 59**
10:30–35, **3, 48, 49, 59**
10:31–32, **108**
10:36, **49, 59**
10:36–37, **49, 57, 59**
10:37a, **49, 52**
10:37b, **49**
11:5–8, **108**
11:16, 29–32, **190**
12:16–21, **108**
11:20, **126**
12:56, **217**
13:2, 4, **215**
13:15, **217**
13:22–23, 33–34, **214**
13:28–29, **190**
14:11, **93**
14:16–24, **108**
14:28–32, **108**
15:1, **39**
15:1–2, **37, 92**
15:1–2, 7, **244**
15:1–3, **40**
15:2, **39**
15:4–7, **38, 40**
15:6, **244**
15:8–10, **38, 40**
15:11, **38, 45**
15:11–32, **40**
15:12–24, **38**
15:23, 32, **39**
15:24, **39**

Luke (continued)
15:24, 32, **39**
15:25–32, **38**
15:28, **39, 215**
15:29, **39**
15:31–32, **39**
15, **37, 40, 41, 42, 43**
16:1–7, **134**
16:1–12, **108**
16:6–7, **215**
16:16, **125–126**
16:19–21, **93**
16:22–25, **94**
16:27–31, **94**
16:31, **94**
17:11, **214**
17:11–19, **240**
17:20–21, **125**
18:1–8, **108**
18:9, **92**
18:10, **90**
18:10–13, **92**
18:14, **92**
18:31, **214**
19:8, **93**
19:11, 28, **214**
19:12, 14, 27, **100**
19:12–26, **100**
19:13, **101**
19:15–19, **101**
19:20–24, **101**
19:23, **104**
19:29–24:53, **214**
20:27–40, **57**
20:41–44, **57**
22:35–36, **130**
22:37–38, 49–52, **130**
23:4, **208**
23:13–15, **208**
23:22, **208**

23:47, **171**
23:53, **233**
24:12, **235, 236**
24:13–33, **3**
24:27, **94**
24:28–30, **94**
24:28–32, **4**
24:31–32, **94**
24:49, **201**
24:52–53, **214, 215**

John
1:1–2, **224**
1:1–18, **221**
1:14, **225**
1:29–34, **124**
1:32–34, **124**
3:1–9, **233**
4, **229**
4:3–6, **240**
4:7–15, **230**
4:9, **61**
4:19, **240, 241**
4:25, 29, **241**
4:25–26, **240**
4:29–30, **240**
4:31–38, **230**
4:39–43, **240–241**
4:42, **241**
4:46–47, **203**
4:46–53, **202**
5:18, **222–223**
6, **229, 235**
6:1–13, **226, 227**
6:5–7, **228**
6:13, **228**
6:14–59, **226, 228**
6:26, **228–229**
6:27, **229**
6:35, **229**

6:35, 42, 48, 51, **235**
6:41, **229**
6:48–50, **229**
6:51, **229**
7:32, 45, **222**
7:50–52, **233**
7–9, **222**
8:44, **223**
8:48, **223**
9:2, **86**
9:40–41, **222**
11, **235**
11:6, **234**
11:17, **234**
11:23–27, **234–235**
11:25, **235**
11:39, **234**
11:44, **234**
11:47, **222**
11:57, **222**
13–17, **237**
14:2, **241**
14:16–17, **237–238**
14:18–19, **238**
14:26, **238**
15:26, **238**
16:7, **239**
16:11, **238**
16:16–19, **238**
17:12, **231**
18:3, **222**
18:3–6, **230**
18:7–8, **231**
18:9, **231**
18:10–11, **230–231**
18:12, **231**
18:28, **143**
18:33–38, **130**
18:35, **130**
18:36, **130, 242**

19:6–7, **223**
19:28–30, **232**
19:38, **233**
19:39–41, **233**
20, **235**
20:1–2, **235**
20:2, **235**, **236**
20:3–9, **235–236**
20:3–10, **235**
20:11–18, **235**
20:13, **236**
20:14–15, **236**
20:16, **236–237**
20:17, **237**
20:19, **237**
20:19–23, **237**
20:22, **237**
20:24, **237**
20–21, **171**

Acts
1:1, **200**
1:1–7:60, **214**
1:2–28:25, **216**
1:4–5, **201**
1:8, **240**
1–7, **240**
2, **201**
5:17–18, **207**
8, **240**
8:1–28:14a, **214**
8:5, **214**
8:5–25, **240**
8:27, **203**
9:31, **214**, **240**
9–28, **240**

10:1–2a, **217**
10:2, 22, 35, **203**
10:2–4, 31, **217–218**
11:19, **214**
13, **207**
13:1–14:6, **214**
13:7, **209**
13:9, **209**
13:12, **209**
13:14–16a, **206**
13:16, **203**
13:16b–41, **206**
13:42–43, **206**
13:43, **203**, **207**
13:43, 50, **203**
13:44–45, **206–207**
13:44–49, **206**
13:50, **203**
13:50–52, **206**
15:3, **240**
15:40–19:41, **214**
16:14, **203**
17, **207**
17:1, 4, **203**
17:1–2a, **206**
17:2b–3, **206**
17:4, **206**
17:4, 17, **203**
17:4–5a, **207**
17:5a, **206**
17:5b–9, **206**
17:17, **203**
18:7, **203**
18:12–17, **209**
19:31, **210**
19:37, **210**

21:17–28:14a, **214**
22:25–29, **210**
23:12–22, **210**
23:23–24, **210**
23:27, **210**
23:29, **210**
24:26, **211**
25:7, **211**
25:18–19, **211**
26:31, **211**
26:32, **211**
28:14b–31, **214**
28:30–31, **211**
28:31, **202**, **214**, **217**

Romans
1:1, **160**
1:9, **160**
11:25, **207**

1 Corinthians 15,
    171

2 Corinthians
4:4, **160**
9:14, **50**
11:25, **210**

Galatians 1:6–9, **160**

Philemon 1:27, **160**

Revelation
19, **250**
19:11, 19, 21, **250**